The SharePoint Shepherd's Guide for End Users: 2010

Robert L. Bogue

AVAILTEK

www.availtekllc.com

The SharePoint Shepherds Guide for End Users: 2010

By Robert L. Bogue

Editor:	Kathi Anderson
Technical Editor:	Amy Dehmer
Cover Design:	Arnel Reynon

ISBN-13: 978-0-9824198-0-9

Printed in the United States of America

For more information about this book including frequently asked questions and corporate licensing please visit us at http://www.sharepointshepherd.com.

About the Author

Robert Bogue, MCT, MCSE (NT4/W2K), MCSA:Security, A+, Network+, Server+, I-Net+, IT Project+, E-Biz+, CDIA+, is a consultant, author, and speaker who is also the president of Thor Projects LLC. Thor Projects LLC provides SharePoint Consulting services to clients around the globe. Robert has contributed to more than 100 book projects and numerous other publishing projects. He has been pleased to be a part of the Microsoft Most Valuable Professional (MVP) program for the past seven years, and was most recently awarded MVP status for Microsoft Office SharePoint Server. Before that, Robert was a Microsoft Commerce Server MVP and Microsoft Windows Servers-Networking MVP. He runs the SharePoint Users Group of Indiana (SPIN, www.spindiana.com), and has been engaged by multiple groups at Microsoft to help support them and to produce content. You'll find his byline on articles and whitepapers across the Internet, and read his blog at http://www.thorprojects.com/blog. You can reach Robert at Rob.Bogue@thorprojects.com.

About the Technical Editor

Amy Dehmer is a SharePoint consultant with Ambassador Solutions with more than 10 years of Information Technology Experience. Her passion is in helping companies maximize their SharePoint value by leveraging out of the box functionality. Her unique understanding of software, business, and people enables her to deliver excellence in the SharePoint solutions she provides. Amy specializes in SharePoint Technologies with a focus on Implementation and Configuration, InfoPath Solutions, and SharePoint Designer Workflows, and has worked with SharePoint Technologies since the 2001 version.

Dedication

One of the benefits of being an author is that you are given the opportunity to recognize a special person – or persons – in your life in the form of a dedication. I can honestly say that my life as I know it would not be possible without the love and support of my wife, Shelley. She doesn't know how beautiful she is to me – inside and out. I keep telling her, but my words are not enough. I love you, dear.

Acknowledgements

Any book project is fraught with challenges. This project is no exception. Thanks to my friends on the SharePoint product team, I found myself working on launch and post-launch materials until well after release. I further found myself blessed by an abundance of clients who wanted my time. The net result of this is that I ended up quite late with the process.

There are numerous folks who've written some of the material here, have rushed edits, done extra reviews, and generally just done what they could to make this book even more spectacular than the previous edition.

One name you won't see in the official acknowledgements page is my friend Brian Proffitt. Brian is responsible for creating and writing most of the task content in the book while I slaved away over the mechanics of publishing, the decision trees, background information, etc. He's truly the juggernaut behind the project.

Amy Dehmer has been putting up with me in the Indianapolis market for years. Through clients and competition, we've always enjoyed a respect for one another, and I'm pleased to say that she did an excellent job of ensuring the technical accuracy of the book. If there are any remaining technical errors despite her careful work, please assume that I reintroduced them after her edits.

Finally, I have to acknowledge the fact that I'm surrounded by a great group of people. I sometimes tell clients I feel like I play *Who Wants to be a Millionaire?* every day. The only exception is that I don't get multiple choice questions and I have a seemingly limitless "Phone a Friend" lifeline. My fellow MVPs and respected members of the SharePoint community who are now accustomed to my instant messages and emails have bailed me out with regularity when I didn't know an answer.

Going further, SharePoint allows you to apply version control to an item. This allows you to keep older versions of the item for review. Consider the case where you have task items for a project. SharePoint can automatically track when updates were made and by whom, by keeping versions of the same record. This means that contributors don't have to be as focused on what each other is doing. They can simply do their work and allow SharePoint to do its job coordinating the activity.

Communications Tool

The ability to work on information together is just one piece of the puzzle. What about how to disseminate that information to the appropriate parties inside the organization? That's a fundamentally different problem than tracking revisions and enabling collaboration. As a communications tool, SharePoint has a set of key features that allow you as the user to control its appearance and how the data is displayed to the consumers.

Building Pages from Parts

Rarely does the user get to create his or her own Web page. While some online portals allow users to select their components and the order that they appear, in most corporate environments, everything is pre-assigned and rigid. That isn't the case in SharePoint. One of SharePoint's key features is the ability for anyone to build a page from a set of components – called Web Parts. Even more impressive is that SharePoint allows you to configure these Web Parts to suit your needs.

Web Parts have what are called properties. These are settings that you – the user – can control; these properties make the Web Part behave the way you want it to. In some cases, the properties allow you to control which view is displayed in the Web Part. Other properties control the title and location of the Web Part on the page.

SharePoint ships with numerous Web Parts, including Web Parts for showing the members of a site, for allowing you to add static content, to insert other pages as a part of your page, etc. Developers in your organization and at third-party companies can write Web Parts which are added to the gallery of available Web Parts that you can then add to a page.

Creating Your Own Pages and Sites

Your control of SharePoint isn't limited to adding parts to pages – you can add pages themselves. You can select from a template and create your own pages. These new pages can have Web Parts placed on them, as well. The benefit of being able to create your own pages is that it allows you a way to show different contents to different people – or to contain different types of content that may not belong on the same page.

For truly separate topics, SharePoint allows you to create your own containers, called sites. Sites can have different security, navigation menus, and pages. Sites are like folders except more powerful. While SharePoint allows you to secure folders, sites allow you to change how users are grouped and assigned security. This allows you to tailor the experience of different groups of consumers based on varying sets of criteria.

Quick Wiki

Wikis derive their name from the Hawaiian word for "quick." The Wiki concept is designed to be quick and easy. There are several implementations of Wiki – perhaps the most popular is Wikipedia, which rivals the information held by traditional encyclopedia companies. Wikis themselves are designed to allow untrained users to quickly create and connect information. Instead of the <A HREF="http://sharepointsheperd.com">SharePoint Shepherd</A> notation that a Web page would require, a Wiki allows you to build links by simply specifying the title that you want for the target. For instance, [[SharePoint Shepherd]] creates a link to a page titled SharePoint Shepherd.

What's better is that Wikis included in a SharePoint implementation will automatically allow you to create the page after you've created (stubbed out) the link. By clicking on the link to SharePoint Shepherd, you'll be given the opportunity to create the page if it doesn't already exist. The net effect is that it takes very little effort to create knowledge repositories that are connected to one another.

SharePoint extends this model by allowing you to add Web Parts to a Wiki page. This means that the content and links that you've created can sit side-by-side with a Web Part, showing the results of a query, the temperature in Alaska, or status from some third-party system.

The benefit of a Wiki is plain in terms of speed to get content into the system. The negative to Wikis is that pages tend not to have the same look and feel, nor does the navigation seem to have any structure to it. .

Structuring Web Content

In communication environments, particularly where you're communicating with the public, the key concern isn't always how quick the content can be generated but is, instead, how easy it is for the consumers to consume. This means that the pages should have a consistent page layout and that the navigation should be architected. SharePoint allows you to publish structured content through a set of features called publishing features. These features allow for the creation of page layouts – page templates – into which content can be added. The page layouts are varied by content type so that some of the pages can have more fields than others. Users can create new pages by selecting a new page and the layout that they want to use. The content is added into the entry boxes in the layout and, when completed, the output is merged into a single page that the user can see.

The beauty of this arrangement is that the page is stored relatively pre-built in the database so it can be returned quickly, but it's also stored in its component parts so that it's easy to change the appearance of the page when the company changes its name or its branding. Power users can create the page layouts themselves so it's easy to create new types of content and layouts for it. It leaves the power of managing the appearance of the site to the user.

In addition to the ability to control – and change – the appearance of content, SharePoint includes several components designed to dynamically build the menus. By dynamically building menus to match the content that has been created, SharePoint minimizes the amount of effort that must be spent considering how to create the navigation and how to keep menus up-to-date. Further, SharePoint includes a page for Manage Content and Structure that allows you to move the content around, thereby changing the structure and menus which are dynamically generated. With all these tools, it's probable that your site will seem navigable. Of course, some users won't know how to navigate through your site's structure and will need another way to find the information they're looking for – that is where search comes in.

Leveraging the Power of Search

Unlike older systems that allowed you to only search for things within special fields, SharePoint includes a full-text search capability that can extract the text from documents and allow you to search that content for information. SharePoint ships with adapters, called IFilters, for several of the most popular file formats, including text, xml, and the Microsoft Office suite of applications. IFilters are available for Adobe's Acrobat PDF file format, as well.

Beyond being able to search content stored in SharePoint, the search engine can be configured to index information in File Shares, Exchange, and nearly every kind of system that you can imagine if you're willing to build the XML file that specifies how to get to that content. The result is that SharePoint can be an enterprise-level tool for finding information.

SharePoint's full-text search capability can even reach out to other systems through federation. This allows you to run the same search on your intranet that you run on the Internet – at the same time. SharePoint also allows for the use of faceted search, using the metadata that SharePoint stores on a document or list item to further refine the result sets.

Consider that you're looking for a specific presentation on the topic of wind power that you know was given to the ABC Corporation in May. You can search for "wind power abc corporation" and receive a relatively large set of results and then click on a link on the set to limit your results to the PowerPoint presentation type. You can further refine the results to those where the client is identified as ABC Corporation by clicking on the dynamic list of customers that was generated from the results. Ultimately, you can even click into a date range to shrink the scope of the search results to a more manageable level. Often, one, two, or three facets will quickly reduce the number of results to a handful (less than a page). The impact of this is that it is easier to find the results that you're looking for – quickly.

Faceted search relies upon the correct metadata being filled out by users as they upload content to the system. That's something that is facilitated by the upload process – and by the Microsoft Office clients themselves.

Adding Office Client Applications

One of the key challenges in any content management system is getting users to apply metadata or storage location consistently. SharePoint is different than most other content management systems because SharePoint leverages the Office client applications to facilitate the addition of the metadata by the users when they're creating the document.

One feature is QuickParts, which allows the user to enter data into the document directly and have that data promoted to metadata properties automatically. Another is the document information panel (DIP), with an InfoPath form that appears at the top of the document to specify properties. Both aid in the capture of metadata in the document. SharePoint promotes the properties in the documents to metadata in the SharePoint document library. This can dramatically simplify the process of capturing the metadata necessary to route documents (SharePoint's Content Organizer can move documents to new locations based on metadata).

Office client integration also includes the ability to take SharePoint data off-line and to synchronize calendars and contacts to Outlook. This means that SharePoint can be your storage repository for your data even if the primary way that you access that data is to leverage office tools like SharePoint Workspace and Outlook.

A Tale of Two SharePoints

It's important to realize that most, but not all, of the features ascribed to SharePoint are available in any version. There are two different SharePoint products. There's the SharePoint Foundation product, whose license is included as a part of your Windows Server license and the SharePoint Server, which is a separate for-pay product.

SharePoint Foundation has all of the Office integration, document management, and list management features, as well as basic search capabilities. SharePoint Server includes the Web content management features for publishing. SharePoint Server itself comes in two versions: Standard and Enterprise. Enterprise includes services like Visio Services, InfoPath Form Services, and others. Refer to your Microsoft licensing expert for more specific details.

The key here is that there is a great deal that can be done with SharePoint Foundation. When you need features like Web Content Management, you'll want to upgrade to SharePoint Server Standard edition. When you want to use enhanced services like Visio services, you'll need to get SharePoint Server Enterprise edition.

What is SharePoint Designer and Do I Need It?

For the most part, SharePoint is a Web-based system. Most of the changes that you do for SharePoint are done from a Web browser. There are some cases, like creating a new page layout or modifying a design, where you need to use a free tool called SharePoint Designer. SharePoint Designer also allows you to create your own workflows so that you can create your own automatic responses to how data flows.

These two key features of SharePoint Designer would cause you to need it. Beyond these two uses, there are other valuable things you can do, which can be done in the Web browser, as well. Creating content types and some other operations available from the Web user interface are much quicker when performed from within SharePoint Designer.

If you're allowed to install software and you're going to use SharePoint, then you should install SharePoint Designer and see if it can help you out.

Conclusion

There are dozens of features not mentioned in this brief introduction to SharePoint. The point here is to give you a flavor – not enumerate every feature. An enumerated feature list can be found at http://www.microsoft.com/sharepoint.

If you have a better way to explain what SharePoint is, please drop me a line at Rob.Bogue@ThorProjects.com

What is a Content Type?

Content types are mentioned more than occasionally in the SharePoint documentation that you see online and hear from experts speaking at conferences. It's one of those things that makes SharePoint very powerful – but in some ways equally confusing.

Let's start with the problem that content types are designed to solve. You have a set of different kinds of documents that you may want to work with that might really be best if stored in the same place. Consider the idea that you are in a sales role and that you work with customers on a variety of projects. Each time you need to do a proposal there are several different kinds of documents that are needed. For instance, you might need to do a PowerPoint file as a face-to-face presentation to the customer. You might also need to develop a pro-forma profit and loss (P&L) analysis for approval by management. Further, you might also need to develop a formal offer letter.

The fact is, the files themselves are different, needing different approval processes and perhaps differing in the amount and type of metadata that is required. For instance, doing a presentation to the customer may not require any approvals. The P&L might require approval by finance. The formal offer letter might require both financial and sales management approval.

On the metadata side, you might require that all the different documents require the customer ID number for the customer that the proposed project is for. You might require a projected one-year and three-year profit from the P&L. The formal offer letter might require an offer date and an offer expiration date.

SharePoint handles the need for different metadata and different approval processes with a content type. A content type collects a set of rules, including the fields and the processes around the content. The formal offer letter might include the fields as well as an approval workflow that includes both finance and sales management.

Content types form a hierarchy; that is, a content type can derive from another content type. So in our example, we might create a content type called customer document which includes the field for the customer ID. The formal offer letter could derive from the customer document type and pick up the customer ID field. In this way, you can make changes to a whole set of content types by modifying their shared parent content type.

The real magic of content types isn't in the ability to define fields and processes. The real magic is in the idea that you can put multiple content types in the same document library (or list). In the management of a list, there's an option to enable content types. Once enabled, you can connect a library to an existing content type – in other words, to an existing definition. When you add the content type to the library, SharePoint automatically adds the fields of the content type to the library. Then when a user saves a document as a specific content type, SharePoint displays the fields that apply to that content type on the edit form.

One benefit of the content type approach is that if you create lists in different sub-sites, you can ensure that all of the libraries have the same definition for the data – because they're using the same content type. Without content types, the creator would have to manually verify the creation of each field and ensure that the processes including workflows are assigned correctly.

With a basic understanding of what content types are, it would be natural to be curious when you might want to use them. Certainly one common scenario was laid out here – where there are several different kinds of documents in the same library with different data storage and processing needs, in other words, when you want to store dissimilar things in the same place. However, the opposite reason is also true.

Consider the idea of forms on your Intranet. Some forms come from IT. Some forms come from HR. Some forms come from Accounting. However, when someone wants a form, they don't want to have to know whether the form is a HR form or an IT form or an Accounting form. They want to be able to get the form they're looking for. By using the same content type in IT, HR, and Accounting, it's possible to leverage search to look only for items matching that content type. The net result is that you can get a searchable list of forms regardless of their source location. In this case, content types are good because they provide a way to bring together the same data located in different areas of the organization.

Content types aren't limited to just the columns, templates, and workflows we've discussed above. Content types are also capable of having event receivers assigned to them. They can have information rights management, custom New/Display/Edits forms, and event receivers applied to them. They're capable of controlling the entire experience.

How Do I Manage Versions?

Most people have struggled with version management at some point in their career. There's been some sort of a snafu where the wrong version of a letter, a presentation, or a spreadsheet was used. Many of us have gone back into email to try to find the "latest" version of some important document. Those of us with battle scars have taken to adding identification to the file itself in the form of a "V1" appendix to the regular file name. Others have settled on adding a suffix of the date to the name of the file. These strategies work when you have multiple versions to look at side-by-side but fail miserably when you can't remember what the last version was and you don't have time to hunt down all of the versions.

Luckily, SharePoint can save you from these challenges. SharePoint supports versioning for both list items and for files. You don't have to rename the file to know which version is which. Once enabled, SharePoint will automatically keep previous versions of the file – up to the limit you set – without any further action from you. This prevents the user errors that sometimes overwrite good versions of the file with bad changes, and makes it easier to be certain that you have the latest version.

Let me sidestep the conversation of document versioning for a moment, since that conversation is more detailed – and more understood. I have said that SharePoint supports versions of list items. This means that you can see who changed what in each item in a list. This can be very handy when you're trying to piece together what happened with a task, issue, or other item. Items support a simple versioning where each new version gets a new, incremental whole number. So the first version of an item is version 1, the second version is version 2, and so on.

The versioning settings are on the list or library settings page. They're important enough to get the second link from the top-left of the settings page. Enabling versioning for the list is as simple as turning on the *Enable version* option. On libraries, the versioning information allows for enhanced features beyond the basic incremental versioning supported on lists.

In addition to basic versioning, files can have major/minor versioning enabled. This versioning takes each draft (non-approved) version and assigns it a new partial number. For instance, the first version of a draft document is 0.1 and the next non-published version is 0.2. Once published, the version number is converted to a whole number. So 0.2 could be come 1.0 if the version is approved.

The implication of major/minor versioning is that the public (those with read permissions) can see the approved versions (whole numbers). Users with contribute access have access to see both the approved version as well as the current draft version.

Consider the scenario of an employee handbook. Most employees in the organization get to see the most recent approved version – and might be allowed to even see the previously approved versions. The HR department can work on the draft versions of the document in the same place that users are getting the previous approved version. When HR approves the latest draft, it immediately becomes available to all of the employees of the organization.

In some cases simply managing versions isn't enough. There are times when it's possible to overwrite the changes of another user. If all the users are connected online to SharePoint when making changes, SharePoint will prevent a second user from opening a file up for edit if another user is editing it. This is very useful because it prevents most situations where there might be problems because of users overwriting each other's work. (If both users have Office 2010, they may be given the option to co-edit the document.)

However, consider for a moment a user who is using SharePoint Workspace to take files offline. They make changes while they are disconnected on an airplane. When they synchronize back, their changes may conflict with changes made on the server while they weren't connected. While Word has a very good set of conflict resolution tools, PowerPoint and Excel – as well as non-Office files – don't have the same benefit. In this case, SharePoint does allow a user to formally check out a file. Once a file is checked out, no other user can modify the file until the file is checked in or someone discards the check out.

It's possible to require checkout on an entire document library so all files must be checked out to be edited. In practice, this is rarely used because it's generally not worth the extra hassle to have to check out the document to edit it; again, SharePoint will handle letting folks know that a document is being edited if everyone is online.

SharePoint is good at notifying users that the file is checked out. It adds a small arrow marker over the bottom right of the document icon to indicates the file is checked out. Additionally, there's a checked out field that will show the name of the user who has the file checked out. Finally, if you attempt to edit a document that is checked out, you'll receive a dialog prompt indicating that the file is checked out and isn't available for edit.

With all these features, it can be hard to decide how to best handle your situation. As a general rule, basic versioning is used in all collaborative cases where you just want to protect yourself from accidentally overwriting someone else's changes. Major/Minor versioning is used when the documents are public documents that are revised by a small group of people. As already mentioned, the require check-out feature is used for special cases where there is zero tolerance for accidentally overwriting things. Finally, every user should check out a document they intend to edit before they go offline to indicate to other users that they're intending to modify it.

The one thing that you won't have to do is append the version number to the file to manually manage the versions yourself.

How Do I Get Notified of Changes?

Knowing when something changes is a trick in any organization. Of course, the person making the change can let you know that they've done it – if they know that you need to know about the change. SharePoint can help if you're interested; neither the data nor the person who updates the data knows that you want to know about the changes. There are three basic ways that you can be notified of changes.

First, you can use Alerts. Alerts are an email that SharePoint can send immediately after a change, once a day, or once a week. The once a day and once a week options allow you to receive an aggregate list of the changes at the end of the day or week; this can be handy if you expect a lot of changes and don't need to know about them immediately. Alert emails can be set up from any list or from search results. There are a few other options, but in short, you'll receive an email notifying you of a change.

Alerts are a powerful feature for SharePoint. This solves the problem of being notified about changes in the most expedient and, in some ways, least elegant way possible. With mailboxes burgeoning with hundreds of messages a day, it isn't necessarily the best idea to add more to that. The good news is that email rules can quite effectively shunt these messages off to special folders for review later.

However, once you've shunted the alert messages off to a special folder, it might be worth asking if you need to be using emails at all. There's another facility that has become popular which can get the same effect without additional pressure on your inbox – that technology is Really Simple Syndication, more frequently referred to by the acronym RSS.

SharePoint lists and searches are capable of providing a RSS feed via a specially formatted link. This becomes a summary of the latest data in the list. It's also possible for search to provide RSS. RSS feeds – as these links are called – can be displayed directly in Internet Explorer, in Microsoft Outlook, or in dedicated news reader software.

The benefit of getting information as an RSS feed is that you can have the immediacy of an immediate alert with the efficiency of a daily or weekly alert. Immediate alerts are sent – surprisingly – immediately. That means that multiple changes will mean multiple emails. It also means that each individual change is found in a separate message. There is no summary view which can show you all of the recent changes together, as would happen with a daily or weekly alert message. An RSS feed allows you to see the summary of changes like those delayed emails with the ability to hit refresh and get immediately updated data.

Internet Explorer and Outlook allow you to track the same feeds in a shared space called the Windows Common Feed list. This means that Outlook can periodically check the RSS feeds and provide access to them offline like you would have with emails.

In short, Alerts are good if you're comfortable with emails and setting up rules. However, once you get comfortable with RSS and how it can be used in Outlook and Internet Explorer, it's likely that you'll migrate to using RSS feeds to manage rapidly changing information.

In addition to SharePoint Alerts and RSS feeds, there are other techniques you can use to get notified that something is changing. You can create workflows in SharePoint Designer which are designed to notify you only when certain criteria are met. For instance, let's say that you're a manager who has given your employees purchase order request signing authority for $1,000, but you want to know any time they submit a purchase order request for more than $250. You can create a workflow on the purchase order request document library. You can set a criterion of amounts more than $250 and have a special email sent to you. That email could contain additional information from the purchase request, including the requestor, the cost center, the vendor, etc. Anything that is promoted to the properties of the file/item can be used to form the message to you. The benefit of this is that you'll be able to better control the information you want to see without looking at the items themselves.

Whatever option you choose, SharePoint makes it easy to be notified of changes.

Choosing the Right Site Template

SharePoint Server 2010 Enterprise Edition offers 24 site templates out of the box. Trying to figure which template is the right template to create is more than a bit challenging, particularly if you've not seen the templates in use. However, after a relatively short list of yes-no decisions, you can generally identify the best fit for a given situation.

The first question to ask yourself is whether you want to configure the site from scratch. That is, do you want to go through the trouble of creating all the lists, libraries, workflow associations, etc., that you want in the site? If you're willing to do all the work yourself, you can start with a blank site. In most cases you can add everything in the other templates to the site via features once the site has been created. That being said, it's not always the best approach to take the time to manually configure things for every site you want to create.

The next key decision to ask yourself is whether the site is going to be a communication site. That is, are more people going to be reading the content than collaborating on its creation? This is sometimes a difficult question because you may want to allow many people to look at the outcome or you may want to ensure that folks have access to see the current thinking. However, in both of these cases, the key purpose for the site is the generation of the content. There's generally no "polishing" that goes on before the information goes to a wider audience. Communication sites are generally designed so that the primary activity in the site is publishing the information – which was developed elsewhere.

One specific type of communications site is a Blog (short for weB LOG). Blogs are like a journal in that they are ordered mostly by chronology, with the latest blog posts being listed first. Blogs are good replacements for emails from senior management, but they're also difficult to organize by categories. If you're trying to capture a sequential chronology then a blog is a good fit, but if not, you'll need to choose between other options.

If you decide that the site that you want is a communication site but not a blog then you must ask yourself whether the information is structured or unstructured. Structured information is important when the key criterion is the ease with which a visitor can consume the information. Structured information is easier for the visitor to consume because it follows a repeatable pattern. Unstructured data is more difficult for the visitor to consume – but sometimes the lack of structure is essential. In some cases it's impractical to create a structured data repository because you don't yet know enough about the data that you're trying to communicate. For instance, consider if you were living in a time before automobiles were common. You would have a hard time figuring out the right kinds of information to store about cars today to organize it in a way that would make sense to the 21st century consumer. If you need to learn more – or if you need to make the creation of the data more important than the possible consumption, you'll need to use some sort of unstructured approach.

On the unstructured side is the Wiki (Hawaiian for "quick"). The benefit of a Wiki is that it's easy for users to form links to other documents in the Wiki. The disadvantage is that its *ad-hoc* nature can make it difficult to locate the specific information you want – even when you know the material exists.

On the structured side of communications sites, you have SharePoint Server's publishing site templates. These templates allow you to control structured web content. The only remaining decision is whether you want the approval workflows to come out-of-the-box or whether you want to create your own approval workflows.

Going back to the top, if the site isn't a communication site then you might ask yourself whether the site is a search site. That is, is the purpose of the site to help users leverage search to find the content they want? This could include the use of facets, advanced metadata searching, or whatever is necessary to help the visitor find what they're looking for. If the site you're creating is a site for search, you'll need to further decide whether it should be a basic search center or whether the site should leverage FAST. If you've got FAST, you're likely to use it – and if you don't, well, it's probably a basic search site for you.

If the site isn't a communication or a search site, then perhaps it's a site that's designed to support a meeting. That is, SharePoint is capable of managing agenda items, action items, issues, and supporting materials for meetings. If you're looking to support a physical meeting, you may want to choose one of the SharePoint meeting templates. Like sites in general, the first question you may want to ask yourself is whether you want to configure features individually. In other words, if you want to customize the meeting site yourself, you may want to select the blank meeting site.

The next key question about meetings is whether the audience will be a large number of parties who will need to register, need directions, etc. For instance, you might decide that the company picnic fits the category of a meeting that contains a large number of people. For these types of situations, you might try the social meeting workspace.

If it is, instead, a meeting that is an operational meeting – and is therefore recurring – you might want to pick the multipage template because it will allow you to break the meetings into meaningful groups on individual pages.

The final decision to make about a meeting site is whether the site will be used primarily for the recording of decisions – a common problem in most organizations – or whether the site will be focused on the execution of the meetings. If the site is for the recording of decisions, then the decisions meeting workspace is probably more appropriate – and if not, the basic meeting workspace will probably work well.

If a site isn't for communication, search, or for a meeting, there are really only two questions left. First, if the site is for the management of a large number of documents (tens or hundreds of thousands), then you might consider a document center which will have automatically activated some of the core features that a large document library might use. Alternatively, you're talking about some sort of site that supports a team or a group of people. In SharePoint terms, a team site should be used to support key teams while the Group Work Site is designed for more transient teams that are formed, dissolved, and forgotten. The Group Work site is prepopulated with a set of lists appropriate for a temporary work team.

The diagram below demonstrates the flow of decisions to lead you to a specific template. It should be noted that this list is not exhaustive. Some templates, like the web database templates, have a very specific use and if they fit your specific needs, then by all means use them as the starting point of your site; however, there are some cases where the sites are not intended to be created directly or are not inherently more useful than one of the sites identified below.

Create a List or Library

With SharePoint's document libraries having so many features that are similar to lists – particularly the ability to store additional metadata with the file – it can be confusing to decide whether you should be creating a list or a library. There are certainly some limitations with creating a document library – but extra features as well.

The key decision to make is the number of files that a given set of data may need. You can often structure the way you look at a problem several ways, but there is generally a way that is more natural than others. In that most natural way possible, do you have situations where you need metadata without an attachment – or a need to associate multiple files with a set of metadata? In either case you'll want to use a list, since only a list can handle a situation which has data and no files – or more than one file. Libraries always store metadata with a single file.

The next set of questions pertains to features that are only available on libraries. WebDAV, or more often referred to as Explorer view, is only available for document libraries. Similarly, if you want major and minor versions – so that visitors can only see approved versions – you'll need to do a document library, since lists support only basic versioning. Similarly, libraries support folders, and while lists can have folders, this is rarely done. If you need folders, you're likely going to want to create a library.

The final considerations are related to Office client and XML. SharePoint has the capability of promoting properties in a Word document or in an XML document to properties in SharePoint automatically. This process even allows you to edit the metadata in SharePoint and have that metadata pushed back into the document. This is a powerful set of features. These features only work with document libraries. Also, the Office client applications, like Word, are only able to open document libraries and not lists – this is, of course, because there is no file to open on a list.

Since InfoPath can now be used to modify list edit forms directly, there's little reason to create a document library for InfoPath forms. If you want to create an InfoPath form to use the rules, validation, and other features of InfoPath, you can try to create the form as a list edit form first, and if the capability isn't available as a list edit form, you can create a document library with a custom InfoPath form.

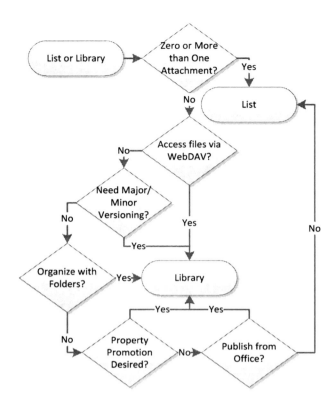

Organize with Folders or Metadata

The decision on whether to organize data with folders or with metadata is a classic problem that's been with SharePoint for many versions. The problem with this decision is that there are key limitations to both approaches, some of which require a difference in the way that you think about the problem.

For instance, in the past, using metadata for storing information in SharePoint meant that you couldn't open the files in the Office client applications because they only understood the folder hierarchy. With Office 2010 and SharePoint 2010, it's possible to see a metadata view of the files – but only if metadata navigation is turned on in SharePoint.

On the other side, there are key limitations which cause issues with file names, including folders and host names that exceed 260 characters. In those cases, the Office client applications will refuse to open the files directly; they'll have to be saved locally then opened in the Office client application – and then re-uploaded to SharePoint. Obviously, this isn't the most efficient way to operate.

The good news is that SharePoint's new features – and the new ability for Office to view metadata navigation when enabled – make it less difficult to find a balance between the two approaches.

The first deciding factor for whether or not you need to use folders for organization is whether you're using a method of access to the document library that doesn't support metadata navigation. The most common reason for this is using the Explorer view of a folder. This simply doesn't support viewing the files by metadata; it only supports a folder concept. Similarly, if users are often opening files from Office client applications directly, folders may be necessary – unless all the locations they navigate to support metadata based navigation and you can train users how to use that in the Office clients – some pretty big ifs.

The second key factor that might lead you to folders is the need to have individual security on files. Often documents in a document library have one set of security, but in some cases, it's necessary to have different permissions for different groups of documents. In this case, it's important to create folders. Performance with large numbers of access control lists falls off quickly. By organizing contents with similar security into folders, the number of unique access control lists is minimized. This can be critical for larger libraries.

There are two factors that might lead to the decision that metadata is required. The first is that not all users navigate to the data in the same way. For instance, assume you're a clothing manufacturer that makes shirts in different colors and in different sizes and styles. If some of your users navigate first by size and others navigate first by style, you'll need something other than a folder structure to allow them to navigate in ways that they're comfortable with – and that's metadata based navigation. Similarly, if you have a folder structure that would lead to more than 260 characters in the URL, you'll need to use metadata, since several problems happen once path lengths – including the host name – exceed 260 characters. Specifically, you won't be able to directly open the file in an Office client application.

If none of these criteria apply to you, then selecting either folders or metadata based navigation should work fine. The bias is that metadata based navigation is better from an information architecture perspective – but it's not enough to pull you away from a folder based structure if that's what your users are able to work with.

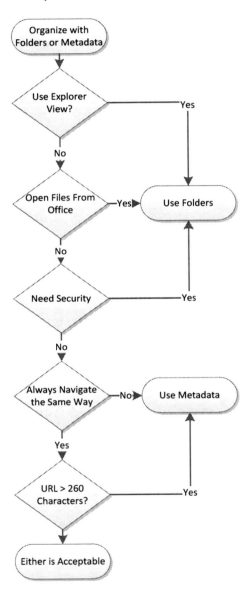

Create a Page or Site

SharePoint offers so many different ways to do things that it's often confusing to pick. This is particularly true of the question of whether to create a new page or a whole new site for something. It doesn't help that creating a page and creating a site can be done from the same dialog in SharePoint. However, there is a distinct difference between the results of creating a page versus creating a site. The decision is also essential because migrating data from one site or page to another site or page can be challenging with out-of-the-box tools.

The first question to ask is whether you're looking for a page to help provide a different view of the same data or whether the data that the page will operate on will be separate from the data in existing sites. SharePoint can easily query and display data in the same site and less easily show data in other sites in the same site collection, and even less easily show data in different site collections on the same farm. As a result, if you're looking for the page to display in a different way some data that already exists, then it's likely you want a page.

Next up is considering the navigation. Inside a site, there's one set of navigation settings. That is, the top navigation and the left navigation (Quick Launch) will be the same. As a result, if you're looking for customized navigation on the new thing that you're creating, you'll need to create a site.

It's possible to secure both a site and a page if you want, but securing the page doesn't secure the content. If there are situations that require that you have a different security structure with different groups, you'll want to create a site – more specifically a site collection. (See the decision tree for selecting a site versus a site collection for more information.)

The final consideration is a bit more difficult to quantify. That consideration is whether what you're trying to create is independent. That is, should the item be on its own because it's different enough. For instance, you might want to create a space for accounts payable inside the accounting department. If you're just listing contacts for accounts payable, it's fine to leave that in the accounting department site. However, if you want to have independent business processes like invoice payment approval, then what you're doing is probably independent enough that it should have its own site because it's going to have a lot of its own data.

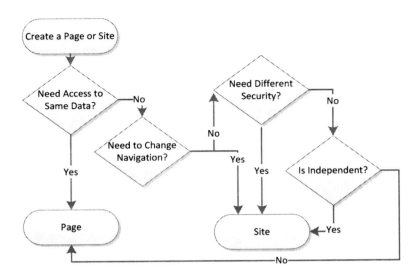

Create a Sub-Site or Site Collection

A frequent question is whether a sub-site or a site collection should be created when trying to address some new need in SharePoint. The answer is often confusing since there are advantages to keeping everything in one site collection – particularly for querying information – but there are also disadvantages, such as the amount of time necessary to backup and restore the site collection. Often you'll find that requirements will lead you to a new site collection, but there are other reasons for having unified navigation, which isn't possible when you have multiple site collections (without custom code).

The first decision to make is whether you can even choose to create a site collection. Because creating site collections requires an administrator, you'll need to have administrative rights on the server or you'll need to be able to request that the site be created. If neither of these is true, you'll need to use a site (sub-site) instead of a site collection. It doesn't matter whether it is the "right" answer or not if you can't do the alternative.

The next set of considerations is whether you need to have the separation that a site collection affords. If you need to have the chargeback for the new entity done separately, you'll need to have a separate site collection since chargebacks are nearly always accomplished at the site collection level. If your organization doesn't do chargebacks, you can answer no and proceed to answering whether you need to have separate quotas (either storage or processing) for the new site. Quotas can only be assigned at a site collection level, so if you need to have quotas set for the new site, you'll have to do a site collection.

The next two questions are about the visibility of other groups and users. In SharePoint all users of a site collection can see all of the groups in the site collection – and all of the users. So in situations where even knowing what the other groups are or who the other users are is a problem, you'll need separate site collections. For instance, it's common to create separate site collections for different customers so that your customers can't see your other customers or their employee names.

The next key question is whether the new site will be large. "Large" is relative, but certainly a site that's expected to consume more than about 20GB of storage would be considered large. Because the smallest unit of backup is the site collection, large sites shouldn't be clumped together; rather, they should remain separated as much as possible to improve recovery performance.

The next question is whether the site is independent. In other words, is the site really related? For instance, accounts payable would potentially be a sub-site of accounting (depending upon the organization's requirements), where manufacturing shouldn't be a sub-site of accounting. In general, smaller sites should be sub-sites and thereby related to the parent.

The final question is whether you need universal – that is consistent – navigation between the site you have and the new site you want to create. Each site collection has its own navigation, and synchronizing navigation across site collections can be challenging. If you need universal navigation, you're more likely to use a sub-site than a new site collection.

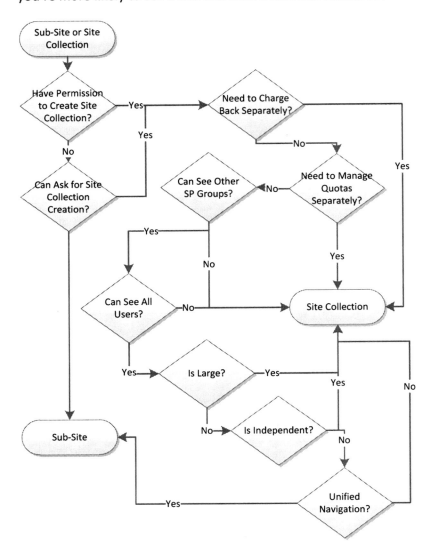

Managing Permissions with Active Directory Groups or SharePoint Groups

A common question about managing security in SharePoint is how to control the users who have – and do not have – access to the system. Obviously, individually managing permissions for individual users can be time consuming and tedious – especially if the users all fall into one or two permission levels. It is much easier to add a user to a group that has the right permissions in the right places than to establish security individually for each user. While this is clear, the question about whether or not site administrators should use SharePoint Groups or Active Directory groups isn't so clear.

It's first important to review the types of groups that SharePoint supports. The first type of group that SharePoint supports is a SharePoint group; that is to say, SharePoint knows the precise membership of the group because every user has to be manually added in SharePoint. The obvious limitation to this approach is that the group is scoped to SharePoint – it can't be used for any other purpose except for security in SharePoint. Less obvious is the fact that a SharePoint group is scoped to the SharePoint site collection it was created in. That means the group cannot be used in another site collection on the same farm.

The second type of group that SharePoint supports is an active directory group. The active directory group looks to SharePoint to be just another user during the setup of security. The group is added to permissions – or to a SharePoint group – just like any other user. The benefit of an active directory group is that it can be used across site collections and can be used outside of SharePoint. The disadvantage of an Active Directory group is that it's not easy to display the membership of the group to a user who is curious about who is in the group. Similarly, in most organizations, not everyone can add/remove members of a group; that is to say, generally, the IT administrators or the help desk must make changes to group membership. Because of this, managing Active Directory groups is generally harder for an end user than managing a SharePoint Group. However, the consistency in being able to use the group in every site collection, and by non-SharePoint applications, may mean that the extra hassle is worth it.

Making the decision between an Active Directory group and a SharePoint group isn't always as simple as it could be. The following decision tree can help you decide between an active directory group or a SharePoint Group.

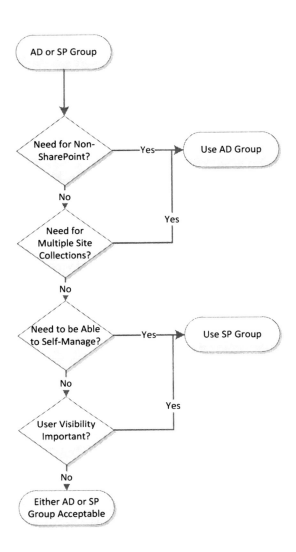

Create a Word form or an InfoPath Form

Let's face it. Most forms in your organization are Microsoft Word forms. They were created by someone to solve a need. That person, however, may not have been the most skilled in creating forms. They may not have been trained in data structures. However, they knew Word and they created a form that worked. But you've heard that InfoPath is a much better forms tool. However, should you convert all of the Word forms that exist in your organization into InfoPath forms? In a word: no.

Why shouldn't you recreate all of your forms in InfoPath? Well, because if there's no compelling reason why you should make extra work for yourself. Your users know Word. They're comfortable with the existing forms. What can you get by changing the forms over to InfoPath?

Of course, one of the benefits of InfoPath is that you can promote fields to SharePoint – but Word has the ability to promote these properties, too. The reality is that most forms aren't using the technology that's already in Word to promote properties – and that's quicker to do than creating a new form to promote properties in InfoPath. If you want to learn how to promote Word properties into SharePoint and how to make those properties easy to enter, see the whitepaper "Managing Enterprise Metadata with Content Types" Don't worry, you don't have to know content types to be able to promote properties from Word.

So let's address the opposite question: "Are there reasons to recreate forms as InfoPath forms?" In a word : yes. While Word supports basic property promotion, there are a lot of things that Word doesn't support. Chief among the benefits of InfoPath support is that Word doesn't handle one-to-many relationships in the form data. In other words, InfoPath can handle rows of data on the form. For instance, expense reports have multiple expenses and invoices have multiple lines. Sure, you won't be able to extract all of those individual lines into SharePoint—but you will be able to summarize them.

In addition, Word property promotion relies on the fields being present in the SharePoint library. This isn't an issue most of the time, but when you have a large amount of data you want to capture from the form—arbitrarily, let's say 30 fields—you may not want to publish those all fields to SharePoint. InfoPath saves its forms in the industry standard XML file format. That means many different systems can reach in and extract data from the InfoPath form – much more easily than fetching the data. If you're going to need the data from the form in another system, InfoPath may be the way to go.

What about validation and formulas? Word isn't setup to do validation—nor is it set up to do calculated values. However, InfoPath can perform these tasks. From conditionally formatting values based on their values, to blocking values that are out of range, requiring values, etc., InfoPath can help validate the information is right – if you need that.

Another situation where InfoPath may be the right answer is when you need to tie the form data to external data. Consider, for instance, that you are doing an expense report and you want to tie the expenses to a customer. It would be great to be able to make sure that the customer name entered on the form exactly matches the customer name in the sales management system. InfoPath can do this by reaching out and getting data from other systems.

There may be other factors in your decision to create an InfoPath form versus creating a Word form. However, all-in-all if you don't have any of these specialized needs you may be better off just creating a quick Word form.

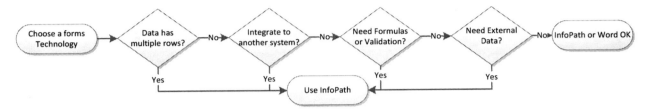

Collaborate on Projects

In any business organization, public or private, the need to effectively communicate and collaborate in a timely manner is very important. Gone are the days of paper memos, and even group e-mail has proved to be a cumbersome method of sharing information. Today, with mobile workers and shifting schedules, the tools of the Internet are the way to go. That's the overall function of SharePoint 2010: to allow users within organizations to collaborate and share work within a commonly accessed Web-site framework. These Web sites are no different than any other Web site you might visit, except that with SharePoint, they can be custom-made to perform exactly the functions you and your team need to get the job done.

The sites that SharePoint creates are designed to be used by workgroups, committees, or a whole department of workers—the choices are entirely flexible to your own organization's needs, and you can organize SharePoint sites however you wish.

Sites can hold lists of things to do, libraries of documents that need work, and discussion boards to share ideas… among other tools.

In this section, you will learn how to handle the basics of collaboration:

- **Create a Team Work Site:** Build a Team Site with which users can work.

- **Add New Users to a Team Site:** Once a new site is created, you need to allow users access to that site.

- **Create a New Group:** While SharePoint provides some basic user groups to which you can assign your users, there may be instances where you will want to create new groups with very specific permissions.

- **Assign Users to a Group:** After groups have been created, users will need to be assigned to these groups.

- **Remove Users from a Group:** In the case of an in-company move or task reassignment, you will need to quickly remove the user from their old group.

- **Edit Group Settings:** Occasionally your group will need certain changes, such as who receives requests to join or leave.

- **Remove a Group:** To prevent site clutter from occurring, you can simply remove obsolete groups from SharePoint.

Task: Create a Place for Teams to Work

Purpose: In any business organization, public or private, the need to effectively communicate and collaborate in a timely manner is very important. Gone are the days of paper memos, and even group e-mail has proved to be a cumbersome method of sharing information. Today, with mobile workers and shifting schedules, the tools of the Internet are the way to go. That's the overall function of SharePoint 2010: to allow users within organizations to collaborate and share work within a commonly accessed Web site framework. These Web sites are no different than any other Web site you might visit, except that with SharePoint, they can be customized to perform exactly the functions you and your team need to get the job done.

SharePoint creates sites that are designed to be used by workgroups, committees, or a whole department of workers. The choices are entirely flexible to your own organization's needs, and you can organize SharePoint sites however you wish.

Sites can hold lists of things to do, libraries of documents that require work or action, discussion boards to share ideas ... or one of several other lists, as well.

Before any of these tools can be put to use, you will need to start with the basics: creating a Team Site where users can start working. If you have the appropriate permissions, you can create a new site fairly easily in SharePoint.

Steps:

1. Start Internet Explorer and type the URL for your organization's SharePoint server. The Start Page will open. If you want your new site located as a sub-site of another site, navigate to that site.

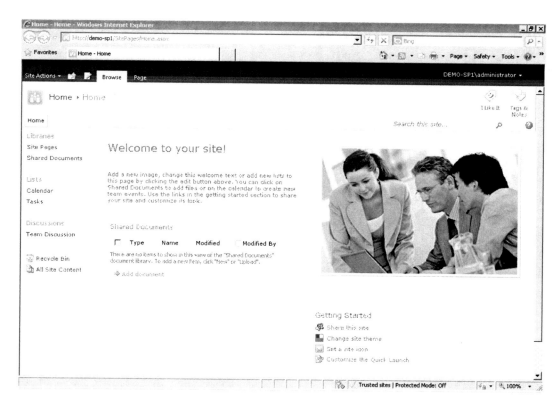

Figure 1: A Start Page for a SharePoint Site

2. Click the Site Actions drop-down control. The Site Actions menu will appear.

Figure 2: The Site Actions Menu

3. Click New Site. The Create site dialog box will open. If you do not see the New Site option, you do not have the proper authorization. Please contact your administrator.

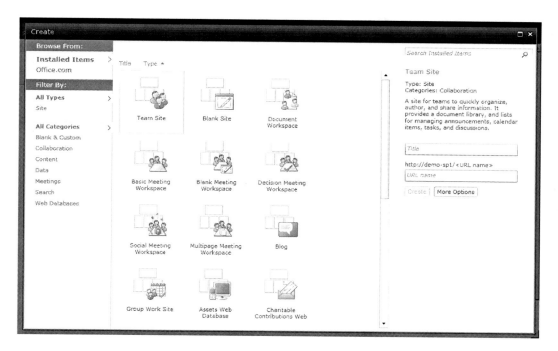

Figure 3: The Create Site Page

4. Type a title for your site in the Title field. The title of your site should be descriptive and can be up to about 50 letters before becoming intrusive. It will appear on the top of your new site, as shown in Figure 5.

5. Type a short, descriptive name for your team in the URL Name field. This will become part of the full Web Site Address for your new Team site. Some features don't work with long URLs, so keeping the names in the URL short but descriptive is recommended.

6. To add more settings for the site, click More Options. The advanced Create site page will appear.

Figure 4: The Advanced Create Site Page.

7. Type a description for your site in the Description field. The description is like a sub-title that will be displayed on some of the pages. It should further clarify the title so that anyone can understand the site's purpose.

8. In the User Permissions field, select the Use same permissions as parent site option. You can change to unique permissions later as shown in "Assign Users to a Group."

   NOTE: If the publishing feature is activated for your site the Display this site on Quick Launch and Display this site on the top link bar of the parent site are not options on the Advanced Create Site page.

9. In the Display this site on the Quick Launch of the parent site field, select the Yes option.

10. In the Display this site on the top link bar of the parent site field, select the Yes option.

11. In the Use the top link bar from the parent site field, select the Yes option.

12. Click Create. The Processing screen will briefly appear, followed by the new Team Site home page.

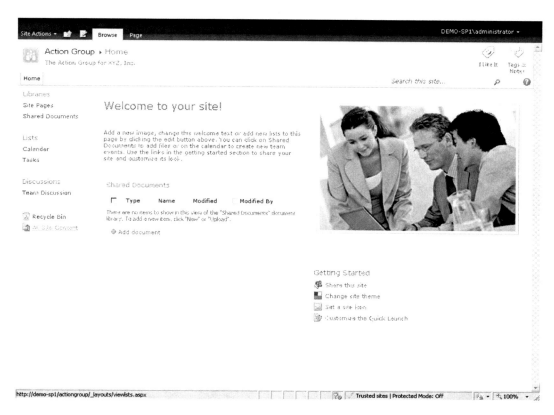

Figure 5: The New Team Site Home Page

Exceptions

The Site Actions menu or Site Settings option don't appear: You may not have permission to create sub-sites. Contact your system administrator for permission.

Task: Add New Users to a Team Site

Purpose: Once a new site is created, you need to allow users access to that site. By default, SharePoint creates three groups

> Owner: Users who can control and administrate all aspects of a team site.
> Member: Users who can contribute to the site by viewing or editing its content.
> Visitor: Users who can only view a site's content.

You can create other groups of users in SharePoint, however, these groups provide a good starting point. For the most part, you will want new users to have Member status; they can create new entries, or read and change existing entries, but they will not be able to change the layout of the pages. Nor will they be able to create new lists.

Example: Once you have created the Action Group team site, the next order of business is to grant access to the site for team members.

Steps:

1. Start Internet Explorer and type the URL for your organization's SharePoint server. The Start Page will open.

2. Navigate to the site where you want to add users. The site's home page will open.

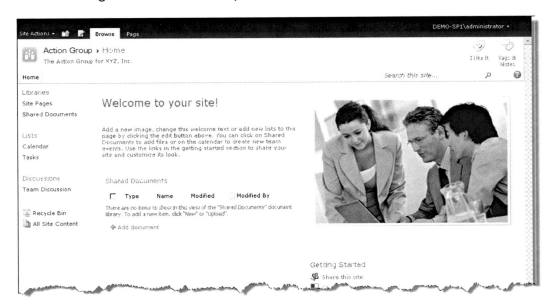

Figure 1: Your Team's Home Page

3. Click the Share this Site link on the right column under Getting Started. The Permission Tools page will open. Like most things in SharePoint, you can reach the

same place in many different ways. You can also use the Site Actions, Site Permissions menu command.

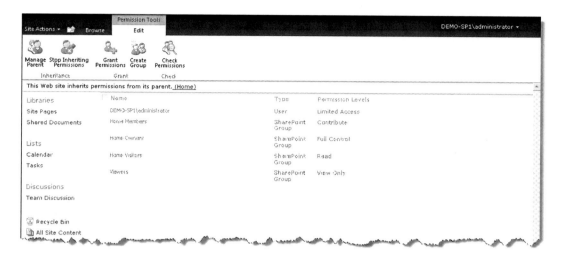

Figure 2: The Permission Tools Page

4. Click the Grant Permissions icon. The Grant Permissions dialog box will open.

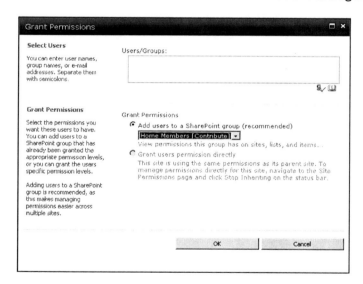

Figure 3: The Grant Permissions Dialog Box

5. At this point, you can add users to the Users/Groups field in one of two ways:

   a. Type in the name of the user in the Users/Groups field and click the Check Names icon, ✍. If the user is part of the authenticated network, their name will be underlined, which means they are authorized.

Figure 4: Authenticated Users are Underlined

b. If you don't know the full name of the user, click the Browse button to open the Select People and Groups dialog box. Type in the portion of the name you can recall and press Enter.

Figure 5: Finding People to Add

6. Select the correct user to add and click the Add button. The user will appear (authenticated) in the Add field.

Figure 6: One or Many Users Can Be Added

7. When finished, click OK to close the Select People and Groups dialog box. The found user(s) will appear in the User/Groups field.

8. Click the Add Users to a SharePoint Group radio button if it's not already selected. The option will be selected.

9. Click the drop-down list and select the <site name> Members [Contribute] group from the list of available options.

10. Click OK.

11. Click the <site name> Members link. The users will now appear on the People and Groups page.

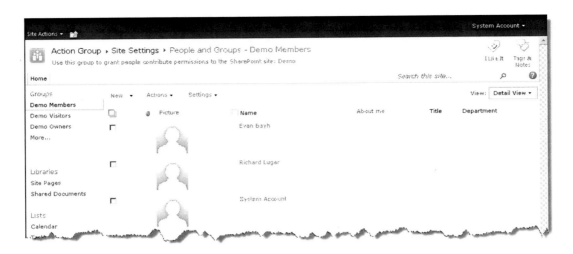

Figure 7: Users Are Now Listed in the Members Group

Exceptions

You cannot find a user: Check the spelling of the user name.

User has the wrong permissions: The user may be part of another group.

Task: Create a New Group

Purpose: While SharePoint provides some basic user groups to which you can assign your users, there may be instances where you will want to create new groups that will have different permissions.

An example of this type of group would be for team members who can only read and edit existing content. Because of your organization's workflow, you might not want them to create documents. Or, perhaps your team has members with specific functions, such as accountants, designers, or writers. You might want the writers to see and edit all of the Word and PowerPoint documents, but not necessarily the Excel spreadsheets.

When these kinds of access issues crop up, it is a big timesaver to create a unique group with specific capabilities and then assign users to that group as needed. You can even add your own permission levels, as demonstrated in "Create a Custom Permission Level."

Example: A few of your team members need to be assigned to a specific group while working with the new team site. But before they can be assigned to this group, it needs to be created.

Steps:

1. Start Internet Explorer and type the URL for your organization's SharePoint server. The Start page will open.

2. Navigate to the site where you want to add a group. The site's home page will open.

3. Click the Site Permissions option on the Site Actions menu. The Permission Tools page will open.

4. Click Create Group. The Create Group page will open.

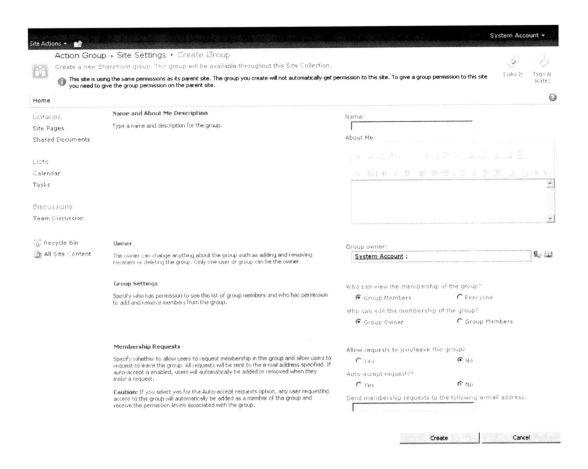

Figure 1: The Create Group Page

5. Type a name for the group in the Name field. When naming the group, consider the people that will be added, not necessarily the permissions that you'll be assigning to them.

6. Type a description for the group in the About Me field. Note that rich text editing tools are present, giving you the capability to format the description however you wish.

7. If the owner of the group is not to be you, delete your user name and enter the appropriate one in the Group Owner field. The owner will always be able to manage group membership. By changing the owner to someone else, you can allow them to modify the group. Users, such as Site Collection administrators, will also be able to modify the group membership.

8. If you want all members of your site to see who's in this group, click the Everyone radio button for the Who can view the membership of this group field. Otherwise,

leave Group Members selected. You might want to make the members private if the confidentiality of the members should be maintained.

9. Indicate who can edit members in the group by clicking the Group Owner or Group Members radio button for the Who can edit the membership of this group field. Typically only the group owner can edit group membership. However, if all of the members are highly trusted, you have the opportunity to allow any of them to modify membership.

10. Click the appropriate option to allow requests to join or leave the group. You may want to allow requests to join or leave the group if you're setting up a volunteer team to support an initiative.

11. Click the appropriate option to auto-accept requests. It is recommended that you keep this option set at No. Auto-accepting could make it difficult to manage the comings and goings of your group. However, if you are working with a volunteer group, such as those helping with the company picnic, auto-accepting requests may be appropriate.

12. If you chose to allow requests, enter the appropriate e-mail address for users to send such requests. Warning: not every server is properly configured to accept inbound email messages.

13. Click Create. The new group will appear in the People and Groups page. You can now add users, as explained in "Assign Users to a Group."

Figure 2: The New Accountant Group

Exceptions

You can't add a group name: Either the group name already exists, or you do not have permission to add a group name. Contact your site administrator for assistance.

Task: Assign Users to a Group

Purpose: After groups have been created, users will need to be assigned to these groups. Unless you have chosen to allow your group to auto-accept requests to join or leave the group, someone will need to quickly add or remove users from the group as the need arises.

Even though this might seem a bit tedious, it's a good idea for someone to act as the "gatekeeper" for a group, if only to make sure that the appropriate people are allowed in.

Example: The new Accountants group has been added to the Action Group's team site, and now you need to assign users to that group.

Steps:

1. Start Internet Explorer and type the URL for your organization's SharePoint server. The Start Page will open.

2. Navigate to the site where you want to manage a group's users. The site's home page will open.

3. Select the Site Actions, Site Settings menu command. The Site Settings page will open.

Figure 1: The Site Settings Page

4. Click the People and Groups link in the Users and Permissions group. The People and Groups page will open.

5. In the Quick Launch, click the link for the group to which you want to add users. That group's list will open.

6. Click the arrow beside New. The New menu will appear.

7. Click Add Users. The Grant Permissions dialog box will open.

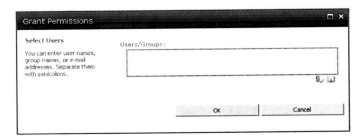

Figure 2: The Grant Permissions Dialog Box

8. Type in the name of the user in the Users/Groups field and click on the Check Names icon, 🖊. If the user is part of the authenticated network, their name will be underlined, which means they are authorized. If a user is not recognized, a red squiggly line will appear. You will need to correct the user name.

NOTE: You can also click the People Picker icon to open a directory of available users.

9. Add additional names, separating the names with semicolons.

10. Click OK. The Grant Permissions dialog box will close and the user will appear in the group list on the People and Groups page.

Figure 3: The New Group Members

Exceptions

A red squiggly line appears under user names added in the Grant Permissions dialog box. This indicated the user cannot be found.

Task: Remove Users from a Group

Purpose: Change is present in every work environment. As new people come in, veterans to an organization may find themselves moving on to different assignments, or even different jobs within the company.

When a user leaves a company altogether, their account will be removed from the various systems by the IT department. In that case, their removal from SharePoint's user roles will be automatic. But in the case of an in-company move or task reassignment, you will need to remove a user from their old group.

Example: One of the members of the Accountant group has transferred to a new team, and will need to be removed from the Action Group team site.

Steps:

1. Start Internet Explorer and type the URL for your organization's SharePoint server. The Start Page will open.

2. Navigate to the site where you want to manage a group's users. The site's home page will open.

3. Select the Site Actions, Site Settings menu command. The Site Settings page will open.

4. Click the People and groups link. The People and Groups page will open.

5. In the Groups list, click the group from which you want to remove a user. The Group page will open.

Figure 1: The Group Page

6. Click the checkbox of the user(s) you want to remove. The user is selected.

7. Click the Actions menu and select Remove Users from Group. A confirmation dialog box will open.

Figure 2: The Actions Menu

Figure 3: The Remove Users from Group Confirmation Dialog Box.

8. Click OK. The user will be removed from the group.

Task: Edit Group Settings

Purpose: Occasionally your group will need to have certain changes made, such as changing the group owner who gets requests to join or leave the group. This doesn't happen very often, but SharePoint's flexibility allows you to make such changes easily.

Example: You have been asked to provide a description to the Accountant group in the team site, to differentiate them from other Accountant groups within the company.

Steps:

1. Start Internet Explorer and type the URL for your organization's SharePoint server. The Start Page will open.

2. Navigate to the site where you want to manage a group's settings. The site's home page will open.

3. Select the Site Actions, Site Settings menu command. The Site Settings page will open.

4. Click the People and groups link. The People and Groups page will open.

5. In the Groups list, click the group you want to edit. The Group page will open.

6. Click the Settings menu and select Group Settings. The Change Group Settings page will open.

Figure 1: The Settings Menu

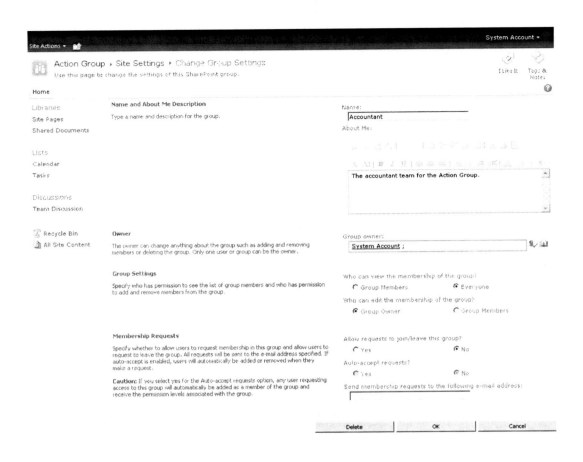

Figure 2: The Change Group Settings Page

7. Make the changes you need, then click OK. You'll find more information about the fields on this page and what they do in "Create a New Group." The changes will be applied to the group.

Task: Create a Group Work Site

Purpose: A new site template within SharePoint 2010 is the Group Work Site. At first glance, this may look and feel very much like a Team site, and there are similarities. The Group Work Site includes a Group Calendar, Circulation, Phone-Call Memo, a Document Library, and other basic lists to get things done. It can be best used as a temporary project site within a Team or company site.

Example: The Action Group has been tasked to put together a marketing campaign for XYZ's newest product. A Group Work Site will allow team members as well as other XYZ employees to collaborate on the project.

Steps:

1. Start Internet Explorer and type the URL for your organization's SharePoint server. The Start Page will open. If you want your Group Work Site located as a sub-site to another site, navigate to that site.

2. Click the Site Actions drop-down control. The Site Actions menu will appear.

3. Click New Site. The Create site dialog box will open.

4. Scroll down and select the Group Work Site icon. Values for the Group Work Site will appear in the right pane.

5. Type a title for the Group Work Site in the Title field. The title of your site should be descriptive and can be up to about 50 letters before becoming intrusive.

6. Type a short, descriptive name for your group in the URL Name field. This will become part of the full Web Site Address for your new Group Work Site. Some features don't work with long URLs, so keeping the names in the URL short but descriptive is recommended.

7. To add more settings for the site, click More Options. The advanced Create site page will appear.

8. Type a description for your site in the Description field. The description is like a sub-title that will be displayed on some of the pages. It should further clarify the title so that anyone can understand the site's purpose.

9. In the User Permissions field, select the Use same permissions as parent site option. You can change to unique permissions later as shown in "Assign Users to a Group".

10. In the Display this site on the Quick Launch of the parent site field, select the Yes option.

11. In the Display this site on the top link bar of the parent site field, select the Yes option.

12. In the Use the top link bar from the parent site field, select the Yes option.

13. Click Create. The Processing screen will briefly appear, followed by the new Group Work Site page.

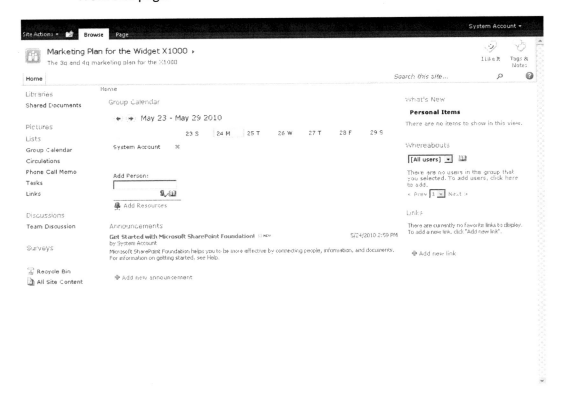

Figure 1: The New Group Work Site Home Page

Exceptions

The desired site template is not listed. You have the wrong permissions, and have a restricted set of site templates. Have your permissions adjusted for publishing sites.

Task: Remove a Group

Purpose: In SharePoint, adding groups is so simple that you might forget to keep old, unused groups from filling up your team site. To prevent such clutter from occurring, you can simply remove obsolete groups from SharePoint.

Example: The Accountant group within the Action Group has been folded into another team within XYZ. Moving forward, there's no need to identify these employees as Accountants in SharePoint, so the group will be removed.

Steps:

1. Start Internet Explorer and type the URL for your organization's SharePoint server. The Start Page will open.

2. Click the site from which you want to remove the group. The site's home page will open.

3. Select the Site Actions, Site Settings menu command. The Site Settings page will open.

4. Click the People and Groups link. The People and Groups page will open.

5. In the Groups list in the Quick Launch, click the group you want to remove. The Group's member page will open. If your group does not appear in the list, click More... to see all groups, then click the group you want to remove.

6. Click the Settings menu, and select Group Settings. The Change Group Settings page will open.

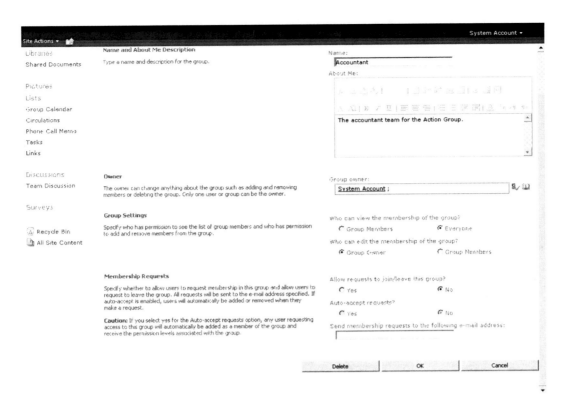

Figure 1: The Change Group Settings Page

7. On the bottom of the page, click Delete. A confirmation dialog box will open.

Figure 2: The Group Deletion Confirmation Dialog Box

8. Click OK. The Group page for the first Group appearing on the Quick Launch menu will open, with the previous group no longer appearing in the Groups list on the Quick Launch bar. Because only 3 groups are listed on the Quick Launch menu, you may need to click the More... link in order to verify that the group has been removed.

Exceptions

You can't delete the group: You may not have the correct permissions. Contact your administrator for assistance.

The SharePoint Shepherd's Guide for End Users: 2010

Discussing and Communicating Ideas

When group projects occur in the workplace, one of the old standbys for communication is the e-mail discussion. Members of a team send e-mails back and forth, going over various approaches and ideas. But e-mails can be cumbersome. Which message had the file you needed for the annual statistics? Who was replying to whom about next week's meeting? Did you hit "reply" or "reply all"?

One good way to avoid these logistical problems is to use SharePoint's discussion board feature. In a discussion board, all of the comments are in one place, for everyone to quickly see and read. Discussions are threaded so their order and flow is easier to follow.

Another useful tool is the SharePoint blog site, which enables team members to highlight events and plans in a timely manner.

In this section, you will learn how to:

- Create a Discussion Board: By default, all new team sites created in SharePoint have a discussion board, but here's how to create one of your own.

- Start a New Discussion: Once a Discussion Board has been created, it is ready to be used by any member of the groups authorized to use the team site.

- Reply to a Discussion: After a discussion is started, you can add your own comments in much the same way you would create a regular e-mail.

- Edit Discussions: From time to time, you may make a comment on a discussion board and then discover that you need to add something or change the original content of that comment.

- Delete Discussions: Once in a while, a comment might be completely in error, or applied to the wrong discussion.

- Remove a Discussion Board: Once the project is completed, you can remove the discussion board from the team site entirely.

- Create a Blog in SharePoint: How to create a Blog site in SharePoint.

- Write a Blog Entry in SharePoint: How to post entries to a SharePoint blog.

- Register a Blog with Word: Connecting a blog site to Word so blog entries can be published from Word.

- Write a Blog Entry in Word: How to post entries to a SharePoint blog from Word.

Task: Create a Discussion Board

Purpose: When group projects occur in the workplace, one of the old standbys for communication is the e-mail discussion. Members of a team send e-mails back and forth, going over various approaches and ideas. But e-mails can be cumbersome. Which message had the file you needed for the annual statistics? Who was replying to whom about next week's meeting? Did you hit "reply" or "reply all"?

One good way to avoid these logistical problems is to use SharePoint's discussion board feature. In a discussion board, all of the comments are in one place, for everyone to quickly see and read. Discussions are threaded so their order and flow is easier to follow. By default, all new team sites created in SharePoint have a discussion board, but here's how to create one of your own.

> **Caution:** SharePoint's discussion board feature isn't a replacement for a full fledged forum management or bulletin board system. It's effective for a relatively small number (less than 100) of original threads. Plan to create many individual discussion boards if you need a large number of topics.

> **NOTE:** If you create a Group Work Site, a Team Discussion board is automatically included within the site.

Example: The Action Group would like to start a discussion board for issues concerning the team's goals. This discussion board should be viewable for all visitors to the Action Group site.

Steps:

1. Start Internet Explorer and type the URL for your organization's SharePoint server. The Start Page will open.

2. Navigate to the site where you want to create a discussion board. The site's home page will open.

3. Click the Site Actions drop-down control. The Site Actions menu will appear.

4. Click More Options... The Create dialog box will appear.

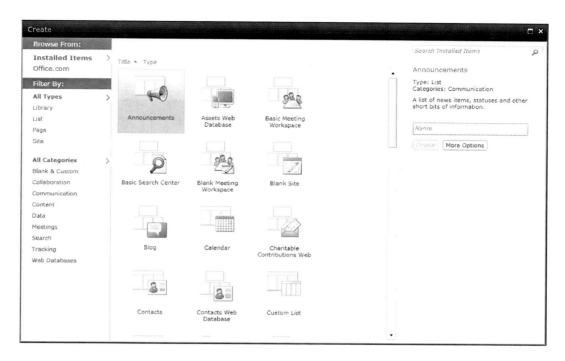

Figure 1: The Create Dialog Box

5. Scroll down and click the Discussion Board icon. The Discussion Board information will appear in the right pane.

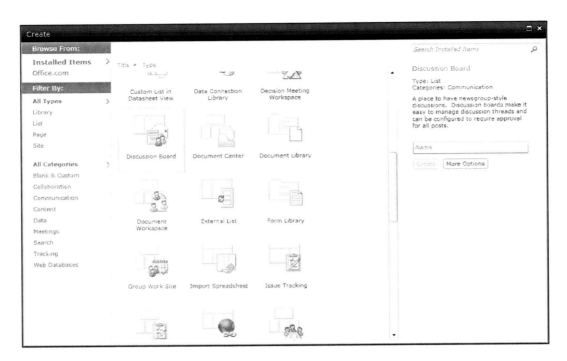

Figure 2: Selecting the Discussion Board

6. Type a name for the discussion board in the Name field.

7. Click More Options. The advanced Discussion Board Create dialog box will appear.

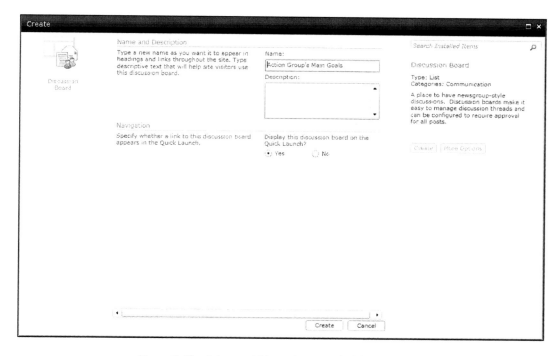

Figure 3: The Advanced Discussion Board Dialog Box

8. Enter a description for the discussion board in the Description field.

9. Click Yes to display the list on the Quick Launch. This will display a link to the discussion board in the Quick Launch.

10. Click Create. The new discussion board will open.

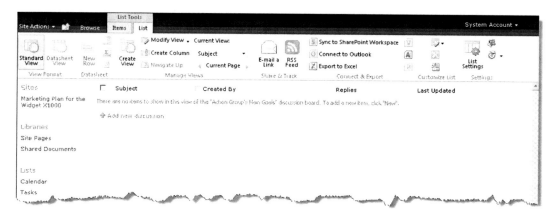

Figure 4: A New Discussion Board

Exceptions

You cannot create a discussion board. You may have the wrong permissions, or there is an existing discussion board with the same name or URL.

Task: Start a New Discussion

Purpose: Once a Discussion Board has been created, it may be used by any user authorized to use the team site. Discussions serve as topics for anyone to jump in and comment. All you need is for someone to get a discussion started.

Example: A new file relating to the yearly goals has been created, and the author wants to post it on the discussion board.

Steps:

1. Start Internet Explorer and type the URL for your organization's SharePoint server. The Start Page will open.

2. Navigate to the site where you want to participate in a discussion. The site's home page will open.

3. Click the discussion board you want to join in the Quick Launch. If the discussion board isn't listed in the Quick Launch bar, click the Discussions heading to see a listing of all discussion boards. The board's home page will open.

4. Click Add new discussion. The New Item dialog box will open.

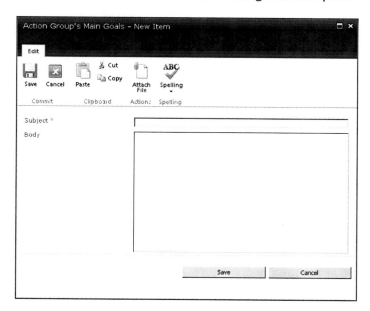

Figure 1: The New Item Dialog Box

5. Type a topic for the discussion in the Subject field. The subject field is the short description that will be displayed in the list.

---

6. Add any message you want in the Body field. The editing tools will appear. You can copy content in from a Word document, Web page, or any other source of content.

7. To attach a file, click the Edit tab, then Attach File. Another New Item dialog box will open. Each discussion item can have multiple files attached if necessary.

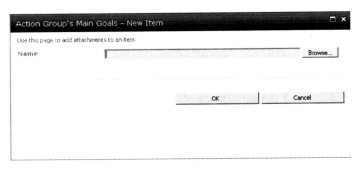

Figure 2: Attaching a New Item Dialog Box

8. Click Browse. The Choose File to Upload dialog box will open.

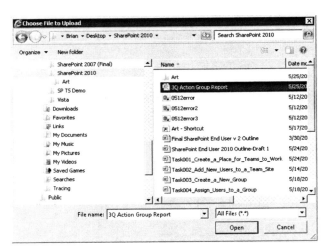

Figure 3: Locate the File to Attach

9. Navigate to the file, click on it to select it, and click Open. The Choose File to Upload dialog box will close, and the file will appear in the Name field on the New Item dialog box. .

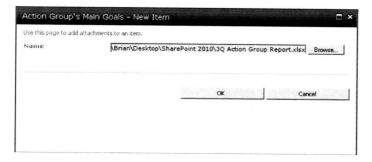

Figure 4: An Attached File on New Item Dialog Box

10. Click OK. The file will appear in the Attachments section of the New Item (discussion) dialog box.

11. Click Save. The new discussion will appear on the discussion board page.

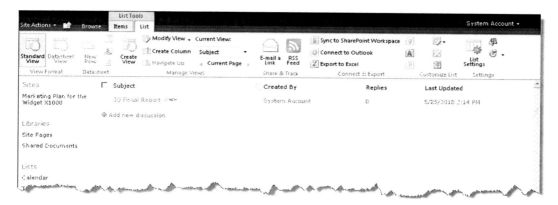

Figure 5: A New Discussion Listed on Discussion Board page

Exceptions

Attachments are disabled: You have no create permission on the discussion board list.

Task: Reply to a Discussion

Purpose: After a discussion is started, you can add your own comments in much the same way you would create a regular E-mail.

Example: As discussions begin, members of the Action Group will want to join in and deliver their own responses.

Steps:

1. Start Internet Explorer and type the URL for your organization's SharePoint server. The Start Page will open.

2. Navigate to the site where you want to participate in a discussion board. The site's home page will open.

3. Click the discussion board you want to join in the Quick Launch.

4. Click the discussion topic to which you want to respond. The discussion page will open.

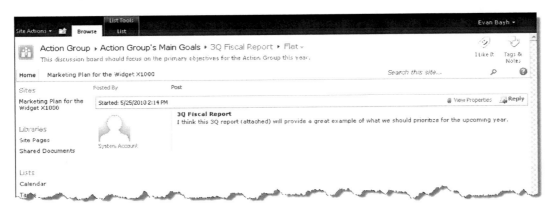

Figure 1: The Discussion Page

5. Click Reply. The New Item dialog box will open.

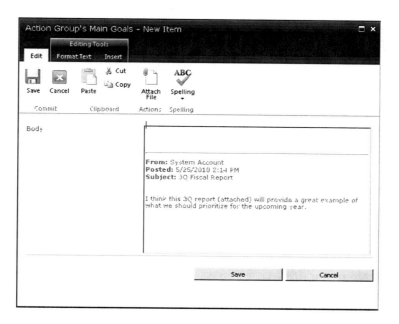

Figure 2: Reply to a Discussion

6. Add any message you want in the Body field.

   NOTE: You can copy and paste text from any source into the Body field. You can also click the Attach File button and add any relevant file to a comment in the discussion.

7. Click Save. The new comment will appear on the discussion page.

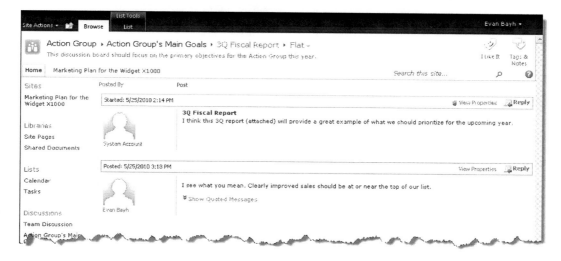

Figure 3: The Discussion Page with New Reply

Exceptions

You can't reply to a discussion: You have read only permissions and cannot create a reply.

Task: Edit Discussions

Purpose: From time to time, you may make a comment on a discussion board and then discover that you need to add something or change the original content of that comment. SharePoint lets you, if need be, edit your own comments after they have been posted.

Example: The most recent comment in the discussion has an error, and the author would like to correct the mistake as soon as possible.

Steps:

1. Start Internet Explorer and type the URL for your organization's SharePoint server. The Start Page will open.

2. Navigate to the site where you want to participate in a discussion board. The site's home page will open.

3. Click the discussion board you want to join in the Quick Launch.

4. Click the discussion topic to join. The discussion page will open.

5. Find the comment you wish to edit and click View Properties for that comment. The View dialog box will open.

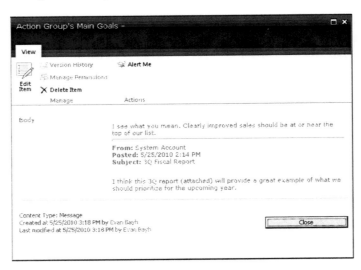

Figure 1: The View Dialog Box

6. Click Edit Item. The Editing Tools will appear.

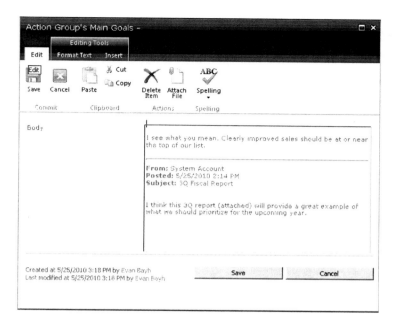

Figure 2: The View Dialog Box with Editing Tools

7. Edit the comment as needed and click Save. The edited comment will now appear in the discussion.

NOTE: If versioning is turned on for the list, prior versions of your comment will be available. Please see "Activate Version Control" for an example of how to access the version history of a SharePoint list item.

Exceptions

You can't edit your response: you have the wrong permissions. The administrator can prevent you from editing your own responses.

Task: Delete Discussions

Purpose: Once in a while, a discussion board comment might be completely in error, or applied to the wrong discussion. In those cases, you may want to remove the comment altogether.

Example: After reviewing his comments, a user decides that he has replied to the wrong discussion topic, and just wants to remove his comment from the wrong thread altogether.

Steps:

1. Start Internet Explorer and type the URL for your organization's SharePoint server. The Start Page will open.

2. Navigate to the site where you want to participate in a discussion board. The site's home page will open.

3. Click the discussion board you want to join in the Quick Launch.

4. Click the discussion topic to join. The discussion page will open.

5. Find the comment you wish to remove and click View Properties for that comment. The View dialog box will open.

6. Click Delete Item. A confirmation dialog box will open.

Figure 1: Delete Item Confirmation Dialog Box

7. Click OK. The comment will be removed from the discussion board.

Exceptions

You cannot delete a discussion: you have the wrong permissions. Contact your administrator for assistance.

Task: Remove a Discussion Board

Purpose: Depending on the activity of a team, you may find that you have to set up specific discussion boards for things like special projects. Once the project is completed, you can remove the discussion board from the team site entirely.

Example: After the feedback for the Action Group's goals has been gathered and analyzed, the site administrator decides to take the board down.

Steps:

1. Start Internet Explorer and type the URL for your organization's SharePoint server. The Start Page will open.

2. Navigate to the site with the discussion board you want to remove. The site's home page will open.

3. Click the discussion board you want to remove in the Quick Launch.

4. Click the List sub-tab in the List Tools tab. The List Tools ribbon will open.

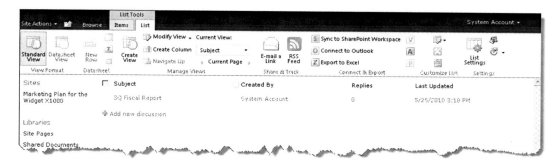

Figure 1: The List Tools Ribbon

5. Click the List Settings button. The Discussion Board Settings page will open.

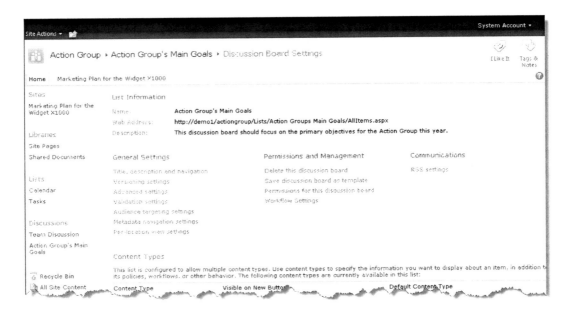

Figure 2: The Discussion Board Settings Page

6. In the Permissions and Management column, click Delete this discussion board. A confirmation dialog box will open.

Figure 3: Delete Discussion Board Confirmation Dialog Box

7. Click OK. The discussion board will be removed from the site.

Exceptions

If you can't remove the discussion board, check to see if you have the correct permissions.

Task: Create a Blog in SharePoint

Purpose: One of the fastest growing aspects of the Internet is the web log, or blog. Blogs serve as a daily (or other interval) diary of your activities, whether business or personal. SharePoint includes a blog management system to get you started on a blog right away.

Example: The Action Group wants to team members to start adding blog entries.

Steps:

1. Start Internet Explorer and type the URL for your organization's SharePoint server. The Start Page will open. If you want your Blog Site located as a sub-site to another site, navigate to that site.

2. Click the Site Actions drop-down control. The Site Actions menu will appear.

3. Click New Site. The Create site dialog box will open.

4. Scroll down and select the Blog icon. Values for the Blog Site will appear in the right pane.

5. Type a title for the Blog in the Title field. The title of your site should be descriptive and can be up to about 50 letters before becoming intrusive.

6. Type a short, descriptive name for your group in the URL Name field. This will become part of the full Web Site Address for your new Blog Site. Some features don't work with long URLs, so keeping the names in the URL short but descriptive is recommended.

7. To add more settings for the site, click More Options. The advanced Create page will appear.

8. Enter information into the appropriate fields.

9. Click Create. The new Blog home page will appear.

Figure 1: The New Blog Home Page

Task: Create a Blog Entry in SharePoint

Purpose: After you have a blog page set up, authorized users can come in and create entries within SharePoint.

Example: The Action Group team members will be writing blog entries in SharePoint.

Steps:

1. Start Internet Explorer and navigate to the Blog site.

2. Click the Create a post link under Blog Tools on the right of the page. The Posts - New Item dialog box will open.

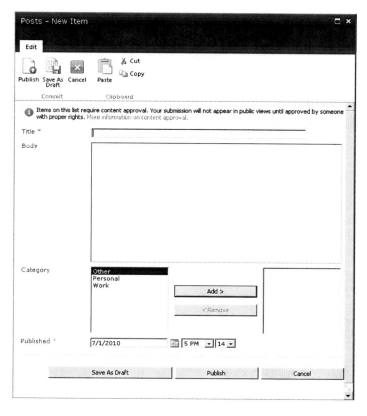

Figure 1: The Posts - New Item Dialog Box

3. Enter information into the appropriate fields.

4. Click Publish. The new blog entry will appear on the Blog home page.

Task: Register a Blog in Word

Purpose: When you create a blog page in SharePoint, you can use Word to write your blog entries, and then post directly to the blog page.

Example: The Action Group team members will be using Word to post blog entries, so they will need to connect Word to the blog page.

Steps:

1. Start Internet Explorer and navigate to the blog site you want to connect to Word. The Blog home page will open.

2. Click the Launch blog program to post link under Blog Tools on the right of the page. Microsoft Word will open with the New SharePoint Blog Account dialog box.

Figure 1: The New SharePoint Blog Account Dialog Blog

3. Click OK. A confirmation dialog box will appear.

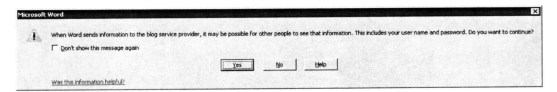

Figure 2: Confirm You Want to Share Account Information

4. Click Yes. A notification dialog box will open.

5. Click OK. The New SharePoint Blog Account dialog box will close and Word will be ready to create a new blog post.

Task: Write a Blog Entry with Word

Purpose: Once you have registered a blog in Word, creating a blog entry is very simple.

Example: Now registered to the Action Group blog, team members will begin creating blog entries in Word.

Steps:

1. In Word, click the File tab. The File window will open.

2. Click New. The Available Templates pane will appear.

3. Click Blog Post, then click Create. A Blog Post tab will open and Word will be ready to create a new blog post.

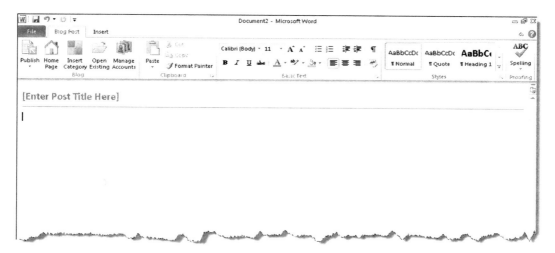

Figure 1: The Blog Post Page in Word

4. Create a blog entry.

5. Click Publish. The entry will be posted to your blog.

Conduct Effective Meetings

Collaboration comes in many forms. In the digital age, many people are encouraged to try online chats, shared document sessions, or e-mail conversations to exchange ideas. Sometimes, though, a good old-fashioned face-to-face meeting is what's needed. SharePoint can create an online home for meetings, allowing attendees to be invited, agendas to be set, and tasks to be assigned.

Before all of this can happen, a new event must be created in the SharePoint calendar. As the event is created, you can designate the creation of a meeting workspace: a special area on your team site where users can get the latest information about the meeting before and after it happens.

In this section, you will learn how to:

- **Create an Event**: The basics of creating an event are reviewed.

- **Create a Recurring Event**: Creating recurring events on your calendar is just a few steps more than creating a one-time event.

- **Create a Meeting Workspace**: Now that you have learned how to create both one-time and recurring events, you can now create a meeting workspace with just a few extra steps.

- **Create Meeting Objectives**: Once the Meeting Workspace is created, you can quickly get things organized by setting the objectives for the meeting.

- **Create a Meeting Agenda**: After you create the objectives for the meeting, it's a simple step to create the agenda for the meeting.

- **Invite Attendees**: Now all you need are the people. Here's how to invite them.

- **Make Sure Everyone's Prepared**: The meeting workspace will let you create a Things to Bring list for your meeting.

- **Assign Issues to Attendees**: As meetings progress, there are invariably assignments and tasks given to attendees.

- **Publish Key Meeting Decisions**: After the meeting is over, the organizers may want to publish some of the important decisions that came out of the get-together, to make sure everyone is communicating on the same page.

Task: Create an Event

Purpose: Collaboration comes in many forms. In the digital age, many people are encouraged to try online chats, shared document sessions, or e-mail conversations to exchange ideas. Sometimes, though, a good old-fashioned face-to-face meeting is what's needed. SharePoint can create an online home for meetings, allowing attendees to be invited, agendas to be set, and tasks to be assigned.

Before all of this can happen, a new event must be created in the SharePoint calendar. As the event is created, you can designate the creation of a meeting workspace: a special area on your team site where users can get the latest information about the meeting before and after it happens.

This task will cover the creation of a one-time event; see "Create a Recurring Event" to make events that occur with regularity. Note, these events will be added to the SharePoint calendar, not the user's calendar.

Example: A client is planning to visit the Action Group offices, and the event needs to be posted on the team's calendar.

Steps:

1. Start Internet Explorer and type the URL for your organization's SharePoint server. The Start Page will open.

2. Navigate to the site where you want to add the event. The site's home page will open.

3. Click the Calendar link in the Quick Launch for your calendar. The Calendar page will open. If the calendar you want to work with doesn't appear on the Quick Launch, you can click the All Site Content link and select the Calendar from the list that appears.

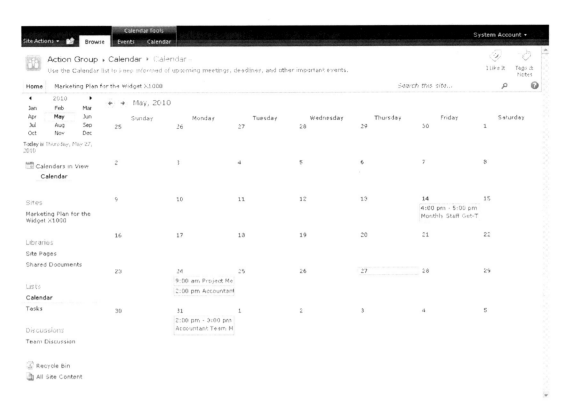

Figure 1: The Calendar Page

4. Hover over the date on which you want add the event and click the Add link when it appears. The Calendar - New Item dialog box will open.

Figure 2: Calendar - New Item Dialog Box

5. Enter the name of the event in the Title field. This description is the one typically used when looking at a summary of events, or at the events in the calendar view.

6. Enter a place for the event in the Location field. This could be the room number for a meeting, or the city, state, and country for larger events.

7. Specify the Start and End Times. It is possible to customize the list such that events don't have times associated with them. If you want to create events without times, click the Make this an all-day activity checkbox.

8. Click Save. The Calendar - New Item dialog box will close and the event will appear in the Calendar on the Calendar page.

Figure 3: The New Event on the Calendar Page

Exception

If you can't add an event to a calendar, check your user permissions.

Task: Create a Recurring Event

Purpose: Some events take place on a regular basis, such as the weekly staff meeting or the quarterly analysts briefing. Creating recurring events on your calendar requires just a few steps more than creating a one-time event.

Example: The Action Group works with several interns during the summer season, and as part of the program, a bi-weekly status meeting is needed to keep up-to-date on all interns' progress.

Steps:

1. Start Internet Explorer and type the URL for your organization's SharePoint server. The Start Page will open.

2. Navigate to the site where you want to add the event. The site's home page will open.

3. Click the Calendar link in the Quick Launch for your calendar. The Calendar page will open. If the calendar you want to work with doesn't appear on the Quick Launch, you can click the All Site Content link and select the Calendar from the list that appears.

4. Hover over the date on which you want add the event and click the Add link when it appears. The Calendar - New Item dialog box will open.

5. Enter the name of the event in the Title field. This should be a succinct description of the meeting's purpose.

6. Enter a place for the event in the Location field. Any venue can be entered here.

7. Specify the Start and End Times.

8. Click the Make this a repeating event checkbox. The recurrence controls will appear.

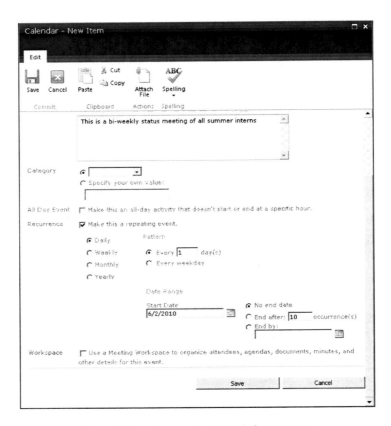

Figure 1: The Recurrence Controls for an Event

9. For a bi-weekly event, click the Weekly option. The Pattern section will change to accommodate a weekly recurrence. Each type of recurrence has its own pattern.

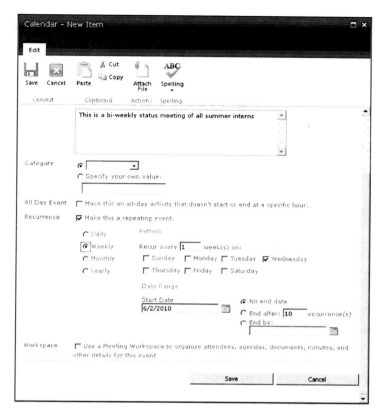

Figure 2: Weekly Recurrence Pattern

10. In the Pattern section, enter 2 in the Recur every __ week(s) field.

11. Select the Start Date for the recurring event. This is the first date when the event should appear.

12. Select an End Date option. In this case, enter a date near the end of summer.

13. Click Save. The new recurring events will appear on the calendar.

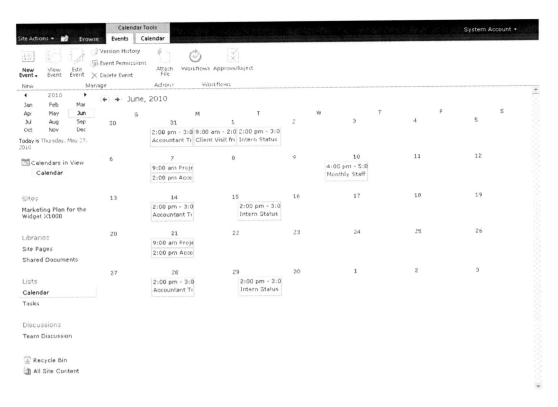

Figure 3: The New Recurring Events on the Calendar Page

Exception

If you can't add a recurring event to a calendar, check your user permissions.

Task: Create a Meeting Workspace

Purpose: The advantages of creating a meeting workspace on your team site are multifold. Ideas, materials, assignments—all are things that can be exchanged far more easily by giving meeting attendees one central place to share information. Most meetings can't stay focused over time, but SharePoint is an excellent place to keep these sorts of records, with the capability to keep track of action items, posting agendas, and creating a log of decisions.

Now that you have learned how to create both one-time and recurring events, you can create a meeting workspace with just a few extra steps.

Example: The Action Group's marketing team needs to deliver a strong marketing plan, and will want to use SharePoint to keep everyone on task.

Steps:

1. Start Internet Explorer and type the URL for your organization's SharePoint server. The Start Page will open.

2. Navigate to the site where you want to add the event. The site's home page will open.

3. Click the Calendar link in the Quick Launch for your calendar. The Calendar page will open. If the calendar you want to work with doesn't appear on the Quick Launch, you can click the All Site Content link and select the Calendar from the list that appears. If no calendars exist in the site you can create one.

4. Hover over the date on which you want to add the event and click the Add link when it appears. The Calendar - New Item dialog box will open.

5. Enter the name of the event in the Title field. This should be a succinct description of the meeting's purpose.

6. Enter a place for the event in the Location field. Any venue can be entered here.

7. Specify the Start and End Times. Remember, any meeting past an hour needs a scheduled break.

8. Add a description and set any recurrence information, if necessary.

9. Click the Use a Meeting Workspace... checkbox.

10. Click Save. The New Meeting Workspace page will open.

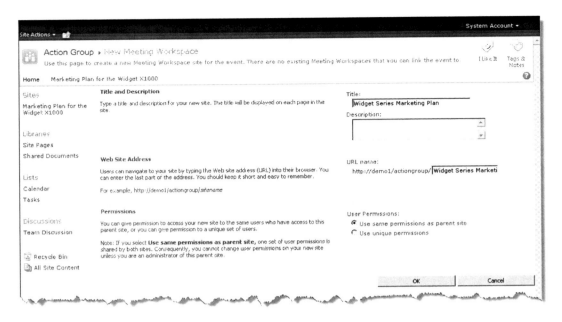

Figure 1: The New Meeting Workspace Page

11. Type a brief synopsis in the Description field.

12. Edit the URL for the Meeting Workspace in the URL name field. Make sure the URL is short and descriptive.

13. Click the Use same permissions as parent site option. You can change to unique permissions for your workspace later.

14. Click OK. The Template Selection page will open.

The SharePoint Shepherd's Guide for End Users: 2010

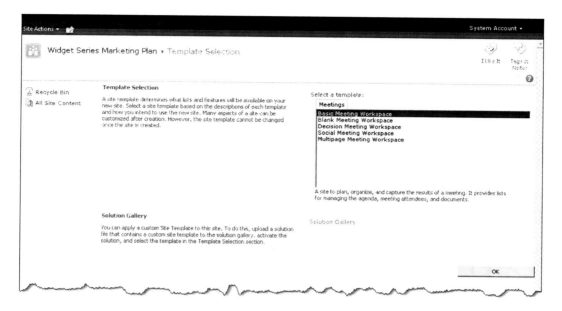

Figure 2: Meeting Workspace Template Selection Page

15. Click on one of the meeting templates:

- Basic Meeting Workspace: This is a site to plan, organize, and capture the results of a meeting. It provides lists for managing the agenda, meeting attendees, and documents.

- Blank Meeting Workspace: This is a blank meeting site for you to customize based on your requirements.

- Decision Meeting Workspace: This is a site for meetings that track status or make decisions. It provides lists for creating tasks, storing documents, and recording decisions.

- Social Meeting Workspace: This is a site to plan social occasions. It provides lists for tracking attendees, providing directions, and storing pictures of the event.

- Multipage Meeting Workspace: This is a site to plan, organize, and capture the results of a meeting. It provides lists for managing the agenda and meeting attendees, in addition to two blank pages for you to customize based on your requirements.

NOTE: Multipage meeting workspaces use a tab control which cannot be used within other sites in SharePoint. Consider carefully using the multipage meeting workspace as it may make it difficult to move or upgrade your meeting workspace.

16. Click OK. The Operation in Progress screen will appear while the new meeting site is being created, and then the Meeting Workspace page will open.

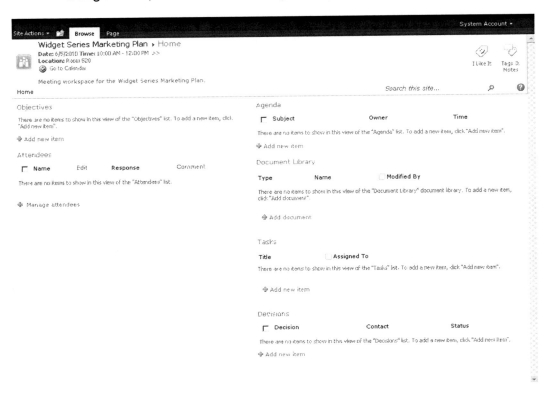

Figure 3: The New Meeting Workspace Page

Exception

If you can't create a meeting workspace, check your user permissions.

Task: Create Meeting Objectives

Purpose: Once the Meeting Workspace is created, you can quickly get things organized by setting the objectives for the meeting. Objectives can be helpful in allowing participants to better prepare for the meeting and for helping to keep participants on-task once the meeting has started.

Steps:

1. Start Internet Explorer and type the URL for your organization's SharePoint server. The Start Page will open.

2. Navigate to the site where you want to edit the meeting workspace. The site's home page will open.

3. Click the Calendar link. The site's calendar will open.

4. Click the meeting's entry on the site calendar. The meeting's calendar dialog box will open.

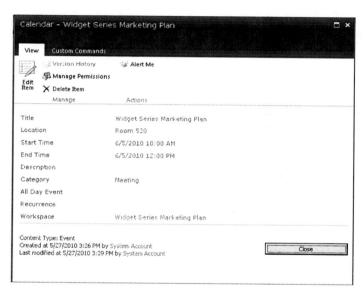

Figure 1: The Meeting's Calendar Dialog Box

5. Click the link in the Workspace section of the dialog box. The Meeting Workspace page will open.

    > **NOTE:** Alternatively, you can type the direct URL of the Meeting Workspace page into your browser, or click Sites in the Quick Launch to see a list of the available workspaces.

6. In the Objectives section, click the Add new item link. The Objectives - New Item page will open.

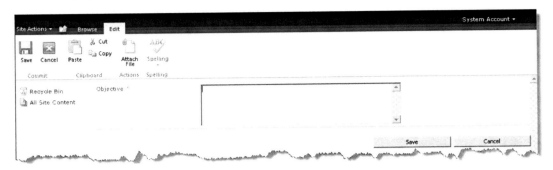

Figure 2: Creating a New Objective

7. Type a description of the goal in the Objective field.

8. Click Save. The workspace page will open, with the new objective added.

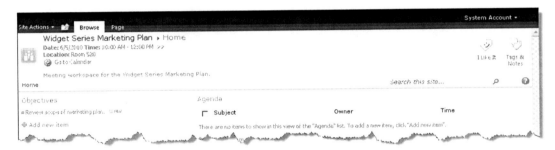

Figure 3: The New Objective on the Meeting Workspace Page

9. Add additional objectives as needed.

Task: Create a Meeting Agenda

Purpose: After you create the objectives for the meeting, it's a simple step to create the agenda for the meeting.

Example: The marketing plan objectives are set, and now a meeting agenda should be created to help facilitate.

Steps:

1. Start Internet Explorer and type the URL for your organization's SharePoint server. The Start Page will open.

2. Navigate to the site where you want to edit the meeting workspace. The site's home page will open.

3. Click the Calendar link. The site's calendar will open.

4. Click the meeting's entry on the site calendar. The meeting's calendar dialog box will open.

5. Click the link in the Workspace section of the dialog box. The Meeting Workspace page will open.

6. In the Agenda section, click the Add new item link. The Agenda - New Item page will open.

Figure 1: Agenda – New Item Page

7. Type a description in the Subject field. It should describe the topic for the agenda in brief detail.

8. Type the name of the person leading this part of the meeting in the Owner field (optional).

9. Type the duration of this section of the meeting in the Time field (optional).

10. Type any remarks in the Notes field (optional).

11. Click Save. The workspace page will open, with the new agenda item added.

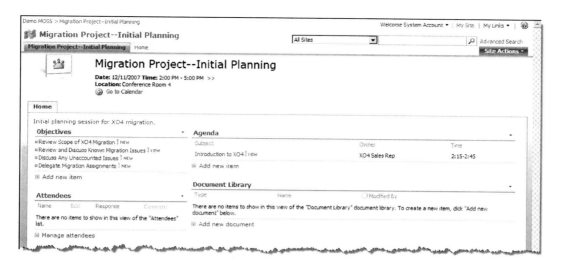

Figure 2: The New Agenda Item on the Meeting Workspace Page

12. Add additional agenda items as needed.

Task: Invite Attendees

Purpose: In a meeting workspace, you invite people to attend meetings. Not only does this let them know about the upcoming meeting so they can put it on their calendars, it also gives them permission to access the meeting workspace site. Here's how to invite users to the meeting and get them started on the meeting workspace site.

Example: You have the objectives. You have the agenda. Now all the marketing plan meeting needs is the people.

Steps:

1. Start Internet Explorer and type the URL for your organization's SharePoint server. The Start Page will open.

2. Navigate to the site where you want to edit the meeting workspace. The site's home page will open.

3. Click the Calendar link. The site's calendar will open.

4. Click the meeting's entry on the site calendar. The meeting's calendar dialog box will open.

5. Click the link in the Workspace section of the dialog box. The Meeting Workspace page will open.

6. In the Attendees section, click the Manage attendees link. The Manage Attendees page will open.

Figure 1: The Manage Attendees Page

7. Click the Items sub-tab in the List Tools tab. The Items Tools ribbon will appear.

Figure 2: The Items Tools Ribbon

8. Click the New Item button. The Attendees - New Item dialog box will open.

Figure 3: The Attendees – New Item Dialog Box

9. Type the name of the attendee in the Name field.

10. Click the Check Names icon, 🕮. The attendee will be validated against the list of users in your organization.

11. Type any notes to the attendee in the Comment field (optional).

12. If you know the attendee's availability already, make a note of it in the Response field.

13. Enter the importance of the attendee's attendance in the Attendance field.

14. Click Save. The new attendee will be added to the list of attendees.

Figure 4: The Attendees List

15. Add additional attendees as needed, starting with Step 8.

Task: Create a Things to Bring List

Purpose: The meeting workspace includes everything related to a meeting, including the ability to create a Things to Bring list.

Example: One thing that's pretty important to most meetings is that everyone arrives fully prepared to discuss the issues at hand -- that means having supporting documents, handouts, and most importantly, food. This list can be created by adding a Things to Bring list on the Meeting Workspace.

Steps:

1. Start Internet Explorer and type the URL for your organization's SharePoint server. The Start Page will open.

2. Navigate to the site where you want to add the Things To Bring list. The site's home page will open.

3. Click the Calendar link. The site's calendar will open.

4. Click the meeting's entry on the site calendar. The meeting's calendar dialog box will open.

5. Click the link in the Workspace section of the dialog box. The Meeting Workspace page will open.

6. Click the Site Actions menu and select More Options... The Create dialog box will open.

7. Scroll down and click the Things To Bring icon. The Things To Bring information will appear in the right pane.

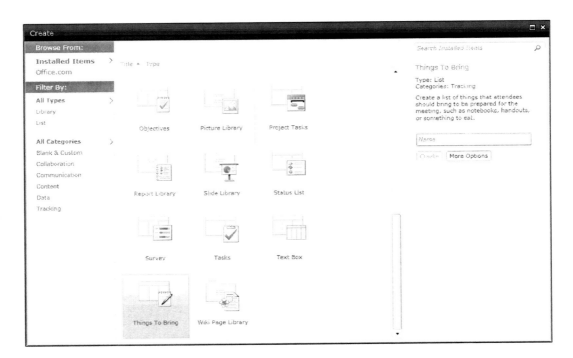

Figure 1: The Create Dialog Box

8. Enter a title for the things to bring list in the Name field. It should describe what the list signifies.

9. Click More Options. The advanced Things To Bring dialog box will appear.

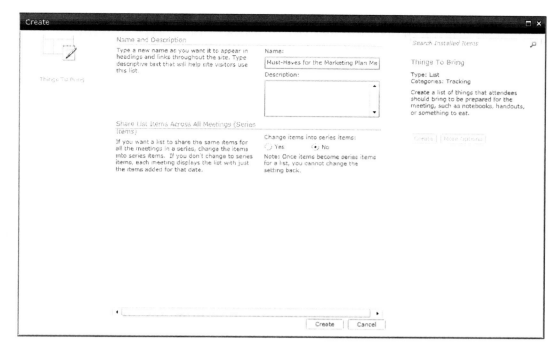

Figure 2: Detailing the Things to Bring List

10. Enter comments for the list in the Description field.

11. If the items in this Things to Bring list will be needed for every related meeting, click Yes in the Change items into series items: field.

12. Click Create. The new things to bring list will open.

Figure 3: The New Things To Bring List

13. Click the Items sub-tab in the List Tools tab. The Items Tools ribbon will appear.

14. Click the New Item button. The New Item dialog box will open.

Figure 5: The New Item Dialog Box

15. Enter a brief name in the Item field.

16. Describe the item in the Comment field (optional). Any additional information is appropriate.

17. Enter the name of the person responsible for the item in the Owner field (optional). You do not need to verify them as a user.

18. Click Save. The item will be added to the Things to Bring list.

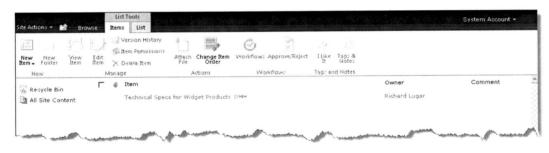

Figure 5: A New Item in the Things to Bring List

19. Add additional new items as needed.

Task: Create an Issue Tracking Page

Purpose: As any meeting progresses, there are invariably tasks given to attendees (or perhaps some lucky fellow not in attendance).

Example: Before the meeting starts, you can set up an Issue Tracking list for tracking assignments. You can then use the list as the meeting progresses to get the assignments tracked in real time.

Steps:

1. Start Internet Explorer and type the URL for your organization's SharePoint server. The Start Page will open.

2. Navigate to the site where you want to add the Issue Tracking list. The site's home page will open.

3. Click the Calendar link. The site's calendar will open.

4. Click the meeting's entry on the site calendar. The meeting's calendar dialog box will open.

5. Click the link in the Workspace section of the dialog box. The Meeting Workspace page will open.

6. Click the Site Actions menu and select More Options... The Create dialog box will open.

7. Scroll down and click the Issue Tracking icon. The Issue Tracking information will appear in the right pane.

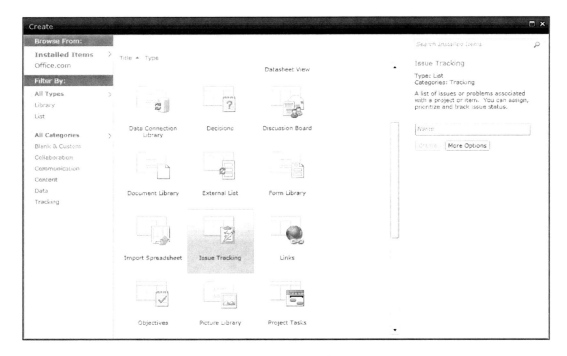

Figure 1: The Create Dialog Box

8. Enter a title for the issue tracking list in the Name field. This will appear at the top of every page for the item in SharePoint.

9. Click More Options. The advanced Issue Tracking dialog box will open.

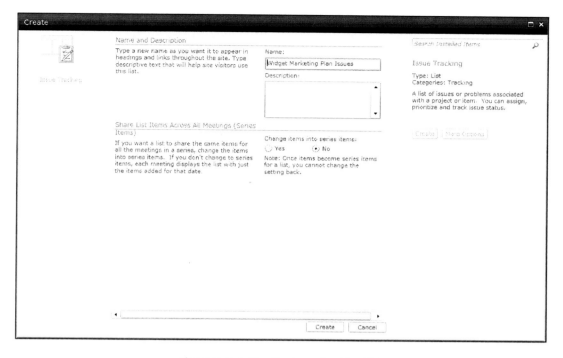

Figure 2: Detailing the Issue Tracking List

10. Enter comments for the list in the Description field. This information will appear in the View All Web Site Content page.

11. If the issues you will add to this list will be assigned in every related meeting, click Yes in the Change items into series items: field.

12. Click Create. The new Issue Tracking list will open.

Figure 3: The New Issue Tracking List

13. Click the Items sub-tab in the List Tools tab. The Items Tools ribbon will appear.

14. Click the New Item button. The New Item dialog box will open.

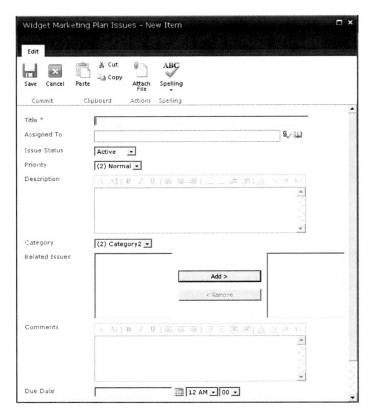

Figure 4: The New Item Dialog Box

15. Enter the issue name in the Title field.

16. If someone needs to be assigned the issue, enter their name in the Assigned To field, and click the Check Names icon, to confirm their username.

17. Select the status of the issue in the Issue Status field. This is commonly used to filter and create views of issues in different statuses.

18. Select the importance of the issue in the Priority field. This will let users know how much attention to devote to this task.

19. Type any instructions or comments about the issue in the Description field.

20. Assign an appropriate category for the issue in the Category field.

21. If there are other issues in this issue tracker related to this one, click on the issue to select, then click the Add > button in the Related Issues field.

22. Enter in additional information in the Comments field.

23. Enter a date in the Due Date field. This is particularly helpful when you're using the Gantt view of a calendar for project management.

24. Click Save. The new task will appear on the task list.

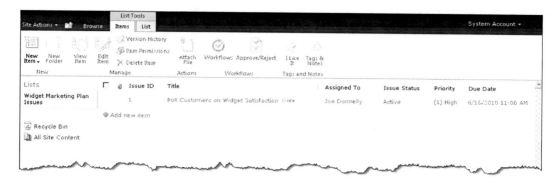

Figure 5: A New Item in the Issues Tracking List

25. Add new tasks as needed.

Task: Create a Decisions List

Purpose: After the meeting is over, the organizers may want to publish some of the important decisions that came out of the get-together, to make sure everyone is on the same page. In a meeting workspace, this is done with another list, the Decisions list.

Example: The marketing plan meeting is over, and now there's work to be done. Add decisions in the meeting workspace to convey these action items to the Action Group.

Steps:

1. Start Internet Explorer and type the URL for your organization's SharePoint server. The Start Page will open.

2. Navigate to the site where you want to add the Decisions list. The site's home page will open.

3. Click the Calendar link. The site's calendar will open.

4. Click the meeting's entry on the site calendar. The meeting's calendar dialog box will open.

5. Click the link in the Workspace section of the dialog box. The Meeting Workspace page will open.

6. Click the Add new item link in the Decisions section. The New Decisions – New Item page will open.

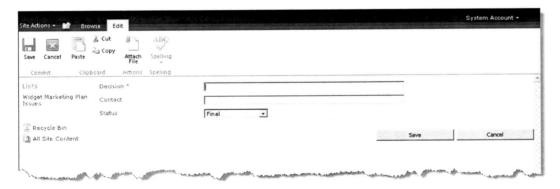

Figure 1: The Decisions – New Item Page

7. Enter the decision name in the Decision field.

8. Enter the name of the responsible person in the Contact field.

9. Select the current status of the decision in the Status field.

NOTE: There are ways to add additional information in any SharePoint item. This is done by adding columns to a list. For more information, see "Create New List Columns."

10. Click Save. The new decision will appear in the decision list on the workspace page.

11. Add new decisions as needed.

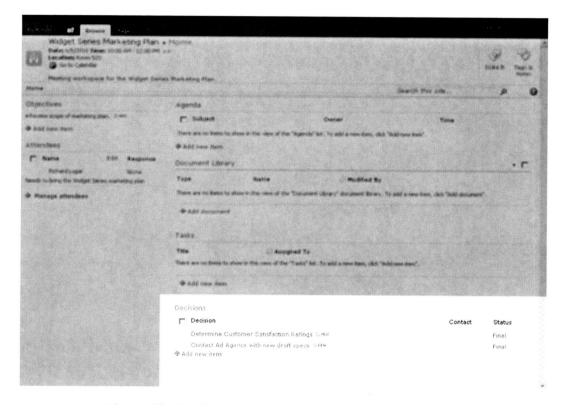

Figure 2: The New Decisions List Item on the Meeting Workspace Page

One of the biggest advantages of using SharePoint is the ability to collaborate on documents using the document workspace. Like the meeting workspace, a document workspace builds an infrastructure on the team site where users can discuss, contribute, and edit any document. SharePoint is also tightly integrated with Microsoft Office - so much so, you can use any Office application to create a document workspace.

And, while it is easy to create document workspace from within Microsoft Office, you may find yourself working on the team site and needing to create such a workspace from there. There are a few steps involved, but it's pretty straightforward. The important thing to remember here is when a new document workspace is created within Office, the document in question is automatically uploaded to the workspace site. In SharePoint, you have to create the workspace first, then upload the correct document(s) to the workspace.

In this section, you'll learn how to:

- **Create a Document Workspace in Office 2007**: The basics of creating a document workspace with Office applications.

- **Create a Document Workspace in SharePoint**: The basics of creating a document workspace within SharePoint.

- **Connect to a Document Workspace in SharePoint Workspace**: How to connect to an existing document workspace with SharePoint Workspace.

- **Open and Save Documents from Office 2010 and 2007**: You can open a document in a SharePoint site and save it again directly from Office 2010 and Office 2007.

- **Open and Save Documents from SharePoint**: You can open a document out on the document workspace, then save your changes back out onto the version on the workspace.

- **Open and Save Documents from SharePoint Workspace**: You use the SharePoint Workspace application to open a document out on the document workspace, then save your changes back out onto the version on the workspace.

- **Add Document Collaborators in Office 2007**: You can grant more users access to a document using the Document Management tools in Office.

- **Add Document Collaborators in SharePoint**: You can also grant more users access to a document in SharePoint itself.

- **Check Out a Document in Office 2010 and 2007**: If many users are working on the same document, it is better to formally check the document out while making edits, to prevent other users from overwriting your changes.

- **Check Out a Document in SharePoint**: How to check out a document from within SharePoint.

- **Check Out a Document in SharePoint Workspace**: How to check out a document from with the SharePoint Workspace application.

- **Check In a Document in Office 2010 or 2007**: After you have completed your edits on a checked out document, you will need to check it back in to the document workspace so other users can see your changes.

- **Check In a Document in SharePoint**: How to check in a document from within SharePoint.

- **Check In a Document in SharePoint Workspace**: How to check in a document from with the SharePoint Workspace application.

- **Sync Documents in a SharePoint Workspace**: Synchronize all documents within a document workspace.

- **Remove a Document Workspace**: Once a project is completed, you will want to remove the document workspace.

- **Create an Approval Workflow Association**: How a site administrator can tag a library, list, or workspace for improvement using the workflow process.

- **Save a Site as a Template**: Learn how to create a template from any site, which can be reused to create other sites.

Task: Create a Document Workspace in Office 2007

Purpose: One of the biggest advantages of using SharePoint is the ability to collaborate on documents using the document workspace. Like the meeting workspace, a document workspace builds an infrastructure on the team site where users can discuss, contribute, and edit any document. SharePoint is also tightly integrated with Microsoft Office. So much so, you can use any Office application to create a document workspace.

Example: The Action Group wants to publish an Excel 2007 spreadsheet on its team site for general viewing.

Steps:

1. Open an existing document in Microsoft Office 2007. It can be a Word, Excel, or PowerPoint document.

2. When the document is ready, click on the Office jewel in the upper-left hand corner and select Publish from the menu. The Publish sub-menu will appear.

Figure 1: The Publish Sub-Menu

3. Click Create Document Workspace. The Document Management pane will appear.

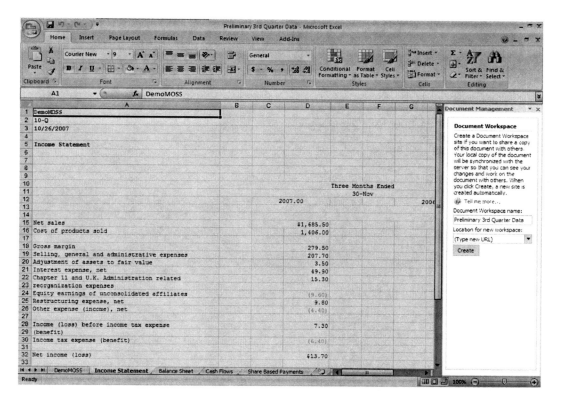

Figure 2: The Document Management Pane

4. Type a name for the document in the Document Workspace name field. This will serve as the title of the document workspace.

5. Enter the location for your new document workspace in the Location for new workspace field. If you have not connected to your SharePoint server yet, you will need to enter the URL for your SharePoint server manually.

6. Click Create. After confirming you want the document to be saved in Office, the new document workspace will be created.

7. To view the new workspace, click the Open Site in Browser link at the top of the Document Management pane. A new browser window will open the new document workspace page.

Figure 3: The New Document Workspace Page

Task: Create a Document Workspace in SharePoint

Purpose: While it is easy to create document workspaces from within Microsoft Office, you may find yourself working on the team site and needing to create such a workspace from there. The important thing to remember here is when a new document workspace is created within Office, the document in question is automatically uploaded to the workspace site. In SharePoint, you have to create the workspace first, then upload the correct document(s) to the workspace.

Example: A document that needs heavy editing should be uploaded to SharePoint, but given the need for collaboration, it should get its own workspace.

Steps:

1. Start Internet Explorer and type the URL for your organization's SharePoint server. The Start Page will open.

2. Navigate to the site where you want to add the document workspace. The site's home page will open.

3. Click the Site Actions menu and select More Options…. The Create dialog box will open.

4. Scroll down and click the Document Workspace icon. The Document Workspace information will appear in the right pane.

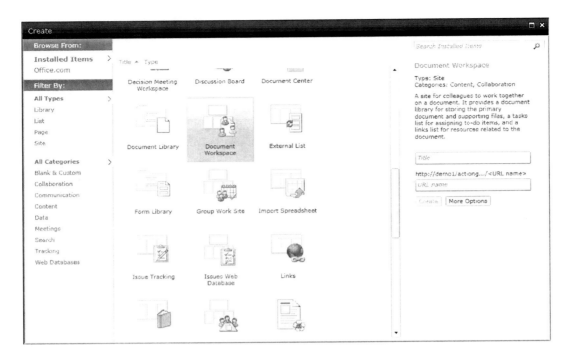

Figure 1: The Create Dialog Box

5. Enter a name for the workspace in the Title field.

6. Enter a brief label for the URL Name field.

7. Click More Options. The advanced Document Workspace create dialog box will appear.

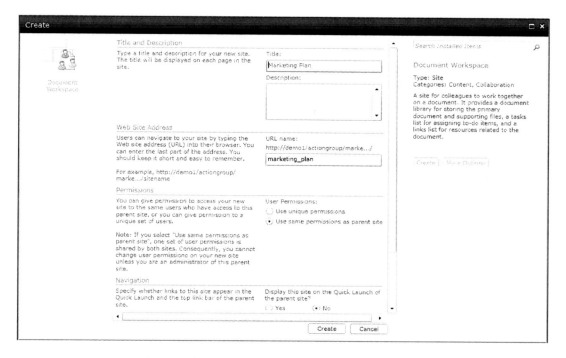

Figure 2: The Advanced Document Workspace Dialog Box

8. Enter comments for the list in the Description field. This description should give users an idea of the purpose of the workspace.

9. Type a short, descriptive name in the URL Name field.

10. In the User Permissions field, select the Use same permissions as parent site option.

11. In the Display this site on the Quick Launch of the parent site field, select the Yes option.

12. In the Display this site on the top link bar of the parent site field, select the Yes option.

13. In the Use the top link bar from the parent site field, select the Yes option.

14. Click Create. The Processing screen will briefly appear, followed by the new Document Workspace home page.

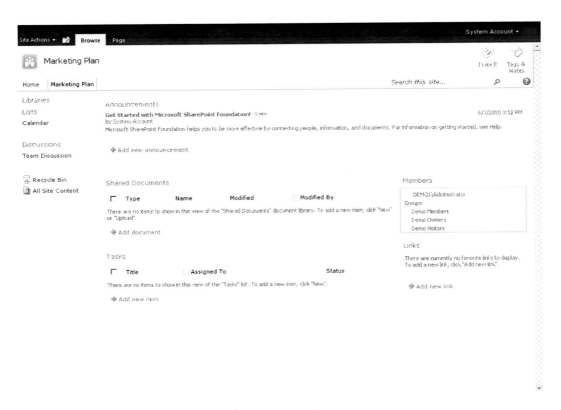

Figure 3: The New Document Workspace Page

15. In the Shared Documents Web Part, click Add document. The Upload Document dialog box will open.

Figure 4: The Upload Document Dialog Box

16. Click Browse. The Choose File to Upload dialog box will appear.

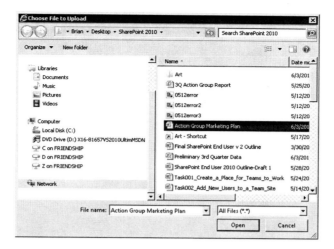

Figure 5: The Choose File to Upload Dialog Box

17. Click the document to upload, then click Open. The Choose File to Upload dialog box will close, and the full path and filename of the document will appear in the Name field of the Upload Document dialog box.

Figure 6: The Full Path and Filename in the Upload Document Dialog Box

18. Click OK. The document now appears in the Shared Documents section of the document workspace.

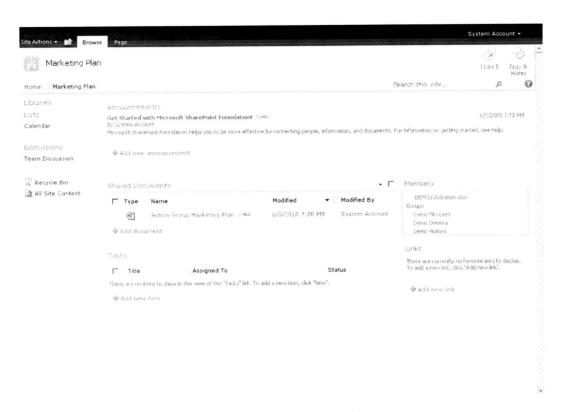

Figure 7: The New Document on the Document Workspace Page

19. Add additional documents as needed. These can be supporting documents, reference materials—any file that you believe your users will need to better create the primary document in the workspace.

Task: Connect to a Document Workspace in SharePoint Workspace

Purpose: While it is easy to create document workspaces from within Microsoft Office, you may find yourself working on the team site and needing to create such a workspace from there. The important thing to remember here is when a new document workspace is created within Office, the document in question is automatically uploaded to the workspace site. In SharePoint Workspace, you have to create the workspace first, then sync to the workspace.

Example: A document workspace has been created in SharePoint, and you would like to sync local copies of the files with SharePoint Workspace.

Steps:

1. Start SharePoint Workspace 2010 by clicking the Start | All Programs | Microsoft Office | Microsoft SharePoint Workspace 2010 menu option. The Launchbar for SharePoint Workspace will open.

Figure 1: The SharePoint Workspace Launchbar

2. Click the New button. The New menu will appear.

Figure 2: The SharePoint Workspace New Menu

3. Click SharePoint Workspace. The New SharePoint Workspace dialog box will open.

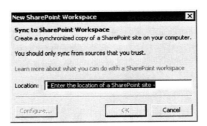

Figure 3: The New SharePoint Workspace Dialog Box

4. Type the URL for the desired workspace and click OK. The Sync to SharePoint Workspace dialog box will appear.

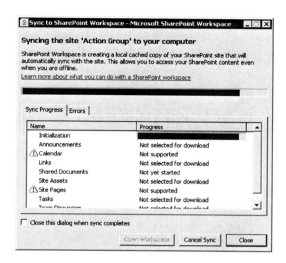

Figure 4: The Sync to SharePoint Workspace Dialog Box

5. Click Close. The Sync to SharePoint Workspace dialog box will close and the document workspace will appear in the Launchbar.

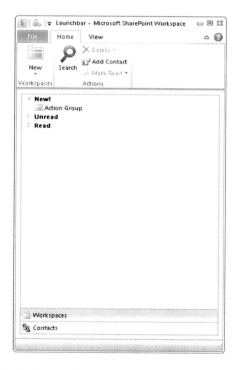

Figure 5: The Synced Document Workspace in the Launchbar

6. Double-click the document workspace name. The main SharePoint Workspace window will open, displaying the contents of the workspace.

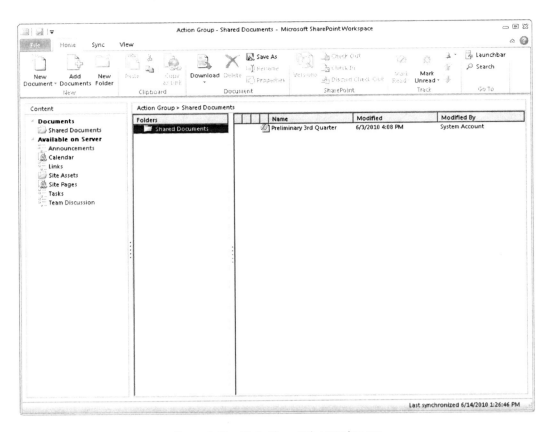

Figure 6: The Main SharePoint Workspace

Task: Open and Save Documents from Office 2010

Purpose: When you are in Office and your system is connected to the Internet, you can open a document out on the document workspace, work with it on your local computer, then save your changes in the workspace.

Example: Open the Action Group's Marketing Plan document from within Word 2010.

Steps:

1. Open an application in Microsoft Office. It can be Word, Excel, or PowerPoint.

2. Click the File tab and select Open from the menu. The Open window will appear.

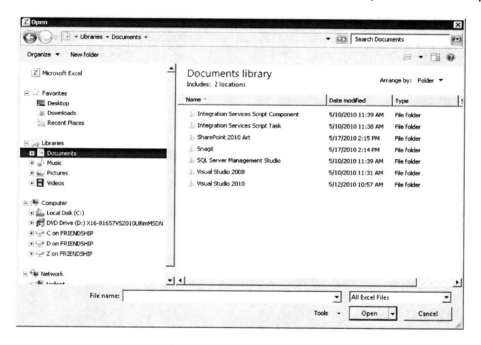

Figure 1: The Open Dialog Box

3. Type the URL for the Document Workspace you want to browse in the File name field. The All Site Content page for your document workspace will open.

4. Click the document library that contains the document you would like to edit. The document library appears in the Open dialog box.

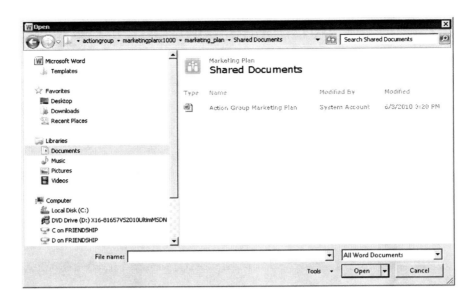

Figure 2: The Shared Documents Library Appears in the Open Dialog Box

5. Click the desired document, then click Open. The document will open in the respective Office application.

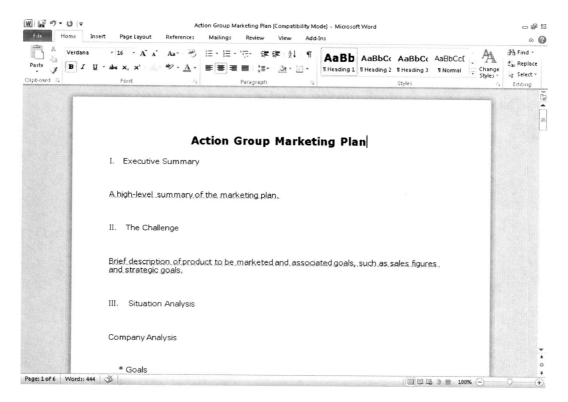

Figure 3: The Opened Document

6. Once the document editing is complete, click the File tab, then click Save. The new version of the document will be saved on the document workspace site, and the document will remain open in the Office application. If version control is activated for your workspace, you will be given a choice to save the document as a draft version or a published major version. For more information, see "Activate Version Control."

    NOTE: If you try save without checking in, you'll get a warning bar to indicate that the document is not checked in.

Task: Open and Save Documents from Office 2007

Purpose: When you are in Office and your system is connected to the Internet, you can open a document out on the document workspace, work with it on your local computer, then save your changes in the workspace.

Example: Open the Action Group's third quarter document from within Excel 2007.

Steps:

1. Open an application in Microsoft Office. It can be Word, Excel, or PowerPoint.

2. Click the Office jewel and select Open from the menu. The Open dialog box will appear.

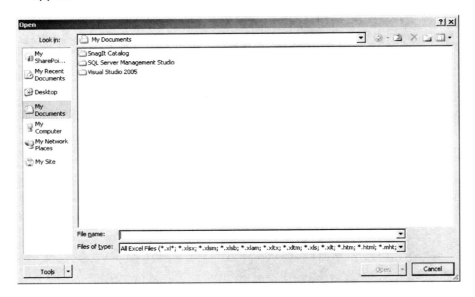

Figure 1: The Open Dialog Box

3. Navigate to the shortcut you have created for the site where your document resides. This site content page will open.

    NOTE: If you are connecting to a site you did not originally create in Office, do not click the My Site icon in the Open dialog box. Instead, click the My Network Places icon and navigate to your workspace to work with documents in a SharePoint workspace. For details on setting up a connection to an existing SharePoint workspace, see "Connect Office to a SharePoint Site or Workspace."

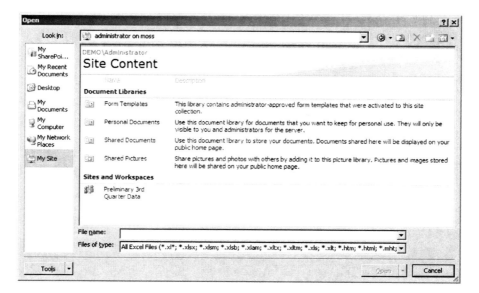

Figure 2: The Site Content in the Open Dialog Box

4. Double-click the document workspace where the document is located. The Site Content page will open.

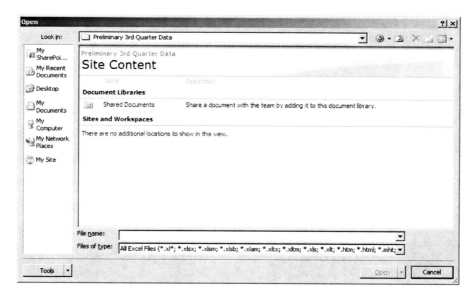

Figure 3: The Document Libraries for Your Site

5. Double-click Shared Documents. The site's Shared Documents page will open.

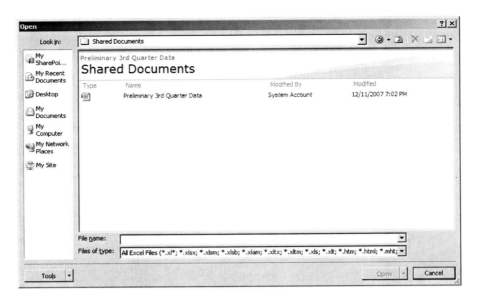

Figure 4: The Shared Documents Page

6. Click the desired document, then click Open. The document will automatically download and open in your Office application.

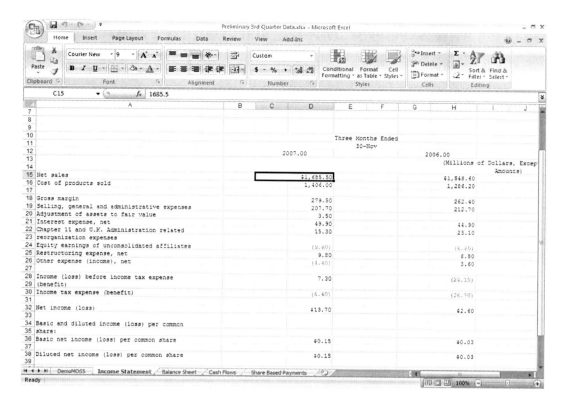

Figure 5: The Opened Document

7. Once the document editing is complete, click the Office jewel and select Save from the menu. The new version of the document will be saved on the document workspace site. If version control is activated for your workspace, you will be given a choice to save the document as a draft version or a published major version. For more information, see "Activate Version Control."

Task: Open and Save Documents from SharePoint

Purpose: If you are already working within a SharePoint site, you can open documents directly from SharePoint and view them right inside your browser.

Example: Open a spreadsheet from within SharePoint to view it, then use Excel to locally edit it.

Steps:

1. Start Internet Explorer and type the URL for your organization's SharePoint server. The Start Page will open.

2. Navigate to the document workspace where you want to edit a document. The document workspace page will open.

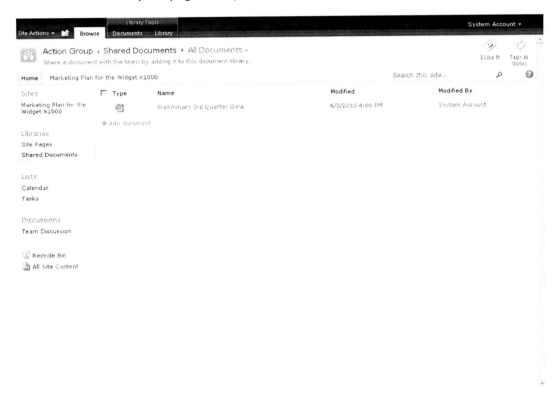

Figure 1: A Document Workspace

3. Click the link for the document. If the document workspace settings are set correctly, the document will open inside the Internet Explorer browser.

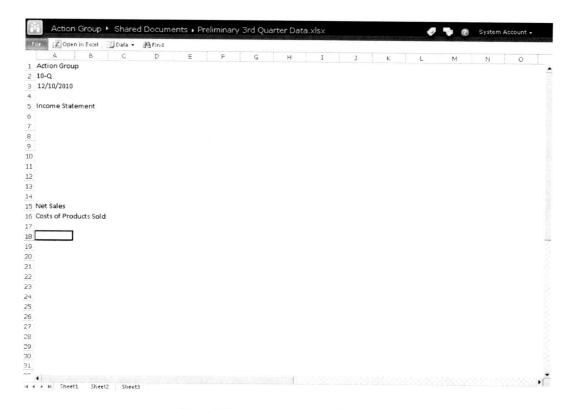

Figure 2: The Document Opened in Browser

4. To make changes, click Open in Excel. The Open Document dialog box will open.

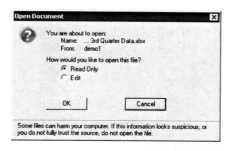

Figure 3: The Open Document Dialog Box

5. Click the Edit option, then click OK. The document will be opened in the appropriate Office application.

6. Once the document editing is complete, click the File tab and Save. The new version of the document will be saved on the document workspace site.

7. Close the document and Office Application, leaving the browser window of the document open.

8. In the browser, click the File | Reload Workbook menu command. The most recent version of the document will be displayed.

Task: Open and Save Documents from SharePoint Workspace

Purpose: If you have SharePoint Workspace 2010 installed on your computer, you can open documents directly from there and edit them inside the appropriate Office application.

Example: Open a spreadsheet from within SharePoint Workspace to view and edit it within Excel.

Steps:

1. Start SharePoint Workspace 2010 by clicking the Start | All Programs | Microsoft Office | Microsoft SharePoint Workspace 2010 menu option. The Launchbar for SharePoint Workspace will open.

2. Double-click the workspace name that contains the document you want to edit. The main SharePoint Workspace window will open, displaying the contents of the workspace.

3. Double-click the link for the document. The document will open inside the appropriate Office application.

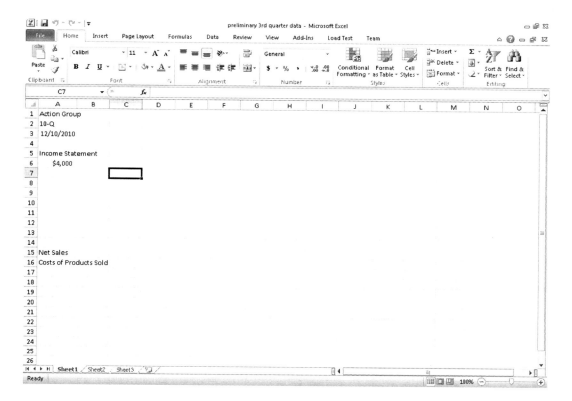

Figure 1: The Document Opened in the Appropriate Office Application

4. Once the document editing is complete, click File | Save. After confirming the Save action, the new version of the document will be saved on the document workspace site.

Task: Add Document Collaborators in Office 2007

Purpose: When a document is assigned to a workspace, the collaborators of the document are typically the same users who were originally granted access to that workspace. You can, however, grant more users access to a document using the Document Management tools in Office 2007.

Example: The third quarter data document is starting to be created, and at this time you only want to allow a few people access to it.

Steps:

1. Open an application in Microsoft Office. It can be Word, Excel, or PowerPoint.

2. Click the Office jewel and select Open from the menu. The Open dialog box will appear.

3. Navigate to the shortcut you have created for the site where your document resides. This site content page will open.

    NOTE: If you are connecting to a site you did not originally create in Office, do not click the My Site icon in the Open dialog box. Instead, click the My Network Places icon and navigate to your workspace to work with documents in a SharePoint workspace. For details on setting up a connection to an existing SharePoint workspace, see "Connect Office to a SharePoint Site or Workspace."

4. Double-click on the document workspace where the document is located. The Site Content page will open.

5. Double-click Shared Documents. The site's Shared Documents page will open.

6. Click the desired document, then click Open. The document will automatically download and open in the appropriate Office application.

7. Typically, the Document Management pane is open when you open a document from a document workspace. If it is, skip to Step 9. If it is not, click the Office jewel, and select Server. The Server sub-menu will appear.

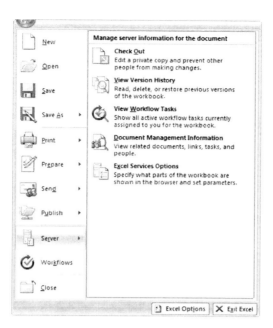

Figure 1: The Server Sub-Menu

8. Click Document Management Information. The Document Management pane will appear on the right side of the Office application.

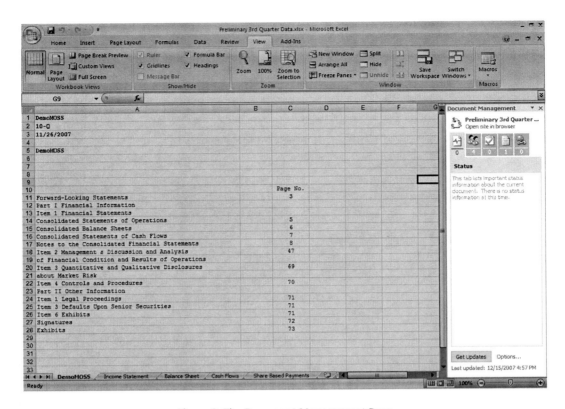

Figure 2: The Document Management Pane

9. Click the Members button. The Members tab will appear.

The SharePoint Shepherd's Guide for End Users: 2010

Figure 3: Members Information for the Document

10. Click the Add new members... link. The Add New Members dialog box will open.

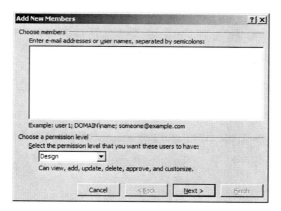

Figure 4: The Add New Members Dialog Box

11. Enter the desired user names or e-mail addresses in the Choose members field.

12. Assign user permissions for the Document Workspace in the Choose a permission level field.

13. Click Next. The confirmation page will appear.

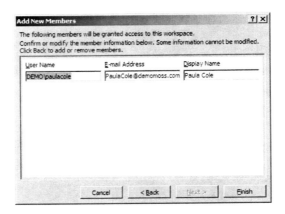

Figure 5: The New Users Confirmation Dialog Box

14. Click Finish. A confirmation dialog box will open.

Figure 6: Confirm Sending a Message to the New Users

15. Click the Send an E-mail… checkbox if you don't want an e-mail sent to the new users welcoming them to the workspace. If you leave this selected, a new window will open allowing you to edit the welcoming message.

16. Edit the welcome message in the Outlook message window and click Send, if you selected this option.

17. Click OK. The new member will appear in the Members tab of the Document Management pane.

Task: Changing Document Permissions on SharePoint

Purpose: When a document is assigned to a workspace, the collaborators of the document are typically the same users who were originally granted access to that workspace. You can, however, grant more users access to a document workspace within SharePoint itself.

Example: The marketing plan document is starting to be created, and at this time you only want to allow a few people access to it. You will want to accomplish this using SharePoint.

Steps:

1. Start Internet Explorer and type the URL for your organization's SharePoint server. The Start Page will open.

2. Navigate to the document workspace site where the document you wish to modify is located. The document workspace page will open.

Figure 1: A Document Workspace

3. Move the mouse over the document you want to edit and click the drop-down list control that appears. The document's properties menu will appear.

Figure 2: The Document Properties Menu

4. Click the Manage Permissions option. The Permissions Tools page will open.

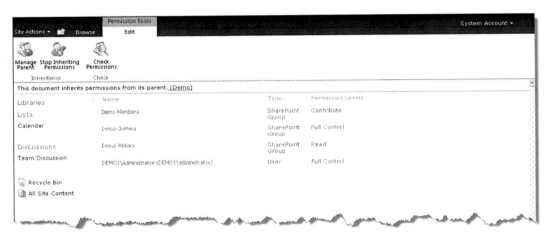

Figure 3: The Permissions Tools Page

5. Click the Stop Inheriting Permissions icon. A confirmation dialog box will appear.

6. Click OK. The confirmation dialog box will close, the document will no longer have the same permissions set, and a new set of tools will appear on the page.

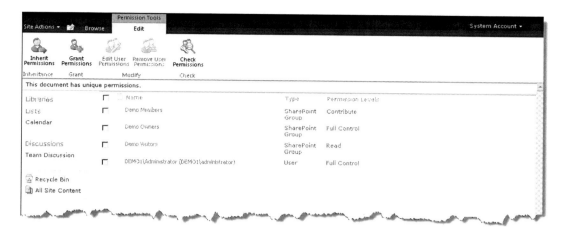

Figure 4: The Permissions Tools Page, Without Permission Inheritance

7. Click the Grant Permissions icon. The Grant Permissions dialog box will open.

8. At this point, you can add users to the Users/Groups field in one of two ways:

    a. Type in the name of the user in the Users/Groups field and click the Check Names icon, 🔍. If the user is part of the authenticated network, their name will be underlined, which means they are authorized.

    b. If you don't know the full name of the user, click the Browse icon to open the Select People and Groups dialog box. Type in the portion of the name you can recall and press Enter.

9. Select the correct user to add and click the Add button. The user will appear (authenticated) in the Add field.

10. When finished, click OK to close the Select People and Groups dialog box. The found user(s) will appear in the User/Groups field.

11. Click the Grant users permissions directly radio button if it's not already selected. The option will be selected.

12. Click permissions you wish to grant this set of users for this document.

13. Click OK. The Grant Permissions dialog box will close and the users will now appear on the Permission Tools page. Repeat Steps 7-13 to grant other users different permission levels.

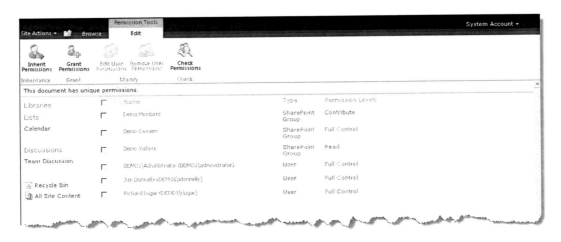

Figure 5: New Users Listed in the Permissions Tools Window.

14. Click the checkboxes for all of the users and groups you do not want to have access. The users and groups will be selected.

15. Click the Remove User Permissions icon. A confirmation dialog box will appear.

16. Click OK. The confirmation dialog box will close and the user(s) will be removed from the user list.

Task: Check Out a Document in Office 2010

Purpose: When a document is being edited from a document workspace, a user can quickly open the document, make changes, and then save the document back into the workspace. If many users are working on the same document, however, it is better to formally check the document out while making edits, to prevent other users from overwriting your changes. You also may be required to check out documents as required by a library's properties. Here's how to check out a document in Office 2010.

Example: When you have a document opened from a SharePoint document workspace, you can check it out from the Office application.

Steps:

1. Open an application in Microsoft Office. It can be Word, Excel, or PowerPoint.

2. Click the File tab and select Open from the menu. The Open window will appear.

3. Type the URL for the Document Workspace you want to browse in the Location field. The All Site Content page for the document workspace will open.

4. Click the desired document, then click Open. The document will open in the appropriate Office application.

5. Click the File tab and select Info from the menu. The Info window will appear.

Figure 1: The Document Info Window

6. Click the Manage Versions button, then click the Check Out option. The document will be checked out to you, but will remain stored on the SharePoint system.

Task: Check Out a Document in Office 2007

Purpose: When a document is being edited from a document workspace, a user can quickly open the document, make changes, and then save the document back into the workspace. If many users are working on the same document, however, it is better to formally check the document out while making edits, to prevent other users from overwriting your changes. You also may be required to check out documents as required by a library's properties. Here's how to check out a document in Office 2007.

Example: When you have a document opened from a SharePoint document workspace, you can check it out from the Office application.

Steps:

1. Open an application in Microsoft Office. It can be Word, Excel, or PowerPoint.

2. Click the Office jewel and select Open from the menu. The Open dialog box will appear.

3. Navigate to the shortcut you have created for the site where your document resides. This site content page will open.

   NOTE: If you are connecting to a site you did not originally create in Office, do not click the My Site icon in the Open dialog box. Instead, click the My Network Places icon and navigate to your workspace to work with documents in a SharePoint workspace. For details on setting up a connection to an existing SharePoint workspace, see "Connect Office to a SharePoint Site or Workspace."

4. Double-click the document workspace icon where the document is located. The Site Content page will open.

5. Double-click Shared Documents. The site's Shared Documents page will open.

6. Click the desired document, then click Open. The document will automatically download and open in the appropriate Office application.

7. Click the Office jewel and select Server from the menu. The Server sub-menu will appear.

8. Click Check Out. The Edit Offline dialog box will appear.

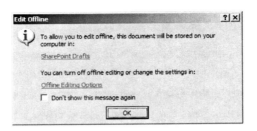

Figure 1: The Edit Offline Dialog Box

9. Click OK. The document will be checked out and a copy saved in the \My Documents\SharePoint Drafts folder on your local system.

Task: Check Out Documents in SharePoint

Purpose: When a document is being edited from a document workspace, a user can quickly open the document, make changes, and then save the document back into the workspace. If many users are working on the same document, however, it is better to formally check the document out while making edits, to prevent other users from overwriting your changes.

Example: Here's how to check out the Action Group Marketing Plan from within SharePoint.

Steps:

1. Start Internet Explorer and type the URL for your organization's SharePoint server. The Start Page will open.

2. Navigate to the document workspace site where the document you wish to modify is located. The document workspace page will open.

3. Move the mouse over the document you want to edit and click the drop-down list control that appears. The document's hover menu will appear.

4. Click Check Out. A notification dialog box will appear.

Figure 1: The Check Out Notification Dialog Box

5. Click OK. The document will be checked out and saved to your \Documents\SharePoint Drafts folder on your local system.

Task: Check Out Documents in SharePoint Workspace

Purpose: When a document is being edited from a document workspace, a user can quickly open the document, make changes, and then save the document back into the workspace. If many users are working on the same document and some have a need to edit offline, however, it is better to formally check the document out while making edits offline, to prevent other users from overwriting your changes.

Example: Here's how to check out the Action Group Marketing Plan from SharePoint Workspace.

Steps:

1. Start SharePoint Workspace 2010 by clicking the Start | All Programs | Microsoft Office | Microsoft SharePoint Workspace 2010 menu option. The Launchbar for SharePoint Workspace will open.

2. Double-click the workspace name that contains the document you want to edit. The main SharePoint Workspace window will open, displaying the contents of the workspace.

3. Select the document you want to check out.

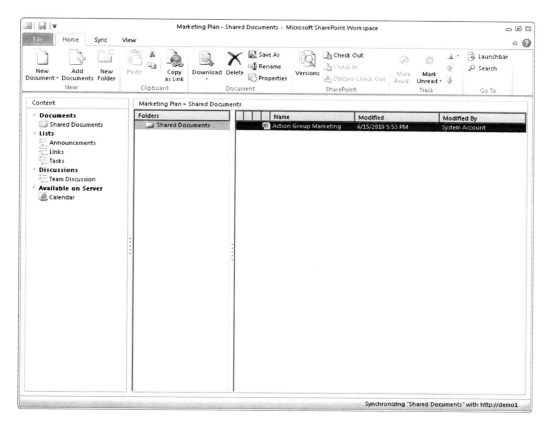

Figure 1: Highlighted Document in SharePoint Workspace Window

4. Click Check Out. The document will be checked out to you.

    NOTE: You can also right-click the document and select the Check Out option.

5. Double-click the document to open it in the appropriate Office application and edit as needed.

Task: Check In a Document in Office 2010

Purpose: After you have completed your edits on a checked out document, you will need to check it back in to the document workspace so others can see your changes, as well as edit the document themselves.

Example: Once the document is edited by you, you can quickly check it in within Office 2010.

Steps:

1. Open an application in Microsoft Office. It can be Word, Excel, or PowerPoint.

2. Click the File tab and select Open from the menu. The Open window will appear.

3. Type the URL for the Document Workspace you want to browse in the Location field. The Site Content page for your shared document site will open.

4. Click the desired document, then click Open. The document will open in your Office application.

5. When your edits are complete, click the File tab and select Info from the menu. The Info pane will appear.

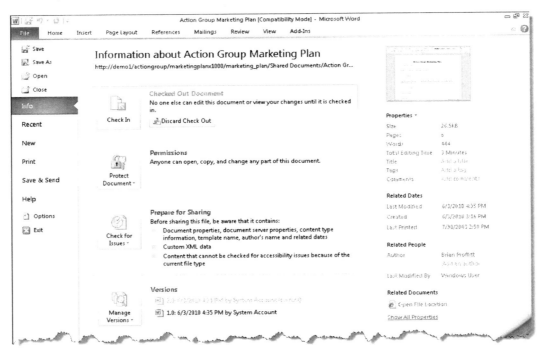

Figure 1: The Document Info Pane

6. Click the Check In icon. The Check In dialog box will appear.

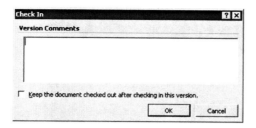

Figure 2: The Check In Dialog Box

7. Enter any notes in the Version Comments field.

8. Click OK. The document will be checked back in to the document workspace. Although the document has been checked in the document will remain open, but read-only.

Task: Check In a Document in Office 2007

Purpose: After you have completed your edits on a checked out document, you will need to check it back in to the document workspace so others can see your changes, as well as edit the document themselves.

Example: Once the document is edited by you, you can quickly check it in within Office 2007.

Steps:

1. Open an application in Microsoft Office. It can be Word, Excel, or PowerPoint.

2. Click the Office jewel and select Open from the menu. The Open dialog box will appear.

3. Double-click the SharePoint Drafts folder in My Documents. The folder's content will appear.

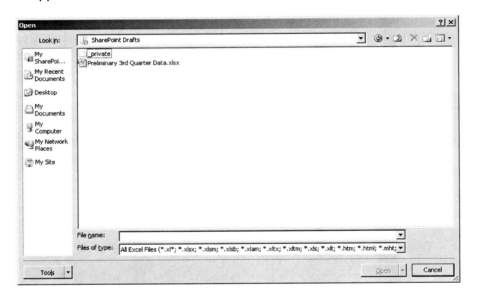

Figure 1: The SharePoint Drafts folder in the Open Dialog Box

4. Click the desired document, then click Open. The document will open in your Office application.

5. When your edits are complete, open the Document Management pane by opening the Office jewel, Server, Document Management Information menu option and click the Check in... link. The Check In dialog box will appear.

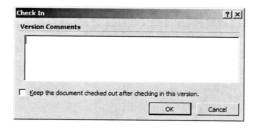

Figure 2: The Check In Dialog Box

6. Enter any notes in the Version Comments field.

7. Click OK. The document will be checked back in to the document workspace.

Task: Check In Documents in SharePoint

Purpose: After you have completed your edits on a checked out document, you will need to check it back in to the document workspace so others can see your changes and/or edit the document themselves.

Example: Here's how to check in the Marketing Plan document from within SharePoint.

Steps:

1. Start Internet Explorer and type the URL for your organization's SharePoint server. The Start Page will open.

2. Navigate to the document workspace site where the document you wish to modify is located. The document workspace page will open.

3. Move the mouse over the document you want to edit and click the drop-down list control that appears. The document's hover menu will appear.

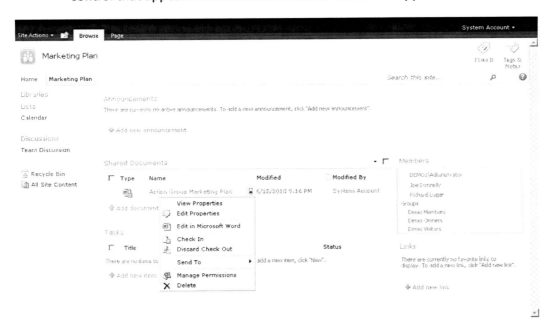

Figure 1: The Document's Hover Menu

4. Click Check In. The Check In dialog box will appear.

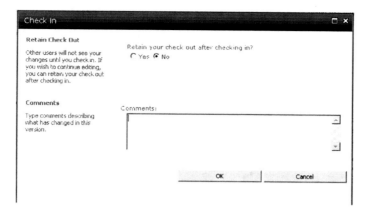

Figure 2: The Check In Dialog Box

5. Choose if you want to keep the document checked out after checking in this version in the Retain Check Out section. You would do this if you made a major change in the document and wanted to be sure that others can see the change while you continue to work.

6. Type any notes about this version of the document in the Comments field.

7. Click OK. A confirmation dialog box will appear.

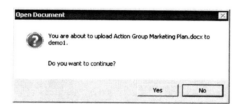

Figure 3: The Confirmation Dialog Box Confirming Upload of the Document

8. Click Yes. The document will be checked in.

Task: Check In Documents in SharePoint Workspace

Purpose: After you have completed your edits on a checked out document, you will need to check it back in to the document workspace so others can see your changes and/or edit the document themselves.

Example: Here's how to check in the Marketing Plan document from within SharePoint Workplace.

Steps:

1. Start SharePoint Workspace 2010 by clicking the Start | All Programs | Microsoft Office | Microsoft SharePoint Workspace 2010 menu option. The Launchbar for SharePoint Workspace will open.

2. Double-click the workspace name that contains the document you want to edit. The main SharePoint Workspace window will open, displaying the contents of the workspace.

3. Select the document you want to check in.

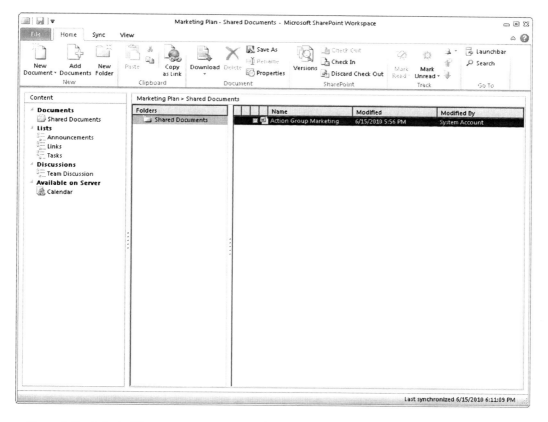

Figure 1: the Selected Document You Want to Check In in the Main SharePoint Workspace Window

4. Click Check In or right click the file and click the Check In option. The Check In dialog box will appear.

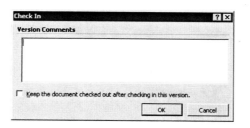

Figure 2: The Check In Dialog Box

5. Type any notes about this version of the document in the Comments field.

6. Click OK. The document will be checked in.

Task: Sync Documents in SharePoint Workspace

Purpose: One of the useful capabilities of SharePoint Workspace is being able to synchronize all documents within a document workspace.

Example: After working offline for quite some time, you will want to synchronize the changes in your local documents with any changes made in the online versions, using SharePoint Workplace.

Steps:

1. Start SharePoint Workspace 2010 by clicking the Start | All Programs | Microsoft Office | Microsoft SharePoint Workspace 2010 menu option. The Launchbar for SharePoint Workspace will open.

2. Double-click the workspace name that contains the document you want to edit. The main SharePoint Workspace window will open, displaying the contents of the workspace.

3. Click the Sync tab. The Sync toolbar will appear.

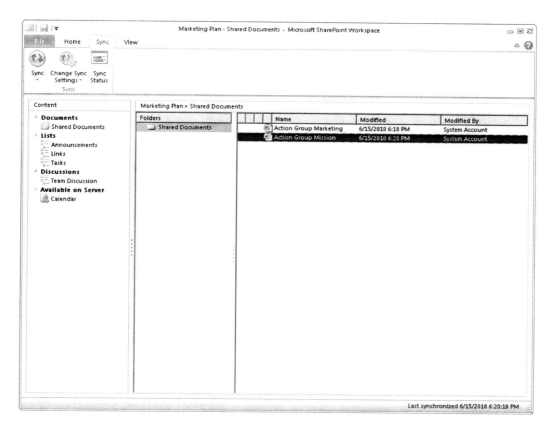

Figure 1: The Sync Toolbar in a Document Workspace

4. Click Sync. All documents within the workspace will be synchronized with their online versions.

Task: Edit SharePoint Workspace Synchronization Settings

Purpose: When creating a SharePoint workspace, you may wish to disconnect from these lists or libraries so that they no longer use storage space on your system, or spend needless resources synchronizing content with the server. This is done by editing the synchronization settings.

Example: The team member will disconnect a list or library from the SharePoint site, removing its downloaded content from the downloaded SharePoint workspace.

Steps:

1. Start SharePoint Workspace 2010 by clicking the Start | All Programs | Microsoft Office | Microsoft SharePoint Workspace 2010 menu option. The Launchbar for SharePoint Workspace will open.

2. Double-click the workspace name to change the synchronization settings. The main SharePoint Workspace window will open, displaying the contents of the workspace.

3. Click the Sync tab. The Sync toolbar will appear.

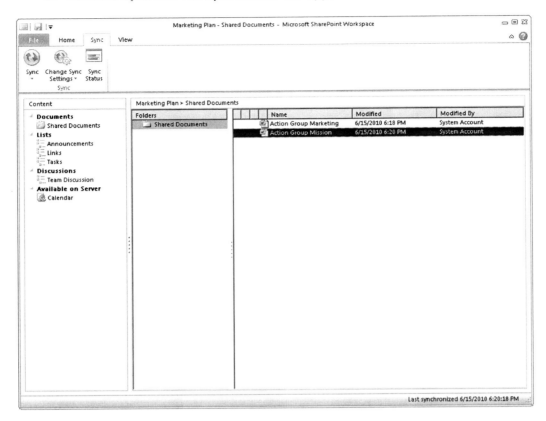

Figure 1: The Sync Toolbar in a Document Workspace

4. Click Change Sync Setting. The Disconnect message will appear.

5. Click the disconnect message. A Warning dialog box will open.

6. Click Yes. The library or list will be disconnected from the Workspace application.

Task: Remove a Document Workspace

Purpose: Once a project is completed, you will want to back up the relevant documents. You can also shift documents to another location on your SharePoint site for archival purposes. Either one of these methods is very important, because you never know when you will need to retrieve a document.

Example: After backing up/archiving your documents, you may also want to remove the document workspace, as shown in this task.

Steps:

1. Start Internet Explorer and type the URL for your organization's SharePoint server. The Start Page will open.

2. Navigate to the document workspace you want to remove. The Document Workspace home page will open.

3. Click the Site Actions menu and select Site Settings. The Site Settings page will open.

Figure 1: The Site Settings Page

4. Click the Delete this site link in the Site Actions section. The Delete This Site page will open.

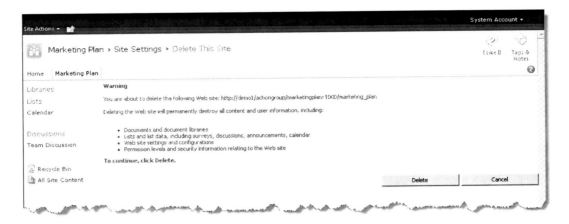

Figure 2: The Delete This Site Page

5. Click Delete. A confirmation dialog box will appear.

6. Click OK. The document workspace and all of the documents stored within it will be removed from the SharePoint site.

NOTE: You will receive an error if sub sites or workspaces exist on the site or document workspace you are trying to delete. Be sure all sub sites and workspaces are deleted before removing the workspace.

Figure 3: The Document Workspace is Deleted

7. Click the Go back to site link. The root site for the site collection will open.

Task: Create an Approval Workflow Association

Purpose: All Web sites need nearly constant revision in order to maintain accuracy and freshness. At any time, a site administrator can tag a library, list, or workspace for improvement using the workflow process.

Example: Documents within the document library need to be assigned a specific workflow so the improvement process can be regulated.

Steps:

1. Start Internet Explorer and type the URL for your organization's SharePoint server. The Start Page will open.

2. Navigate to the document library that needs a workflow started.

3. In the Library Tools tab, click the Library sub-tab. The Library Tools ribbon will open.

4. Click the Library Settings button. The Document Library Settings page will open.

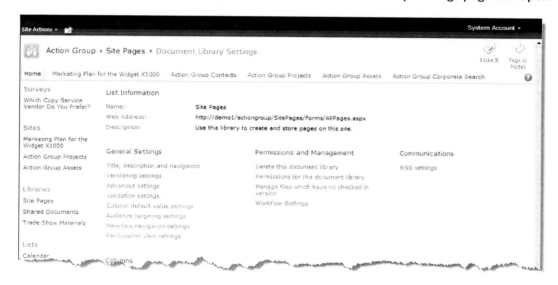

Figure 1: The Document Library Settings Page

5. Click the Workflow Settings link. The Add a Workflow page will open.

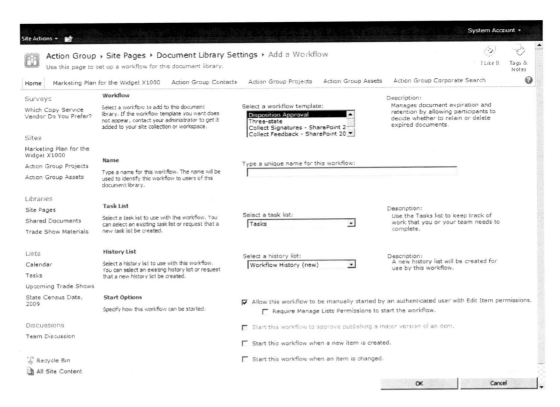

Figure 2: The Add a Workflow Page

6. Click the Approval – SharePoint 2010 option in the Workflow section.

    NOTE: Workflows for sites must be set up by the system administrator. If you do not have any workflows available, contact the administrator and discuss what workflow templates you would like to have activated.

7. Enter a title for the workflow in the Name field.

8. Select New task list in the Task List section.

9. Click the Start this workflow when a new item is created checkbox.

10. Click OK. The Change a Workflow page will open.

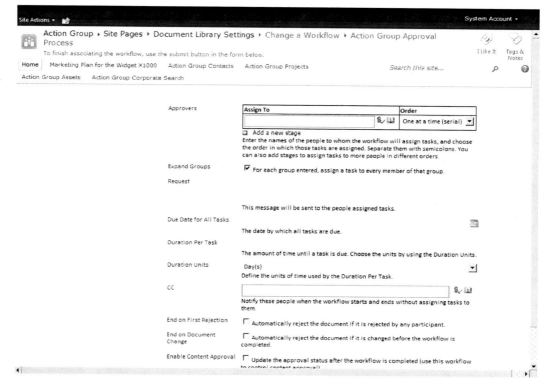

Figure 3: The Change a Workflow Page

11. Type in the name of any users or group you want to follow along in the approval process in the Approvers field and click on the Check Names icon, 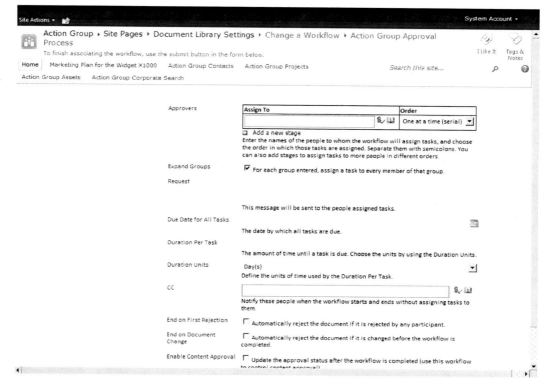. If the user or group is part of the authenticated network, their name will be underlined, which means they are authorized. If a user or group is not recognized, a red squiggly line will appear. You will need to correct the user or group name.

12. Set the Duration Per Task value to 2.

13. Click the Automatically reject the document if it rejected by any participant checkbox.

14. Click the Update the approval status after the workflow is completed… checkbox.

15. Click Save. The Workflow Settings page will appear with the new workflow added.

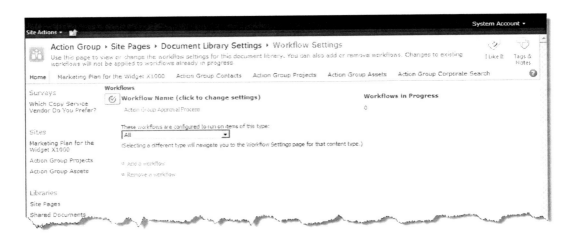

Figure 4: The Workflow Settings Page

The SharePoint Shepherd's Guide for End Users: 2010

Task: Save a Site as a Template

Purpose: Once you have a site created to your specifications, you can save the site as a template to use for future site projects.

Example: The Action Group will save their site as a template to use later for other teams in the XYZ Corporation.

Steps:

1. Start Internet Explorer and type the URL for your organization's SharePoint server. The Start Page will open.

2. Navigate to the site to be templated. The site's home page will open.

3. Click the Site Actions menu and select Site Settings. The Site Settings page will open.

4. In the Site Actions section, click the Save site as template link . The Save as Template page will open.

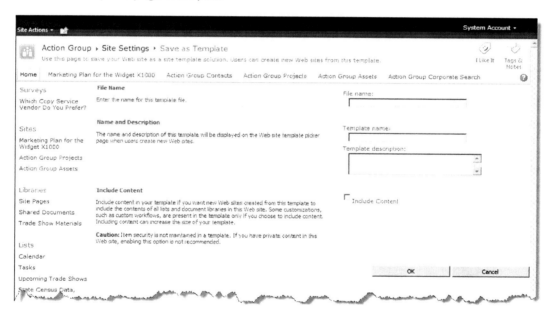

Figure 1: The Save as Template Page

5. Enter the pertinent information in the Name and Description fields.

6. Unless the site's content is highly specialized, click the Include Content checkbox.

7. Click OK. The site will be saved as a template for later use in SharePoint.

Manage Lists

Like a library, a list in SharePoint is a valuable tool for organizing data. Many of the tools built into SharePoint are specialized lists: Announcements, Contacts, Calendar, Tasks, and Surveys are just a few. But if none of the existing tools work for you, you can quickly build a new, custom list that collects exactly the kind of data you need.

In this section, you'll learn how to:

- Create a Custom List: The basics of creating a custom list.

- Import a Spreadsheet to Create a List: Rather than retyping all of the data into SharePoint, you can quickly import an Excel spreadsheet and create a list.

- Create a New List Item: Once you have a list created, you can add items to that list fairly quickly.

- Create New List Columns: When you add columns to the list, you are also providing additional fields to enter information.

- Edit Existing List Columns: Besides adding new columns to a list, you can also edit existing columns in case you need to make a correction or change.

- Delete List Columns: If a column in your list proves to be unnecessary, you can remove it from the list altogether.

- Edit a List in Datasheet View: You can shift to Datasheet view, which looks and functions very similarly to a spreadsheet, allowing you to edit a lot of list data at once.

- Subscribe to a List RSS Feed: If you are interested in a list, they can subscribe to an RSS feed that will notify them or other users when a list's content has changed.

- View List Item Properties: You can easily see a list item's information on the item's properties page.

- Edit List Item Properties: When you need to edit one item in a list, you don't have to use the datasheet view.

- Manage List Item Permissions: Occasionally, you may need to adjust an item's permissions to make sure only the right people are allowed to edit it.

- Edit a List View: By default, lists are displayed in a certain way within SharePoint. You can change these aspects of a list's view very easily.

- **Add a List View**: It is possible to create whole new list views, just the way you want them, rather than heavily modifying the All Items view.

- **Delete a List Item**: If you need to remove an item from a list, it's a quick operation.

Task: Create a Custom List

Purpose: Like a document workspace, a list in SharePoint is a valuable tool for organizing data. Many of the tools built into SharePoint are specialized lists: Announcements, Contacts, Calendar, Tasks, and Surveys are just a few examples of specially-formatted SharePoint lists. But if none of the existing tools work for you, you can quickly build a new, custom list that collects exactly the kind of data you need.

Example: The Action Group wants to create a collaborative list of trade shows that team members will be attending or participating in during the coming year.

Steps:

1. Start Internet Explorer and type the URL for your organization's SharePoint server. The Start Page will open.

2. Navigate to the site where you want to add a custom list. The site's home page will open.

3. Click the Site Actions menu and select More Options... The Create dialog box will open.

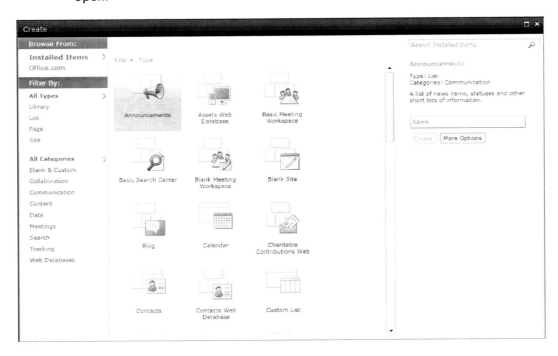

Figure 1: The Create Dialog Box

4. Click the Custom List icon. The Custom List information pane will appear.

5. Enter a title for the new list in the Name field. This is used to identify the list throughout SharePoint.

6. Click More Options. The Advanced Custom List Create dialog box will appear.

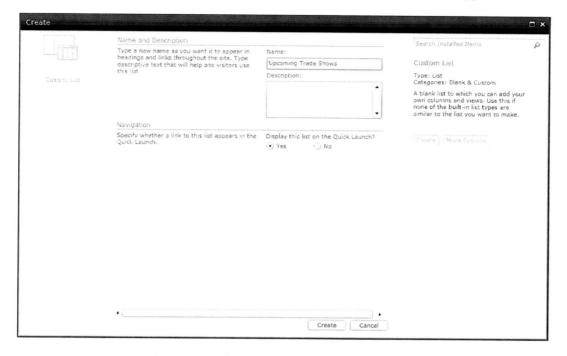

Figure 2: The Advanced Custom List Create Dialog Box

7. Enter any notes about the new list in the Description field. This appears as a sub-heading when your list is open in SharePoint.

8. If you want to have a link to the list in your site's Quick Launch section, leave the Navigation option set to Yes.

9. Click Create. The new list will be created.

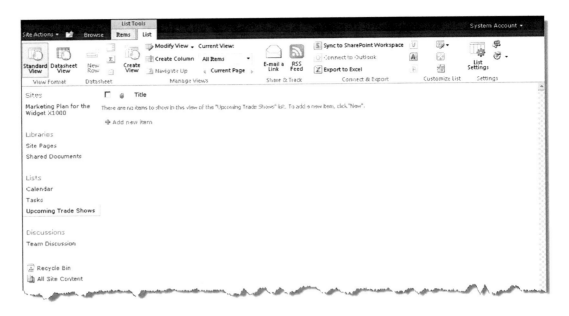

Figure 3: The New List

NOTE: When a custom list is created, it initially has just a few columns. For more information on adding columns to your list, see "Create New List Columns."

Exceptions

If you don't see the option to create a custom list, you may not have the right permissions.

Task: Import a Spreadsheet to Create a List

Purpose: Lists are essentially collections of data that SharePoint lets you publish for other users to see and change, if necessary. In many organizations, such collections of data already exist in the form of Excel spreadsheets. Rather than retyping all of the data into SharePoint, you can quickly import an Excel spreadsheet and create a list from it.

Example: This procedure, it should be noted, works best for simple worksheets. Complex worksheets, with many formulas and tables, may not always translate well into a SharePoint list.

Steps:

1. Start Internet Explorer and type the URL for your organization's SharePoint server. The Start Page will open.

2. Navigate to the site where you want to add a custom list. The site's home page will open.

3. Click the Site Actions menu and select More Options... The Create dialog box will open.

4. Scroll down and click the Import Spreadsheet icon, then click Create. The New list page will open.

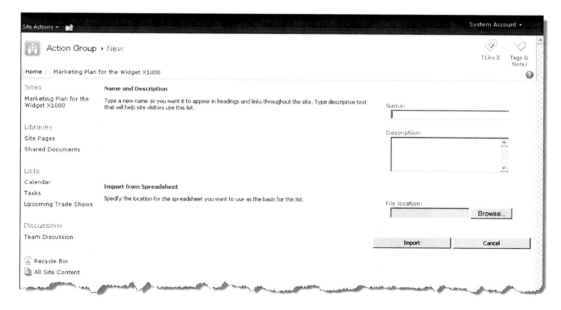

Figure 1: The New List Page

5. Enter a title for the new list in the Name field. This will be the title of the list shown in any of the Site Content pages.

---

6. Enter any notes about the new list in the Description field. This should be a good description of what the list contains.

7. Click Browse in the Import from Spreadsheet section. The Choose File to Upload dialog box will appear.

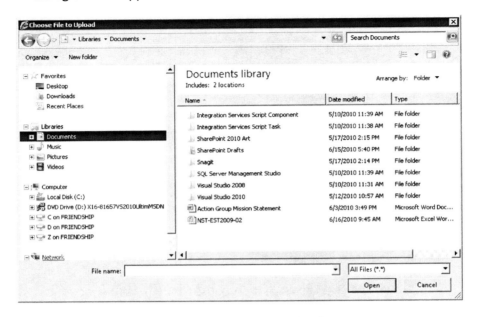

Figure 2: The Choose File to Upload Dialog Box

8. Click the spreadsheet to import, then click Open. The Choose File to Upload dialog box will close and the file name and path for the spreadsheet will appear in the File Location field on the New list page.

9. Click Import. The spreadsheet will open in Excel and the Import to Windows SharePoint Services list dialog box will appear.

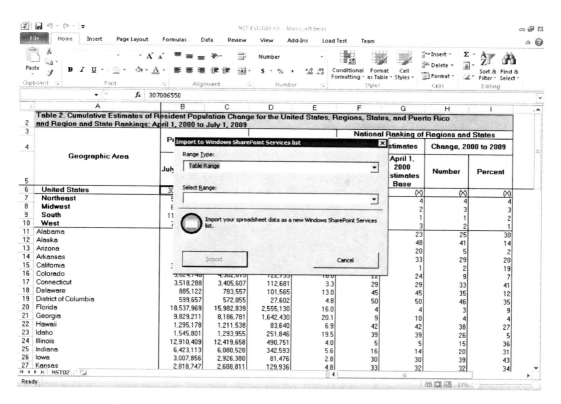

Figure 3: The Import to Windows SharePoint Services List Dialog Box

10. If you have a specified table range or named range, choose the appropriate option in the Range Type field and the desired range in the Select Range field.

11. If no range has been pre-defined, select Range of Cells in the Range Type field and click the control in the Select Range field. Use the keyboard arrows to highlight an appropriate range on the spreadsheet and press Enter. Alternatively, enter the cell range in the Select Range field.

Figure 4: The Configured Range of Cells Range Type in the Import Dialog Box

12. Click Import. The Import to Windows SharePoint Services list dialog box will close and the new list with the imported data will appear.

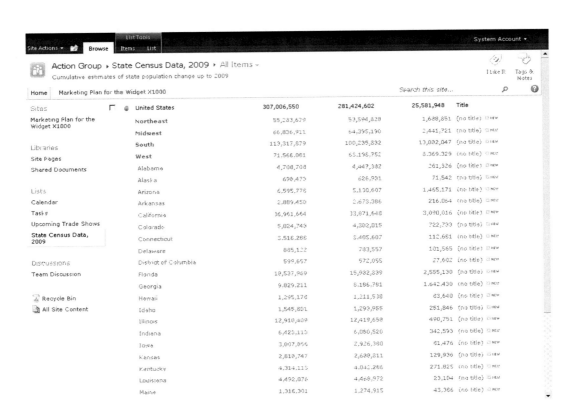

Figure 5: The New Imported List

Task: Create a New List Item

Purpose: Once you have a list created, you can add items to that list fairly quickly.

Example: The Action Group will be presenting a seminar at this year's TechWorld show in New York, and it needs to be put on the Upcoming Trade Show list.

Steps:

1. Start Internet Explorer and type the URL for your organization's SharePoint server. The Start Page will open.

2. Navigate to the list to which you want to add an item. The list page will open.

3. Click Add new item. The New Item dialog box will open.

    NOTE: The New Item dialog box may have a different appearance if the list properties dictate different required fields.

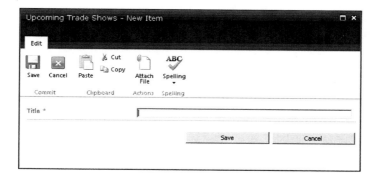

Figure 1: The New Item Dialog Box

4. Enter a name for the new item in the Title field (and enter information for any additional fields that may be listed)..

    NOTE: When a custom list is created, it initially has just a few columns, which is why your item may not require a lot of information to be entered. Different lists will have different required fields. For more information on adding columns to your list, see "Create New List Columns."

5. Click Save. The item will be added to the list.

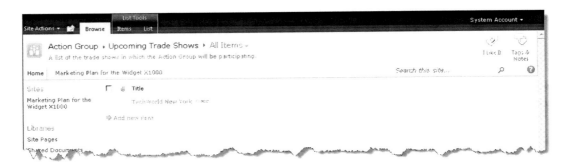

Figure 2: A New Item Added on the List Page

The SharePoint Shepherd's Guide for End Users: 2010

Task: Add New List Columns

Purpose: In the "Create a New List Item" task, you may have noted a conspicuous absence of fields in which to put information. You can change this by customizing the list to include columns that you want to use. When you add columns to the list, you are also providing additional fields to enter information.

Example: Much more information is needed to complete the Upcoming Trade Shows list, in the form of columns for the list.

Steps:

1. Start Internet Explorer and type the URL for your organization's SharePoint server. The Start Page will open.

2. Navigate to the list you want to modify. The list page will open.

3. In the List Tools tab, click the List sub-tab. The List ribbon will open.

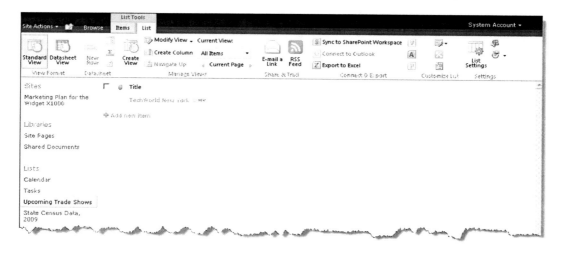

Figure 1: The List Tools Ribbon

4. Click Create Column. The Create Column dialog box will open.

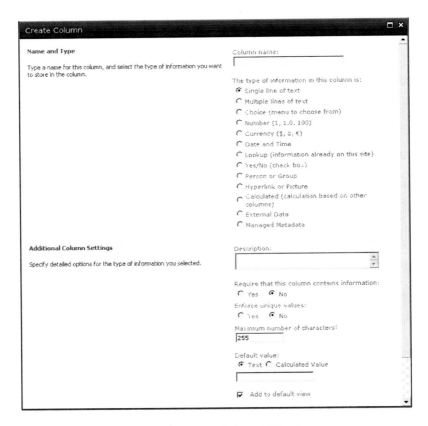

Figure 2: The Create Column Dialog Box

5. Enter a name for the new column in the Column name field.

6. Specify the type of information that will be contained in the list column. This could include text; number; currency values; dates and times; or information already within your SharePoint site.

7. Add notes for the column in the Description field. This will appear in the New and Edit Item pages to tell users what information is needed.

8. Specify if the column is required to contain information. If it is required, the field will be denoted as such in the New and Edit Item pages.

9. Depending on the type of information selected in Step 5 above, additional settings may be needed. Set them as desired.

10. Click OK. The column will be added to the list.

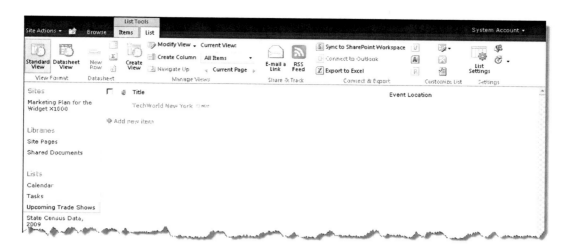

Figure 3: The New Column Added to the List Page

Task: Editing Existing List Columns

Purpose: Besides adding new columns to a list, you can also edit existing columns in case you need to make a correction or change.

Example: Instead of "Title" as primary column in the Upcoming Trade Shows list, you prefer to use the label "Event."

Steps:

1. Start Internet Explorer and type the URL for your organization's SharePoint server. The Start Page will open.

2. Navigate to the list you want to edit. The list page will open.

3. In the List Tools tab, click the List sub-tab. The List tools ribbon will open.

4. Click the List Settings button. The List Settings page will open.

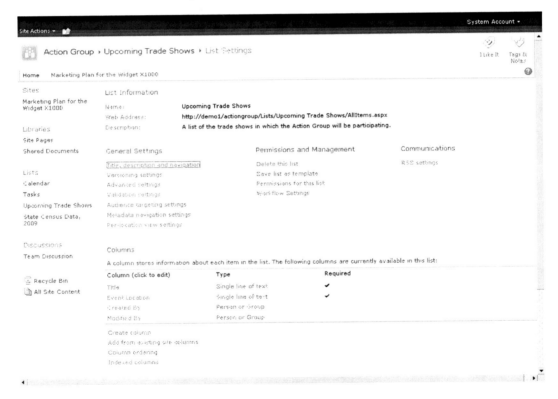

Figure 1: The List Settings Page

5. In the Columns section, click on the name of the title you want to edit. The Change Column page will open.

The SharePoint Shepherd's Guide for End Users: 2010

NOTE: The Change Column page will vary, depending on what column/field you are trying to edit. You may also note that depending on the column selected, your editing choices might be rather limited. One common surprise: you may not be able to change the actual name of the column.

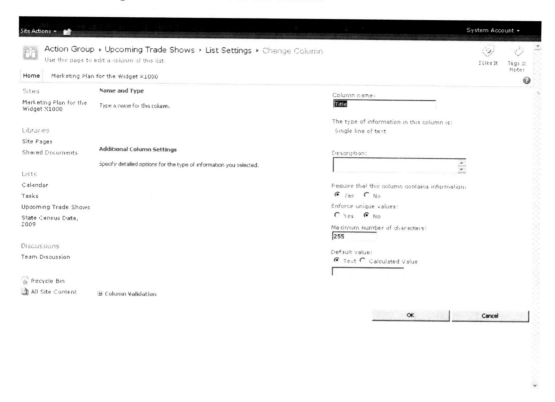

Figure 2: The Change Column Page

6. Enter or add the information you want to change about the column in the appropriate field.

7. Click OK. The List Settings page will open again, with the changes indicated in the Columns section.

Task: Delete List Columns

Purpose: If a column in your list proves to be unnecessary, you can remove it from the list altogether. An important thing to note, however, is that you can only remove certain columns. Some columns, including the default columns used by SharePoint, such as "Title," "Created By," "Modified By," and "Modified" are special fields that cannot be removed. Columns that users have added can always be removed.

Example: Initially the Action Group wanted to track which departments were attending events, but have decided that is no longer necessary, so the column will be removed.

Steps:

1. Start Internet Explorer and type the URL for your organization's SharePoint server. The Start Page will open.

2. Navigate to the list you want to edit. The List page will open.

3. In the List Tools tab, click the List sub-tab. The List tools ribbon will open.

4. Click the List Settings button. The List Settings page will open.

5. In the Columns section, click on the name of the field you want to remove. The Change Column page will open.

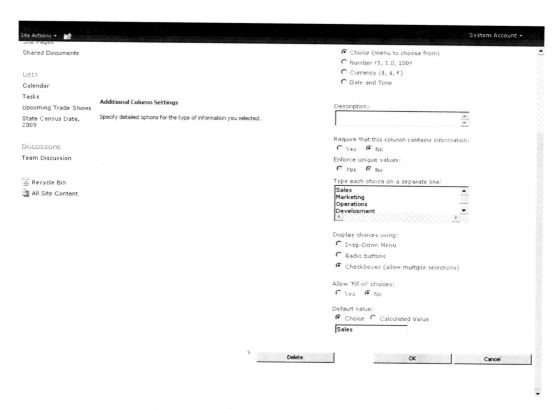

Figure 1: The Change Column Page with Delete Button

6. Near the bottom of the page, click Delete. A confirmation dialog box will open.

Figure 2: The Delete Column Confirmation Dialog Box

7. Click OK. The List Settings page will open again, with the column removed from the Columns section.

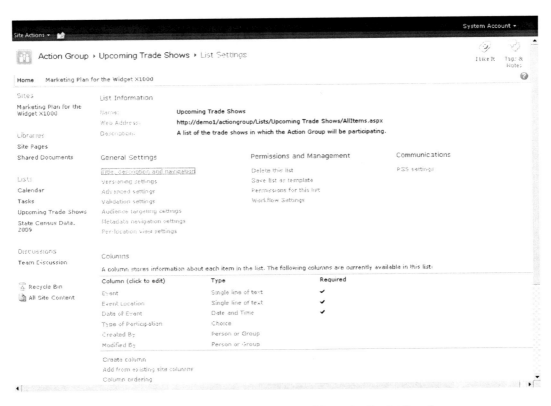

Figure 3: The Specified Column is Removed from the List Settings Page

Task: Edit a List in Datasheet View

Purpose: As you work with lists, you will note a distinct similarity to another collection of data: the spreadsheet. This is made even clearer if you have imported a spreadsheet from Excel to SharePoint. But editing information in a SharePoint list can be tricky if you have to open up one item at a time. Fortunately, you can shift to Datasheet view, which looks and functions very similarly to a spreadsheet, allowing you to edit a lot of list data at once.

Example: Some of the data that was imported into the Census list is not consistent, and will need to be edited quickly.

Steps:

1. Start Internet Explorer and type the URL for your organization's SharePoint server. The Start Page will open.

2. Navigate to the list you want to edit. The list page will open.

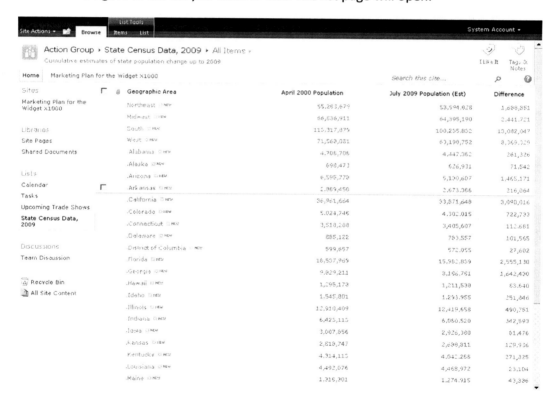

Figure 1: A List in Standard View

3. In the List Tools tab, click the List sub-tab. The List tools ribbon will open.

4. Click the Datasheet View button. The list will now appear in the Datasheet view.

NOTE: Datasheet View will only work if you are using Internet Explorer, and have Office installed on your local computer. 64-bit versions of Office will need a patch to display datasheet view.

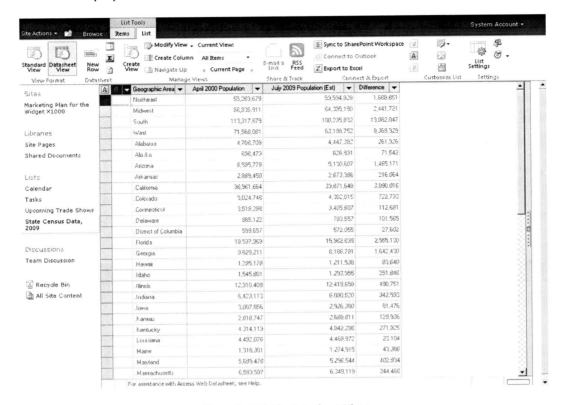

Figure 2: A List in Datasheet View

5. Click a datasheet cell you want to edit to select the cell and make any changes that are needed.

6. Repeat step 5 to edit other cells as needed.

   NOTE: There is an indicator in the status area that pending changes are being committed to the server. If you try to exit the page before changes are committed, you will be prompted about losing your changes.

7. Click the Standard View button. The list will change back to the Standard view.

Task: Subscribe to a List RSS Feed

Purpose: Lists in SharePoint are great, especially if they are updated frequently. But the best list in the world isn't going to do much good if no one actually comes back to look at it. If you are interested in a list, they can subscribe to an RSS feed that will notify them or other users when a list's content has changed.

Example: Now that the Upcoming Trade Shows list has been created, you can subscribe to the list's RSS feed using your preferred feed reader.

Steps:

1. Start Internet Explorer and type the URL for your organization's SharePoint server. The Start Page will open.

2. Navigate to the list in which you are interested. The list page will open.

3. Click the List sub-tab in the List Tools tab. The List Tools ribbon will open.

4. Click the RSS Feed button. The list will appear as an RSS feed page in your browser or in your preferred RSS reader client.

Figure 1: A List RSS Feed

5. Click the Subscribe to this feed link. If you have no other feed readers installed, the Subscribe to this Feed dialog box will appear.

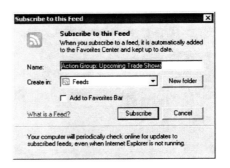

Figure 2: Subscribing to this Feed Dialog Box

6. Click Subscribe. The feed will be added to your browser's feed list.

Task: View List Item Properties

Purpose: Not all information needs to be in a list view or you may want to view all of the details of the items in your list. For example, calculated columns don't appear on the edit page so you'll need to view the item's properties--or add calculated columns to the view. Also, an announcements list would be a good example of such a list.

Example: For quick reference, pull out a list item's information by viewing the item's properties page.

Steps:

1. Start Internet Explorer and type the URL for your organization's SharePoint server. The Start Page will open.

2. Navigate to the list in which you are interested. The list page will open.

3. In the List Tools tab click the Items sub-tab. The Item Tools ribbon will open.

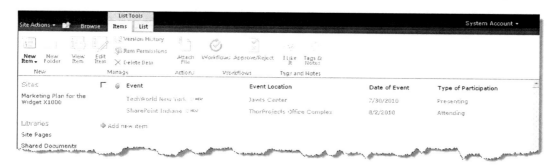

Figure 1: The Item Tools Ribbon

4. Select a list item, then click the View Item button. The item's properties dialog box will open if the list properties allow it.

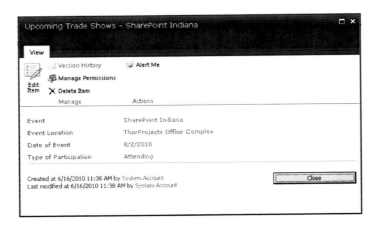

Figure 2: An Item's Properties Dialog Box

5. Click Close when finished. The list page will appear.

    NOTE: Alternatively, simply click on the item in the list to bring up its properties page. This works for items in lists, though not documents in libraries.

Task: Edit List Item Properties

Purpose: When you need to edit one item in a list, you don't have to use the datasheet view. You can quickly change the properties, as well as take advantage of better tools by editing the item's properties directly.

Example: In scanning the Upcoming Trade Shows list, you note an error in one of the item's dates and need to fix it.

Steps:

1. Start Internet Explorer and type the URL for your organization's SharePoint server. The Start Page will open.

2. Navigate to the list in which you are interested. The list page will open.

3. In the List Tools tab, click the Items sub-tab. The Item Tools ribbon will open.

4. Select a list item, then click the Edit Item button. The edit item dialog box will open .

Figure 1: The Edit Item Dialog Box

NOTE: The Edit Item dialog box may look different depending on the settings of your list.

5. Make the changes you want and click Save. The list page will appear with the updated item information.

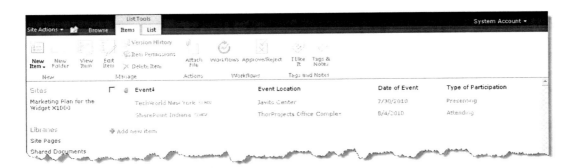

Figure 2: The Updated Item on the List Page

Task: Manage List Item Permissions

Purpose: Occasionally, you may need to adjust an item's permissions to make sure only the right people are allowed to edit it.

Example: A new trade show, hosted by XYZ Corp., has been added to the Upcoming Trade Shows list, and because it is the Action Group's own company, it is preferred that not just anyone can edit the event's entry.

Steps:

1. Start Internet Explorer and type the URL for your organization's SharePoint server. The Start Page will open.

2. Navigate to the list in which you are interested. The list page will open.

3. In the List Tools tab, click the Items sub-tab. The Item Tools ribbon will open.

4. Select a list item, then click the Item Permissions button. The Permission Tools page will open.

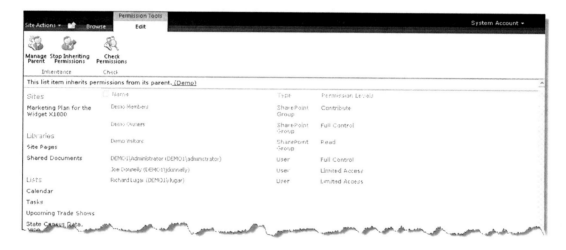

Figure 1: The Permission Tools Page

5. Click the Stop Inheriting Permissions button. A confirmation dialog box will appear.

6. Click OK. The confirmation dialog box will close, the document will no longer have the same permissions set, and a new set of tools will appear in the ribbon on the Permission Tools page.

   NOTE: These steps will break the inherited permissions from the parent list and any changes made later to the list permissions may need to be repeated for individual items.

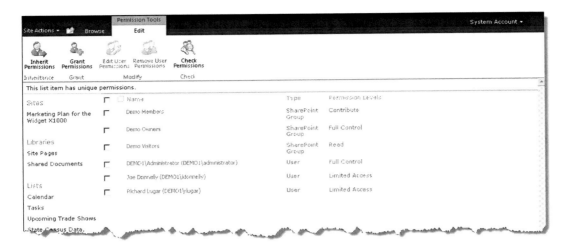

Figure 2: The Permissions Tools Page Without Permission Inheritance

7. Click the Grant Permissions icon. The Grant Permissions dialog box will open.

8. At this point, you can add users to the Users/Groups field in one of two ways:

    a. Enter users

        1)Type in the name of the user in the Users/Groups field and click the Check Names icon, 🔍✓. If the user is part of the authenticated network, their name will be underlined, which means they are authorized.

    b. Browse users

        1)If you don't know the full name of the user, click the Browse button to open the Select People and Groups dialog box. Type in the portion of the name you can recall and press Enter.

        2)Select the correct user to add and click the Add button. The user will appear (authenticated) in the Add field.

        3)When finished, click OK to close the Select People and Groups dialog box. The found user(s) will appear in the User/Groups field.

9. Click the Grant users permissions directly radio button if it's not already selected.

10. Check the permissions you wish to grant this set of users for this document.

11. Check the email option to deselect it if you have several items' permissions to change and don't want users to be emailed every time.

The SharePoint Shepherd's Guide for End Users: 2010

12. Click OK. The Grant Permissions dialog box will close and the users will now appear on the Permission Tools page. Repeat Steps 7-11 to grant different permission levels to additional users.

Task: Edit a List View

Purpose: The default view of a SharePoint list may not be very useful in your business processes. . Each added column is viewed on the right edge of the list, and the items are sorted in the order the items were created.

Example: You can change any aspect of a list's view very easily.

Steps:

1. Start Internet Explorer and type the URL for your organization's SharePoint server. The Start Page will open.

2. Navigate to the list in which you are interested. The list page will open.

3. In the List Tools tab, click the List sub-tab. The List Tools ribbon will open.

4. Click the Modify View button. The Edit View page will open.

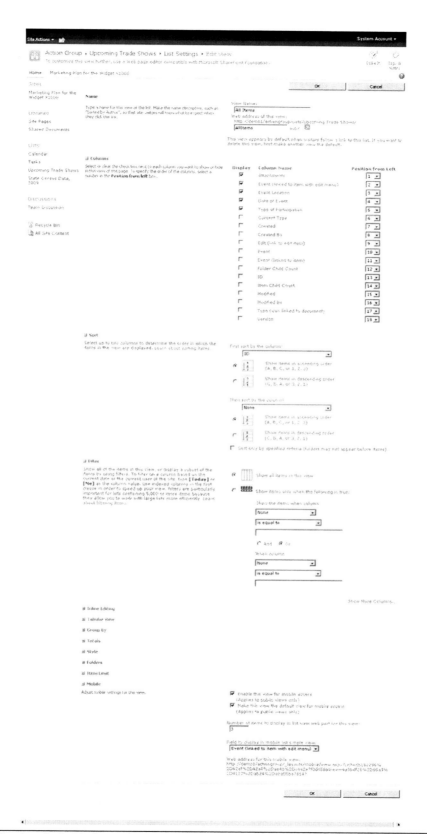

5. In the Columns section, click the Display checkbox for any fields you wish to be visible in the view.

   NOTE: Some column names aren't really completely new columns but instead are columns with additional information or formatting. This is important because you don't want both Name of Event and Name of Event (Linked to Item) to appear.

6. To move a column's position, select a new Position from Left value for that column. The other values will adjust automatically.

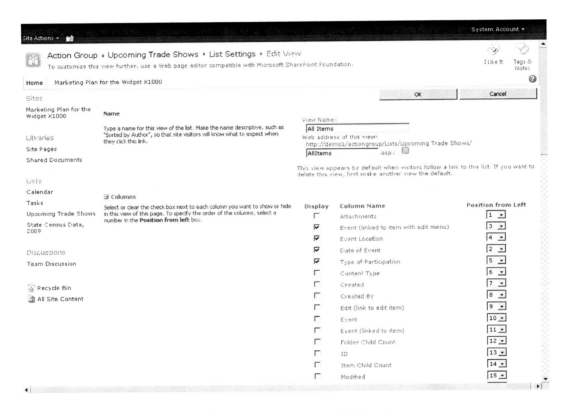

Figure 2: The Column Order on the Edit View Page.

7. In the Sort section, select the column by which you want to sort the items. Typically you'll sort by the columns that you've placed in the left-most position.

8. In the Filter section, set the criteria for which items you want to display. You can display all items, or set some to be removed when a criteria is met, such as when dated events pass. You can also click the Show More Columns to add additional filter criteria.

9. In the Group By section, you can group items by their values within a column and choose to show the groups expanded or collapsed by default.

10. In the Totals section, you can determine if you want to display the totals of any of the columns' content.

11. In the Style section, select a pre-determined style for your list.

12. In the Folders section, choose if you want to display items inside folders.

13. In the Item Limit section, determine what, if any limits you want to impose on the number of items displayed.

14. In the Mobile section, click the options to make the list more readily viewable on a mobile device's browser.

15. Click OK. The list page will open with the new view configuration.

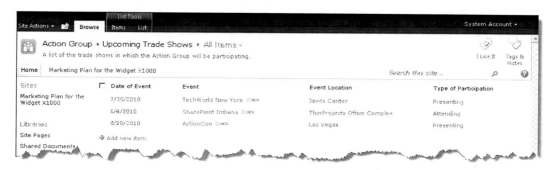

Figure 3: The New View of the List Page

Task: Add a List View

Purpose: SharePoint lists are typically displayed in the All Items view, but that's not the only view available.

Example: It is possible to create whole new list views, just the way you want them, rather than heavily modifying the default All Items view.

Steps:

1. Start Internet Explorer and type the URL for your organization's SharePoint server. The Start Page will open.

2. Navigate to the list in which you are interested. The list page will open.

3. Click the List sub-tab in the List Tools tab. The List Tools ribbon will open.

4. Click the Create View button. The Create View page will open.

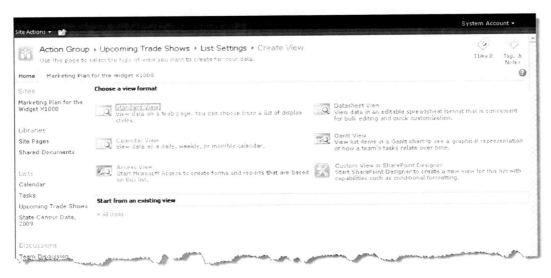

Figure 1: The Create View Page

NOTE: There are five view formats provided with SharePoint: Standard, Calendar, Datasheet, Access database, and the Gantt project management view. A sixth option allows you to create a custom view in SharePoint Designer.

5. Click a view format. The Create View page for that format will open.

NOTE: For more information on the different views available in SharePoint, see Appendix D, "Views."

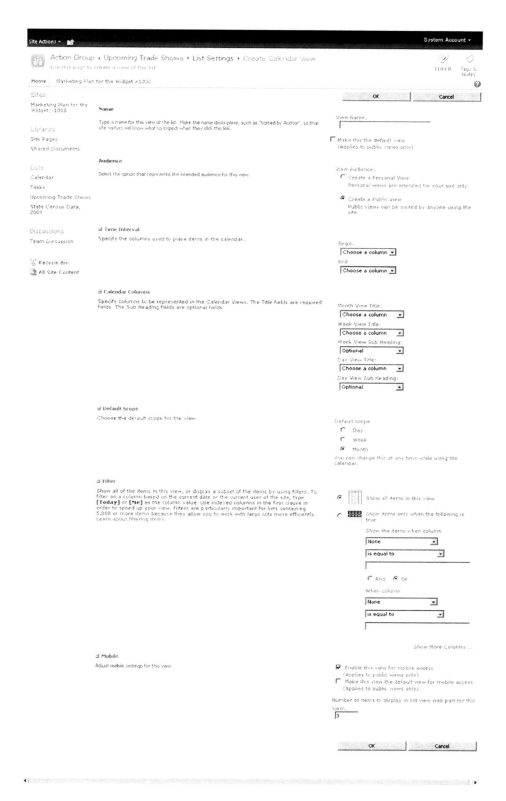

Figure 2: The Create Calendar View Page

6. Enter a title for the view in the View Name field. This is the name that users will see in the view drop down.

7. Select the Make this the default view option. By selecting a view as a default, the previous default view will automatically be unselected.

8. In the Audience section, choose whether to make this view available to the public or just you.

9. Specify which column will provide the begin and end dates for events on the calendar in the Time Interval section.

10. In the Calendar Columns section, specify which columns the Month, Week, and Day View Titles will retrieve. The Week and Day View Sub Heading fields are optional.

11. In the Default Scope section, specify which view (Day, Week, or Month) will be the default view for the calendar.

12. In the Filter section, set the criteria for which items you want to display. You can display all items, or set some to be removed when a criteria is met, such as when dated events pass.

13. Click OK. The list page will open with the new view configuration.

Figure 3: The New View of the List Page

Task: Delete a List Item

Purpose: If you need to remove an item from a list, it's a quick operation. Technically items removed from a list are not deleted but are instead sent to the Recycle Bin. If you accidentally delete an item that you need to get back, see "Recovering Items from the Recycle Bin."

Example: One of the trade shows has been cancelled, so it needs to be removed from the list.

Steps:

1. Start Internet Explorer and type the URL for your organization's SharePoint server. The Start Page will open.

2. Navigate to the list in which you are interested. The list page will open.

3. In the List Tools tab, click the Items sub-tab. The Item Tools ribbon will open.

4. Select a list item, then click the Delete Item button. A confirmation dialog box will open.

Figure 1: The Delete Item Confirmation Dialog Box

5. Click OK. The item will be removed from the list.

Manage Libraries

In SharePoint, a library is simply a specialized list that contains, instead of just items of data, items with separate documents and files. These files can be photos, audio clips, Office documents… anything you can use on a PC, only better. That's because with a SharePoint server hosting your files, you get the added benefits of version control, being able to multiple views of your data, and the capability to add metadata to your content that will enable you and other users to quickly find the file you are seeking.

In this section, you will learn how to:

- Create a Library: The basics of creating a library.

- Create a New Library Item: Once you have a library created, you can add items to that library fairly quickly.

- Create a New Library Folder: Instead of just listing library items in a flat list, you can organize the library's contents by creating folders for the items.

- Create New Library Columns: When you add columns to the library, you are also providing additional fields to enter information.

- Edit Existing Library Columns: Besides adding new columns to a library, you can also edit existing columns in case you need to make a correction or changes.

- Delete Library Columns: If a column in your library proves to be unnecessary, you can remove it from the library altogether.

- Upload a Single Library Item: Not only can you create a document and save it directly to a document library, you can also upload existing documents from your local PC to the SharePoint library.

- Upload Multiple Library Items: If you have a lot of documents to upload, you don't have to upload them one at a time. You can simply upload them all at once.

- Edit a Library in Datasheet View: You can shift to Datasheet view, which looks and functions very similar to a spreadsheet, allowing you to edit a lot of library data at once.

- Export a Library to an Excel 2010 or 2007 Spreadsheet: Rather than retyping all of the data from SharePoint into Excel, you can quickly export a library to an Excel spreadsheet.

- **Subscribe to a Library RSS Feed**: If you are interested in a list, they can subscribe to an RSS feed that will notify them or other users when a list's content has changed.

- **View Library Item Properties**: You can easily see a library item's information on the item's properties page.

- **Edit Library Item Properties**: When you need to edit one item in a library, you don't have to use the datasheet view. It's just as fast to edit the item's properties directly.

- **Manage Library Item Permissions**: Occasionally, you may need to adjust an item's permissions to make sure only the right people are allowed to edit it.

- **Edit a Library View**: You can change the aspects of a library's view very easily.

- **Add a Library View**: It is possible to create whole new library views, just the way you want them, rather than heavily modifying the default views.

- **Delete a Library Item**: If you need to remove an item from a library, it's a quick operation.

- **Edit a Library Item in a Preferred Application**: In this task, you will learn how to edit compatible documents directly from SharePoint, just like opening a file from your local hard drive.

- **Download a Library Item to Edit Locally**: Occasionally, you will have files in your document library that are important to the context of the library, but they may not be in a SharePoint-compatible format.

- **Check Out a Library Item**: Here's how to check out a document from within a document library.

- **Check Out a Library Item in Office 2010 or 2007**: Here's how to check out a document from within Office 2010 or 2007.

- **Check Out a Library Item in SharePoint Workspace**: Here's how to check out a document from within the SharePoint Workspace application.

- **Check In a Library Item**: After you have completed your edits on a checked out document, you will need to check it back in to the document library so others can see the changes or edit the document.

- **Check In a Library Item in Office 2010 or 2007**: Here's how to check in a document from within Office 2010 or 2007.

- **Check In a Library Item in SharePoint Workspace**: Here's how to check in a document from within the SharePoint Workspace application.

- **Send a Copy of an Item to Another Library**: You can use the Send To command to get a document copied to another library anywhere on your SharePoint site.

- **E-mail a Link to the Item**: If you want to get many users involved in the editing/creation process for a document, an efficient way is to send a link to the document in an e-mail.

- **Recover Items from the Recycle Bin**. How to retrieve deleted items from the library Recycle Bin.

Task: Create a Library

Purpose: In SharePoint, a library is simply a specialized list that contains, instead of just items of data, items with separate documents and files. In other words, it's a list of items with one, and only one, attachment. These attachments can be photos, audio clips, Office documents ... almost anything you can use on a PC.

Example: For each trade show the Action Group plans to attend, certain materials (presentations, handouts, videos) will be required. To keep them all in one accessible place, you can create a library on SharePoint.

Steps:

1. Start Internet Explorer and type the URL for your organization's SharePoint server. The Start Page will open.

2. Navigate to the site where you want to add a library. The site's home page will open.

3. Click the Site Actions menu and select More Options... The Create dialog box will open.

4. Click the Library option in the Filter By section. The libraries will be displayed.

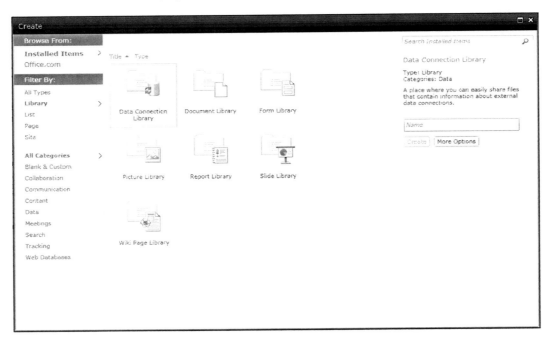

Figure 1: The Create Dialog Box

5. Click the Document Library icon. The Document Library information pane will appear.

---

6. Enter a title for the new library in the Name field. This will appear in any list of libraries in SharePoint.

7. Click the More Options button. The Advanced Document Library Create Dialog dialog box page will appear.

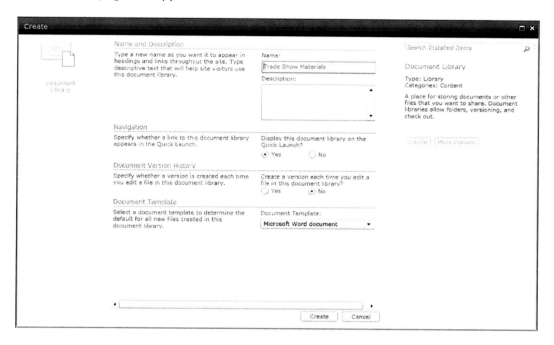

Figure 2: The Advanced Document Library Create Dialog Box

8. Enter any notes about the new library in the Description field.

9. If you want to have a link to the list in your site's Quick Launch, leave the Navigation option set to Yes. This will allow faster navigation by including a link to the library on the left column of most pages.

10. Click the option to determine the tracking of a document's version history. This will track basic versions of documents placed in the library.

11. Select a default Document Template option.

12. Click Create. The new library will be created.

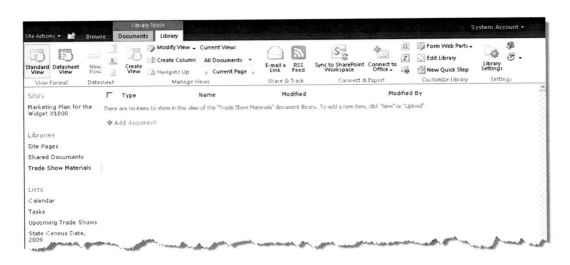

Figure 3: The New Library Page

Task: Add a File to a Document Library

Purpose: Once you have a library created, you can add items to that library fairly quickly. In this example, we will create a new document for a document library using the default document type defined for a library. You can directly upload documents to a library, which is covered in "Upload Existing Documents to a Workspace."

Example: The first of many trade show documents needs to be uploaded to the new library.

Steps:

1. Start Internet Explorer and type the URL for your organization's SharePoint server. The Start Page will open.

2. Click the link in the Quick Launch for the library where you want to add an item. The document library page will open.

3. In the Library Tools tab, click the Documents sub-tab. The Documents tools ribbon will appear.

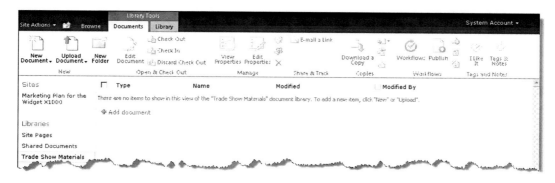

Figure 1: The Documents Tools Ribbon

4. Click the New Document button. A confirmation dialog box will open.

NOTE: The New Document button's drop-down list will reveal multiple content types if they are associated with the library.

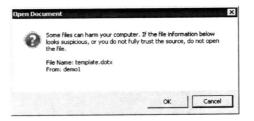

Figure 2: The Open Document Confirmation Dialog Box

5. Click OK. The Office application will open to the basic document template or the library's default template.

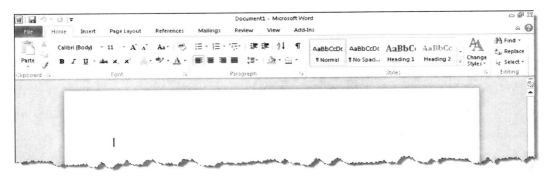

Figure 3: The New Document Opened using the Basic Document Template

6. Create the document in the Office application.

7. When ready, click Save. The Save As dialog box will open to the document library on your SharePoint server.

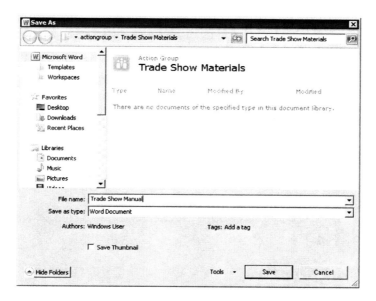

Figure 4: The Save As Dialog Box Opened to the Document Library

8. Enter a file name in the File Name field.

9. Click Save. The document will be saved directly to the SharePoint library instead of your local hard drive.

10. Exit the Office application. The document library page will refresh and the document library will now contain the created document.

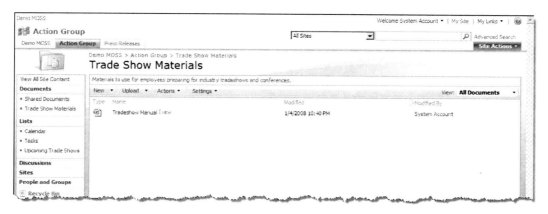

Figure 4: The New Document on the Document Library Page

Task: Create a New Folder in a Library

Purpose: Instead of just listing library items in a flat list, you can organize the library's contents by creating folders for the items just like you would on a local hard drive or network drive.

Example: The IT team would like to have its documents organized separately from the general trade show documents. Creating a folder could be the quickest solution. For the best solution, see the folders or metadata decision tree.

Steps:

1. Start Internet Explorer and type the URL for your organization's SharePoint server. The Start Page will open.

2. Click the link in the Quick Launch for the library where you want to add an item. The document library page will open.

3. Click the Documents sub-tab in the Library Tools tab. The Documents tools ribbon will appear.

4. Click the New Folder button. The New Folder dialog box will open.

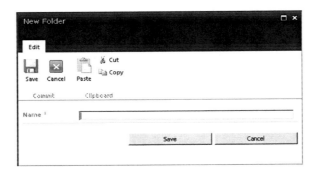

Figure 1: The New Folder Dialog Box

5. Type a label for the folder in the Name field.

6. Click Save. The folder will appear in the document library.

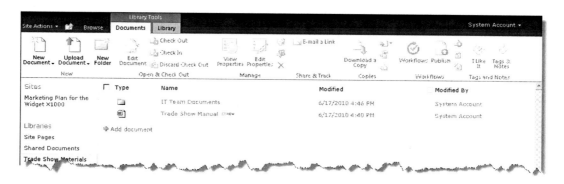

Figure 2: The New Folder on the Document Library Page

Task: Create New Columns in a Library

Purpose: The default library view lacks columns that could describe the library item more fully. You can change this by customizing the library to include any columns that you want to use. When you add columns to the library, you are also providing additional fields to enter information, which can be used as additional attributes to find information later. These steps are identical to those used to add columns to a list.

Example: Much more information is needed to complete the Trade Show Materials library, in the form of columns for the library.

Steps:

1. Start Internet Explorer and type the URL for your organization's SharePoint server. The Start Page will open.

2. Click the link in the Quick Launch for the library you want to modify. The document library page will open.

3. In the Library Tools tab, click the Library sub-tab. The Library tools ribbon will open.

Figure 1: The Library Tools Ribbon

4. Click the Create Column button. The Create Column dialog box will open.

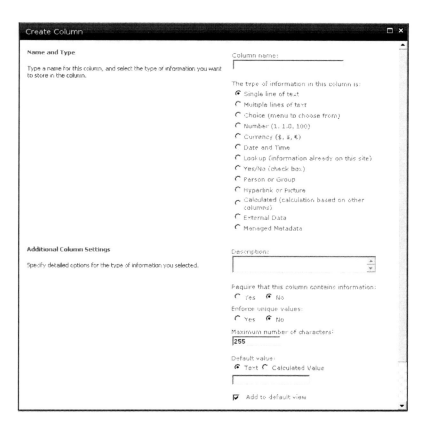

Figure 2: The Create Column Dialog Box

5. Enter a name for the new column in the Column name field.

6. Specify the type of information that will be contained in the library column. This could include text; number and currency values; dates and times; or information already within your SharePoint site.

   NOTE: For more information on column types, see Appendix B, "List Definitions."

7. Add notes for the column in the Description field. This will appear in the New and Edit Item pages to tell users what information is needed.

8. Specify if the column is required to contain information. If it is required, the field will be denoted as such in the New and Edit Item pages.
   NOTE: Files uploaded through Windows Explorer and through the upload multiple files menu will still not be required to enter this information.

9. Depending on the type of information in the column, additional settings will be needed. Set them as desired.

10. Click OK. The column will be added to the library.

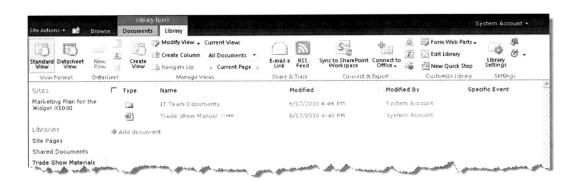

Figure 3: The New Column Added to the Document Library Page

Task: Edit Existing Library Columns

Purpose: Besides adding new columns to a library, you can also edit existing columns in case you need to make a correction or changes.

Example: The Type of Event column was initially set as a text field, but you would like it to present specific choices.

Steps:

1. Start Internet Explorer and type the URL for your organization's SharePoint server. The Start Page will open.

2. Navigate to the library you want to edit. The document library page will open.

3. In the Library Tools tab, click the Library sub-tab. The Library Tools ribbon will open.

4. Click the Library Settings button. The Document Library Settings page will open.

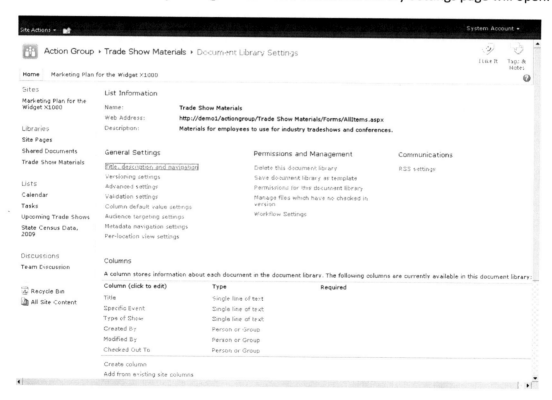

Figure 1: The Document Library Settings Page

5. In the Columns section, click on the name of the column you want to edit. The Change Column page will open.

Figure 2: The Change Column Page

6. Enter or add the information you want to change in the appropriate field.

7. Click OK. The Document Library Settings page will open again and the changes will have been updated for the Column. Changes to the Column name field, type of information or whether the field is required will be reflected in the Columns section.

Task: Delete Library Columns

Purpose: If a column in your library proves to be unnecessary, you can remove it from the library altogether. An important thing to note, however, is that you can only remove columns that users have added. Some columns, including the built-in columns used by SharePoint, such as "Title", "Checked Out To," "Created By," or "Modified By" cannot be removed. You should also be aware that any data that was in a deleted column cannot be recovered.

Example: Initially the Action Group wanted to track the type of event, but have decided that is no longer necessary, so the column will be removed.

Steps:

1. Start Internet Explorer and type the URL for your organization's SharePoint server. The Start Page will open.

2. Navigate to the library you want to edit. The library page will open.

3. In the Library Tools tab, click the Library sub-tab. The Library Tools ribbon will open.

4. Click the Library Settings button. The Library Settings page will open.

5. In the Columns section, click on the name of the title you want to remove. The Change Column page will open.

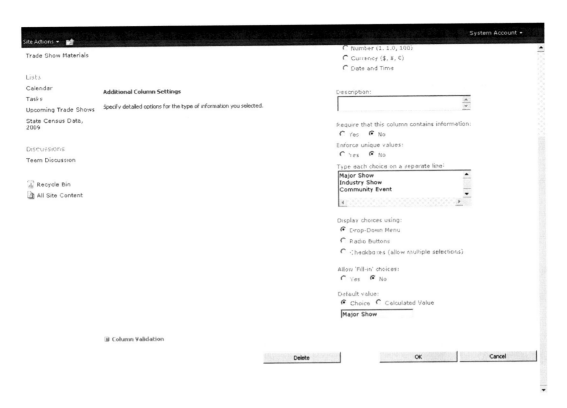

Figure 1: The Change Column Page, with Delete Button

6. Click Delete. A confirmation dialog box will appear.

Figure 2: The Delete Column Confirmation Dialog Box

7. Click OK. The Document Library Settings page will open again, with the desired column removed from the Columns section.

Task: Upload a Single Library Item

Purpose: Not only can you create a document and save it directly to a document library, you can also upload existing documents on your local PC to the SharePoint library.

Example: It's now time to collect existing documents for the Trade Show Materials library.

Steps:

1. Start Internet Explorer and type the URL for your organization's SharePoint server. The Start Page will open.

2. Click the link in the Quick Launch for the library where you want to add an item. The document library page will open.

3. Click Add document. The Upload Document dialog box will open.

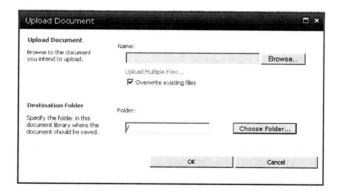

Figure 1: The Upload Document Dialog Box

4. Click the Browse button. The Choose File to Upload dialog box will appear.

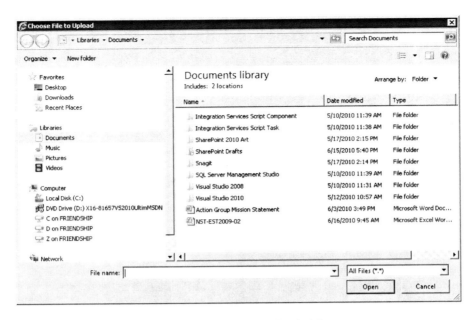

Figure 2: The Choose File to Upload Dialog Box

5. Select a file and click Open. The file and its file path will appear in the Name field of the Upload Document dialog box.

6. Add any notes about the document in the Version Comments field if you have Versioning enabled on the library.

7. Click OK. The Document Properties dialog box will open.

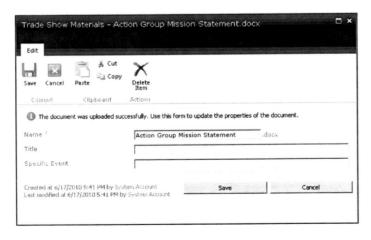

Figure 3: The Document Properties Dialog Box

8. Change any of the document's attributes, as desired.

9. Click Save. The file will be uploaded and will appear on the document library page.

Figure 4: The New Uploaded Document on the Document Library Page

Task: Upload Multiple Library Items

Purpose: If you have a lot of documents to upload, you don't have to upload them one at a time. You can simply upload them all at once, without prompting to enter required fields of information. One important note: multiple file upload only works with the Internet Explorer browser and only when you have Office installed. Firefox, Chrome, and other browsers do not support this action.

Example: Multiple documents will need to be uploaded to the document library.

Steps:

1. Start Internet Explorer and type the URL for your organization's SharePoint server. The Start Page will open.

2. Navigate to the library where you want to upload documents. The document library page will open.

3. In the Library Tools tab, click the Documents sub-tab . The Documents Tool ribbon will open.

4. Click the Upload Documents menu control and select the Upload Multiple Documents sub-menu. The Upload Multiple Documents dialog box will open.

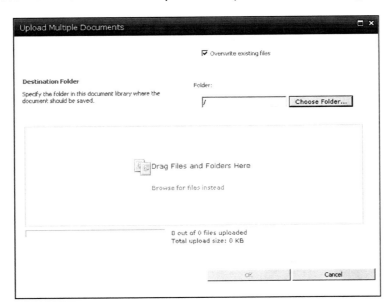

Figure 1: The Upload Multiple Documents Dialog Box

5. Open Windows Explorer and navigate to the files you want to upload.

6. Drag and drop the documents into the Drag Files and Folders Here section. The files will be selected for upload.

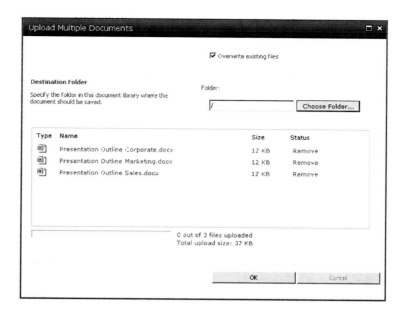

Figure 2: Choosing Files to Upload

7. Click OK. The files will be uploaded.

8. Click Done. The files will appear on the document library page.

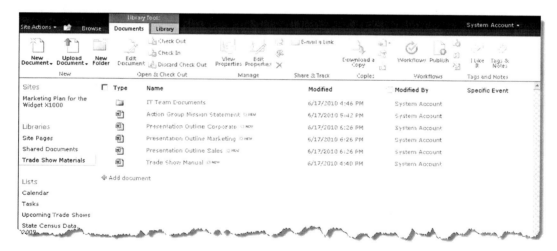

Figure 3: The New Uploaded Documents on the Document Library Page

Task: Edit a Library in Datasheet View

Purpose: Editing information in a SharePoint library can be time-consuming if you have to open up the properties one item at a time. Fortunately, you can shift to Datasheet view, which looks and functions very similar to a spreadsheet, allowing you to edit a lot of library metadata at once. This can be particularly useful with office documents because SharePoint and Office cooperate to update properties in Office documents when the properties are updated in SharePoint.

Example: Several of the documents in the Trade Show Materials library are specifically for one event, so their entries will need to be edited accordingly.

Steps:

1. Start Internet Explorer and type the URL for your organization's SharePoint server. The Start Page will open.

2. Navigate to the library you want to edit. The document library page will open.

3. In the Library Tools tab, click the Library sub-tab. The Library Tools ribbon will open.

4. Click the Datasheet View button. The items will now appear in the Datasheet view.

   NOTE: The Datasheet view is available if Internet Explorer is being used. Microsoft Office must also be installed.

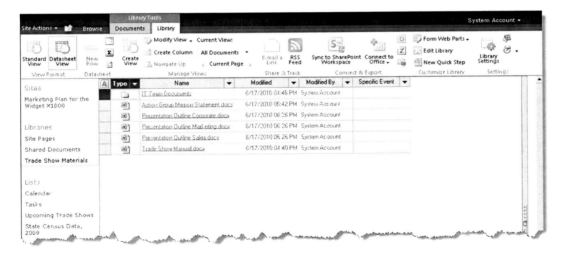

Figure 1: A Document Library in Datasheet View

5. Click a datasheet cell you want to edit. The cell will be selected.

6. Click within the cell and make any changes that are needed.

7. Repeat Steps 5 and 6 to edit other cells as needed.

NOTE: There is an indicator in the status area that pending changes are being committed to the server. If you try to exit the page before changes are committed, you will be prompted about losing your changes.

8. Click the Standard View button. The document library will change back to the Standard view.

Exception

If you can't see the Datasheet view, you may not have Office installed.

Task: Export a Library to an Excel 2010 Spreadsheet

Purpose: Libraries are essentially collections of data that SharePoint lets you publish for other users to see and change, if necessary. In many organizations, such collections of data already exist in the form of Excel spreadsheets.

Example: Rather than retyping all of the library data from SharePoint into Excel 2010, you can quickly export the library to an Excel spreadsheet.

Steps:

1. Start Internet Explorer and type the URL for your organization's SharePoint server. The Start Page will open.

2. Navigate to the library you want to edit. The document library page will open.

3. Click the Library sub-tab in the Library Tools tab. The Library Tools ribbon will open.

4. Click the Export to Excel button. A File Download dialog box will appear.

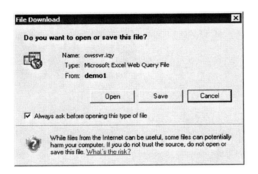

Figure 1: The File Download Dialog Box

5. Click Open. One or more security warnings may appear, depending on your personal computer's settings. Be very sure this is the file you wanted to download, and it is from a trusted source. If you accept these warnings, the file will be downloaded to your local machine and opened in Excel as a data table.

NOTE: Changes made in the exported spreadsheet file will not be reflected in the library.

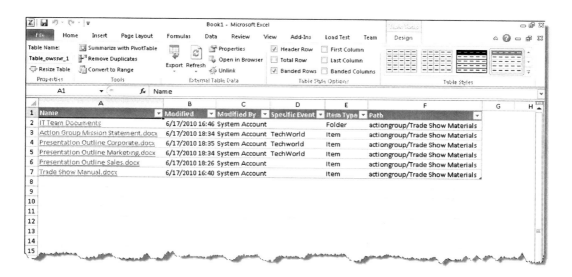

Figure 2: The Exported Spreadsheet

Task: Export a Library to an Excel 2007 Spreadsheet

Purpose: Libraries are essentially collections of data that SharePoint lets you publish for other users to see and change, if necessary. In many organizations, such collections of data already exist in the form of Excel spreadsheets.

Example: Rather than retyping all of the library data from SharePoint into Excel 2007, you can quickly export the library to an Excel spreadsheet.

Steps:

1. Start Internet Explorer and type the URL for your organization's SharePoint server. The Start Page will open.

2. Click the library from which you will export a spreadsheet. The document library page will open.

3. In the Library Tools tab, click the Library sub-tab. The Library Tools ribbon will open.

4. Click the Export to Excel button. A File Download dialog box will appear.

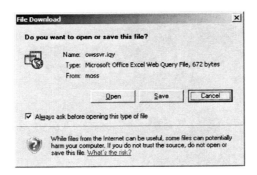

Figure 1: The File Download Dialog Box

5. Click Open. One or more security warnings may appear, depending on your personal computer's settings. Be very sure this is the file you wanted to download, and it is from a trusted source. If you accept these warnings, the file will be downloaded to your local machine and opened in Excel as a data table.

    NOTE: Changes made in the exported spreadsheet file will not be reflected in the library.

6.

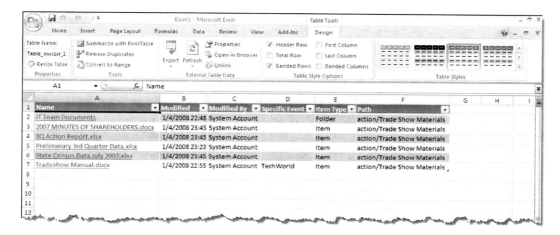

Figure 2: The Exported Spreadsheet

Task: Subscribe to a Library RSS Feed

Purpose: Libraries in SharePoint are great, especially if they are updated frequently. But the best collection of documents in the world isn't going to do much good if no one actually comes back to look at it. If you are interested in a library, they can subscribe to an RSS feed that will notify them or other users when a library's content has changed.

Example: Now that the Trade Show Materials library has been created, you can subscribe to the library's RSS feed using your preferred feed reader.

Steps:

1. Start Internet Explorer and type the URL for your organization's SharePoint server. The Start Page will open.

2. Navigate to the library in which you are interested. The document library page will open.

3. In the Library Tools tab, click the Library sub-tab. The Library Tools ribbon will open.

4. Click the RSS Feed button. The list will appear as an RSS feed page in your browser.

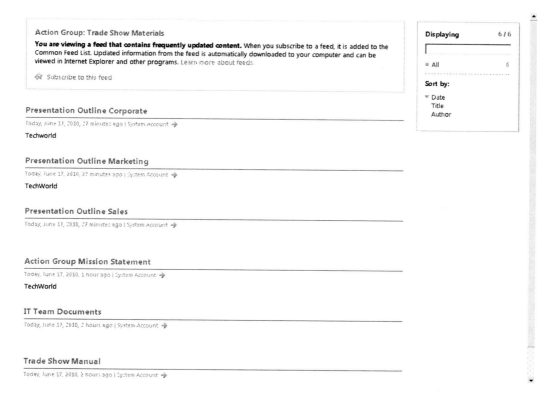

Figure 1: A Library RSS Feed Page

5. Click Subscribe to this feed. If you have no other feed readers installed, the Subscribe to this Feed dialog box will appear.

Figure 2: Subscribe to this Feed Dialog Box

6. Click Subscribe. The feed will be added to your browser's feed list.

Task: View Library Item Properties

Purpose: If a library has a lot of columns, it may be a bit hard on the eyes to read all of the relevant information across the page. Also, you might want to just view the properties of a document in a document library without taking the time to open the document in its native application. This works both ways; because SharePoint can synchronize properties with Office applications, properties that appear in SharePoint as columns may also appear in the document as properties.

Example: You can easily pull out a library item's information by viewing the item's properties page.

Steps:

1. Start Internet Explorer and type the URL for your organization's SharePoint server. The Start Page will open.

2. Navigate to the list in which you are interested. The list page will open.

3. In the Library Tools tab, click the Documents sub-tab. The Documents tools ribbon will open.

4. Select a library item, then click the View Properties button. The item's properties dialog box will open.

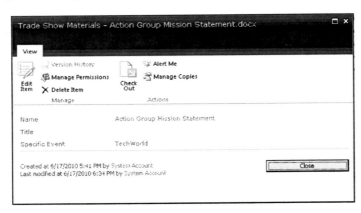

Figure 1: An Item's Properties Dialog Box

NOTE: The item properties dialog box may look different, depending on the properties set for the library.

5. Click Close when finished. The view from which you started will open.

Task: Edit Library Item Properties

Purpose: When you need to edit one item in a list, you don't have to use the datasheet view. It's just as fast to edit the item's properties directly.

Example: In scanning the Trade Show Materials library, you note an error in one of the items and need to fix it.

Steps:

1. Start Internet Explorer and type the URL for your organization's SharePoint server. The Start Page will open.

2. Navigate to the library in which you are interested. The document library page will open.

3. In the Library Tools tab, click the Documents sub-tab. The Documents tools ribbon will open.

4. Select a library item, then click the Edit Properties button. The item's properties dialog box will open in edit mode.

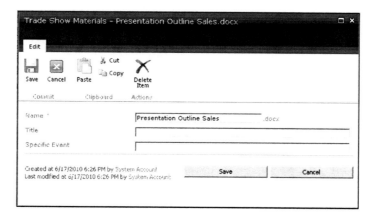

Figure 1: The Edit Item's Properties Dialog Box

NOTE: The item properties dialog box may look different, depending on the properties set for the library.

5. Make the changes you want and click Save. The document library page will appear, with the updated item information.

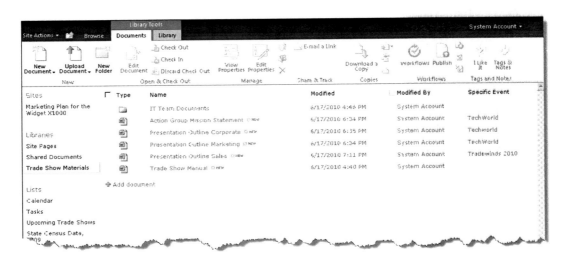

Figure 2: The Updated Item on the Document Library Page

The SharePoint Shepherd's Guide for End Users: 2010

Task: Manage Library Item Permissions

Purpose: Occasionally, you may need to adjust an item's permissions to make sure only the right people are allowed to edit it. This is fairly common in a library, since folders in a library usually need tighter security policies.

Example: The XYZ corporate office would like to limit access to one of the documents in the Trade Show Materials library.

Steps:

1. Start Internet Explorer and type the URL for your organization's SharePoint server. The Start Page will open.

2. Navigate to the library in which you are interested. The document library page will open.

3. In the Library Tools tab, click the Documents sub-tab. The Documents tools ribbon will open.

4. Select a library item, then click the Document Permissions button. The Permissions Tools page will open.

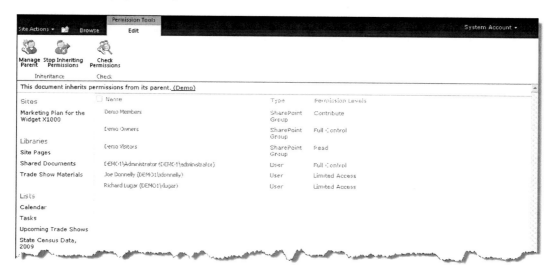

Figure 1: The Permissions Tools Page with Inherited Permissions

5. Click the Stop Inheriting Permissions button. A confirmation dialog box will appear.

6. Click OK. The confirmation dialog box will close, the document will no longer have the same permissions set, and a new set of tools will appear in the ribbon.

NOTE: These steps will break the inherited permissions from the parent list and any changes made later to the list permissions may need to be repeated for individual items.

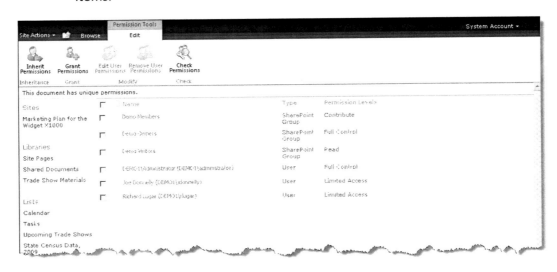

Figure 2: The Permissions Tools Page with Unique Permissions

7. Click the Grant Permissions button. The Grant Permissions dialog box will open.

8. At this point, you can add users to the Users/Groups field in one of two ways:

  a. Enter users

     1) Type in the name of the user in the Users/Groups field and click the Check Names icon, ✅. If the user is part of the authenticated network, their name will be underlined, which means they are authorized.

  b. Browse users

     1) If you don't know the full name of the user, click the Browse button to open the Select People and Groups dialog box. Type in the portion of the name you can recall and press Enter.

     2) Select the correct user to add and click the Add button. The user will appear (authenticated) in the Add field.

     3) When finished, click OK to close the Select People and Groups dialog box. The found user(s) will appear in the User/Groups field.

9. Click the Grant users permissions directly radio button if it's not already selected.

10. Click permissions you wish to grant this set of users for this document.

11. Click the e-mail checkbox to deselect it so the permitted user is not notified for every item changed.

12. Click OK. The Grant Permissions dialog box will close and the users will now appear on the Permission Tools page. Repeat Steps 7-10 to grant other users different permission levels.

    NOTE: For more information on permission levels, see Appendix E, "Permissions in SharePoint."

Task: Edit a Library View

Purpose: The default view of a SharePoint library may not be very useful in your business processes. Each added column is viewed on the right edge of the library, and the items are sorted in the order the items were created.

Example: You can change any aspect of a library's view very easily.

Steps:

1. Start Internet Explorer and type the URL for your organization's SharePoint server. The Start Page will open.

2. Navigate to the library in which you are interested. The document library page will open.

3. In the Library Tools tab, click the Library sub-tab. The Library Tools ribbon will open.

4. Click the Modify View button. The Edit View page will open.

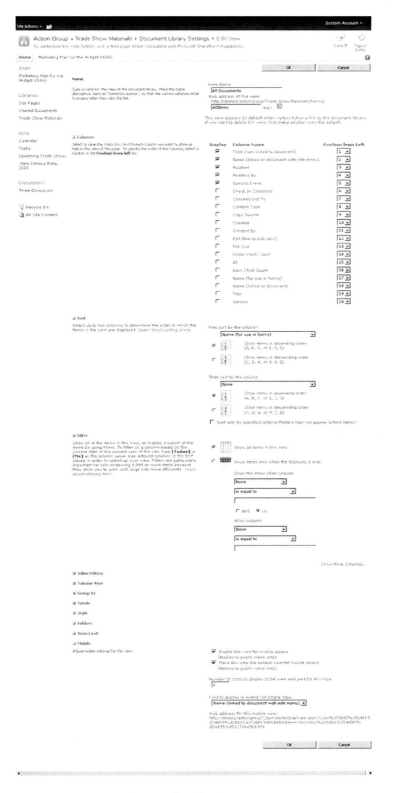

Figure 1: The Edit View Page

5. In the Columns section, click the Display checkbox for any fields you wish to be visible in the view.

6. To move a column's position, select a new Position from Left value for that column. The other values will adjust automatically.

7. In the Sort section, select the column by which you want to sort the items.

    NOTE: Some column names aren't really columns but are instead columns with additional formatting. This is important because you don't want Name of Event and Name of Event (Linked to Item) both to appear.

8. Click OK. The document library page will open with the new view configuration.

Figure 2: The New View of the Document Library Page

Task: Add a Library View

Purpose: SharePoint document libraries are typically displayed in the All Documents or Explorer views.

Example: It is possible to create new library views, just the way you want them, rather than heavily modifying the default views.

Steps:

1. Start Internet Explorer and type the URL for your organization's SharePoint server. The Start Page will open.

2. Navigate to the library in which you are interested. The document library page will open.

3. In the Library Tools tab, click the Library sub-tab. The Library Tools ribbon will open.

4. Click the Create View button. The Create View page will open.

Figure 1: The Create View Page

NOTE: There are five view formats provided with SharePoint: the Standard list, Calendar, Datasheet, Access database, and the Gantt project management view.A sixth option allows you to create a custom view in SharePoint Designer. For more information about views in SharePoint, see Appendix D, "Views."

5. Click a view format or existing view. The Create View page for that format will open.

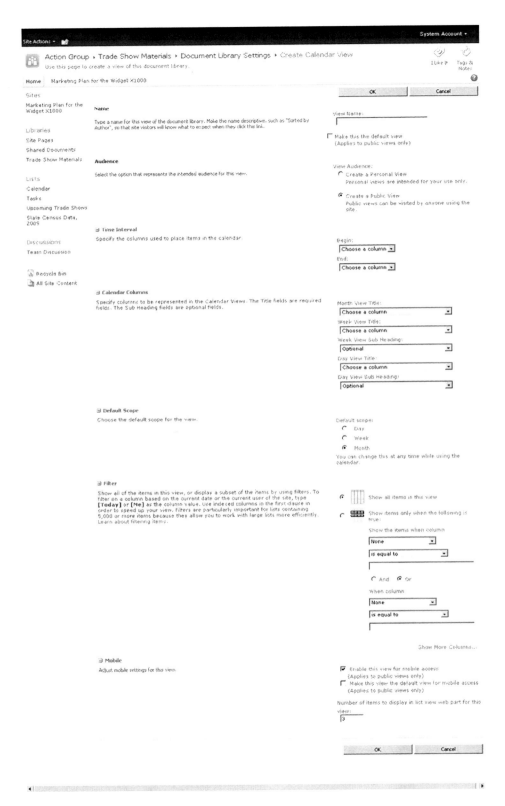

Figure 2: The Create View Page

6. Enter a title for the view in the View Name field.

7. Select the Make this the default view option. This will make this view the standard opening view for this library.

8. Depending on the type of view you are creating, select the appropriate values to configure the view.

9. Click OK. The library will be displayed in the new view.

Task: Delete a Library Item

Purpose: If you need to remove an item from a library, it's a quick operation. And if you mistakenly delete a library item, it will be placed in the site's Recycle Bin, ready to be recovered. For more information, see "Recover Items from the Recycle Bin."

Example: One of the documents is now outdated, so it needs to be removed from the library.

Steps:

1. Start Internet Explorer and type the URL for your organization's SharePoint server. The Start Page will open.

2. Navigate to the library in which you are interested. The document library page will open.

3. In the Library Tools tab, click the Documents sub-tab. The Documents tools ribbon will open.

4. Select a library item, then click the Delete Document button. A confirmation dialog box will open.

Figure 1: The Delete Document Confirmation Dialog Box

5. Click OK. The item will be removed from the library.

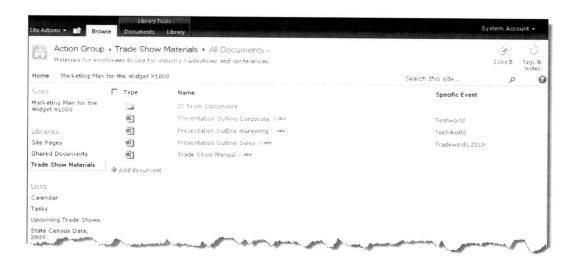

Figure 2: The Item is Removed from the Document Library Page.

Task: Edit a Library Item in a Preferred Application

Purpose: Editing a document in a document library can be done in one of two ways: editing the document using SharePoint-compatible applications (such as Office), or checking the document out of the library for long-term editing.

Example: In this task, you will edit compatible documents directly from SharePoint, just like opening a file from your local hard drive. This is only recommended if you know you are the only user who will be working with the document. If there are multiple users working with the same document, then it's important to use the check out/in capabilities of SharePoint.

Steps:

1. Start Internet Explorer and type the URL for your organization's SharePoint server. The Start Page will open.

2. Navigate to the library in which you are interested. The library page will open.

3. Click the right end of an item you want to view. The item's hover menu will appear.

Figure 1: An Item's Hover Menu

4. Select the Edit in... option. A confirmation dialog box will appear.

   NOTE: You can also directly click the item to begin the opening process.

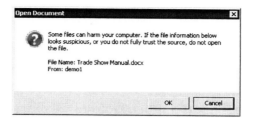

Figure 2: The Open Document Confirmation Dialog Box

5. Click OK. The document will be opened in the appropriate compatible application.

6. When finished editing, click Save. All changes will be saved to the SharePoint document library.

Task: Download a Library Item to Edit Locally

Purpose: Occasionally, you will have files in your document library that are not be in a SharePoint-compatible format. In such a case, you can download a copy of the files to edit on your local PC. Once finished, you can upload the copy back to the document library, replacing the older version that's there. This is only recommended if you know you are the only user who will be working with the file. If there are multiple users working with the same file, then it's important to use the check out/in capabilities of SharePoint.

Example: You need to download a copy of the Trade Show Manual document, to work on it offline over the weekend.

Steps:

1. Start Internet Explorer and type the URL for your organization's SharePoint server. The Start Page will open.

2. Navigate to the library in which you are interested. The library page will open.

3. Click the right side of an item you want to edit. The item's hover menu will appear.

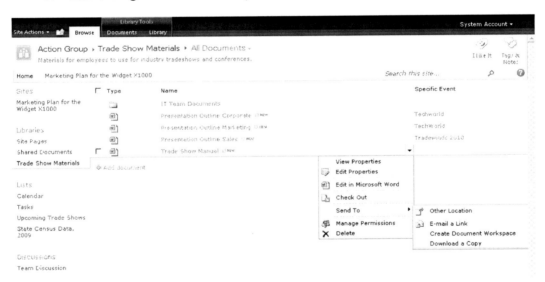

Figure 1: An Item's Hover Menu

4. Select *Send To*. The Send To sub-menu will appear.

5. Select *Download a Copy*. A File Download dialog box will appear.

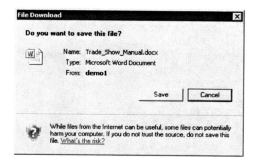

Figure 2: The File Download Dialog Box

6. Click Save. The Save As dialog box will appear.

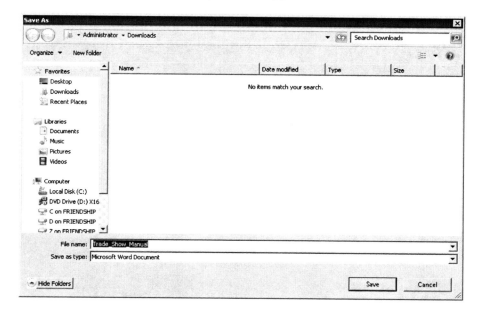

Figure 3: The Save As Dialog Box

7. Navigate to the location where you want to save the document and click Save. The file will be saved to the specified location.

8. Navigate to the specified location to edit and save changes to your copy of the file. When you have edited and saved the changes to your copy of the file, return to the document library in SharePoint.

9. Click the Documents sub-tab in the Library Tools tab. The Documents tools ribbon will open.

10. Click the Upload menu and select the Upload Document option. The Upload Document dialog box will open.

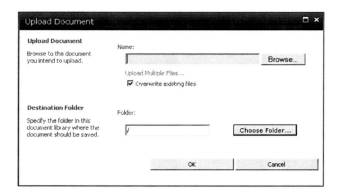

Figure 4: The Upload Document Dialog Box

11. Click the Browse button. The Choose File to Upload dialog box will appear.

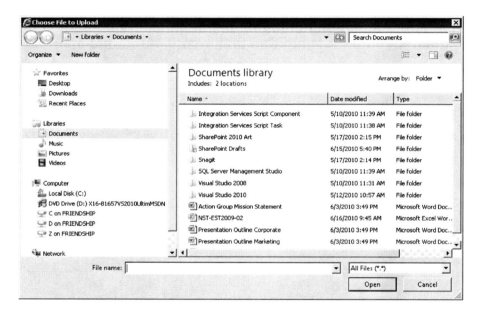

Figure 5: The Choose File to Upload Dialog Box

12. Select the local copy of the file and click Open. The file and its filepath will appear in the Name field.

13. Add any notes about the document in the Version Comments field.

14. Click OK. The Document Properties dialog box will open.

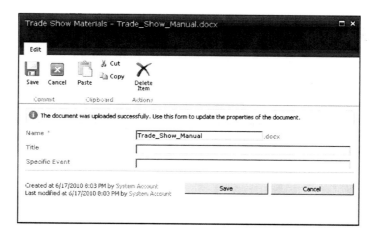

Figure 6: The Document Properties Dialog Box

15. Click Save. The file will be uploaded and will appear in the library.

16. Click the right side of the previous version of the file. The item's context menu will appear.

Figure 7: The Item's Context Menu

17. Click Delete. A confirmation dialog box will appear.

18. Click OK. The older item will be removed from the library.

Task: Check Out a Library Item

Purpose: When a document is being edited from a document library, a user can quickly open the document, make changes, and then save the document back into the workspace. If many users are working on the same document, however, it is better to formally check the document out while making edits, to prevent other users from overwriting your changes. Indeed, some libraries will require check out to edit items.

Example: Here's how to check out the Trade Show Manual from within SharePoint.

Steps:

1. Start Internet Explorer and type the URL for your organization's SharePoint server. The Start Page will open.

2. Navigate to the document workspace site where the document you wish to modify is located. The document workspace page will open.

3. Move the mouse over the document you want to edit and click the drop-down list control that appears. The document's hover menu will appear.

4. Click the Check Out option. A confirmation dialog box will appear.

Figure 1: The Check Out a Document Confirmation Dialog Box

5. Click OK. The document will be checked out and saved to your \My Documents\SharePoint Drafts folder on your local PC.

   NOTE: If you deselected the Use my local drafts folder option, you will be given the opportunity to save the document to a location of your choice on your PC.

Task: Check Out a Library Item in Office 2010

Purpose: When a document is being edited from a library, a user can quickly open the document, make changes, and then save the document back into the library. If many users are working on the same document, files will be locked while someone else has it open, so it is better to formally check the document out while making edits, to prevent other users from overwriting your changes. Here's how to check out a document from Office.

Example: When you have a document opened from a SharePoint library, you can check it out from the Office application.

Steps:

1. Open an application in Microsoft Office. It can be Word, Excel, or PowerPoint.

2. Click the File tab and select Open from the menu. The Open window will appear.

3. Type the URL for the library you want to browse in the Location field. The Site Content page for your library will open.

4. Click the desired document, then click Open. The document will open in your Office application.

5. Click the File tab and select Info from the menu. The Info pane will appear.

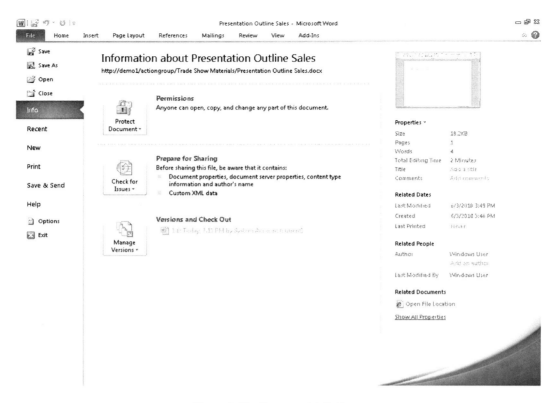

Figure 1: The Document Info Pane

6. Click the Manage Versions icon, then click the Check Out option. The document will be checked out to you, and will remain stored on the SharePoint system.

Task: Check Out a Library Item in Office 2007

Purpose: When a document is being edited from a library, a user can quickly open the document, make changes, and then save the document back into the library. If many users are working on the same document, files will be locked while someone else has it open, so it is better to formally check the document out while making edits, to prevent other users from overwriting your changes. Here's how to check out a document from Office 2007.

Example: When you have a document opened from a SharePoint library, you can check it out from the Office 2007 application.

Steps:

1. Open an application in Microsoft Office. It can be Word, Excel, or PowerPoint.

2. Click the Office jewel and select Open from the menu. The Open dialog box will appear.

3. Type the URL for the library you want to browse in the Location field. The Site Content page for your library will open.

4. Click the desired document, then click Open. The document will open in your Office application.

5. Click the Office jewel and select Server from the menu. The Server sub-menu will appear.

6. Click the Check Out option. The Edit Offline dialog box will appear.

Figure 1: The Edit Offline Dialog Box

7. Click OK. The document will be checked out.

Task: Check Out Library Items in SharePoint Workspace

Purpose: When a document is being edited from a library, a user can quickly open the document, make changes, and then save the document back into the library. If many users are working on the same document, however, it is better to formally check the document out while making edits, to prevent other users from overwriting your changes.

Example: Here's how to check out a document from SharePoint Workspace.

Steps:

1. Start SharePoint Workspace 2010 by clicking the Start | All Programs | Microsoft Office | Microsoft SharePoint Workspace 2010 menu option. The Launchbar for SharePoint Workspace will open.

2. Double-click the library name that contains the document you want to edit. The main SharePoint Workspace window will open, displaying the contents of the library.

3. Select the document you want to check out.

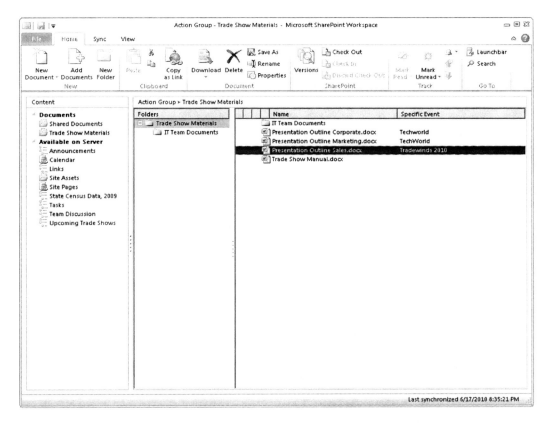

Figure 1: The Selected Item to Check Out in SharePoint Workspace

4. Click the Check Out button. The document will be checked out to you.

5. Double-click the document to open it in the appropriate Office application and edit as needed.

Task: Check In a Library Item

Purpose: After you have completed your edits on a checked out document, you will need to check it back in to the document library so others can edit the document.

Example: Here's how to check in a document to a document library within SharePoint.

Steps:

1. Start Internet Explorer and type the URL for your organization's SharePoint server. The Start Page will open.

2. Navigate to site where the document you have modified is located. The document workspace page will open.

3. Move the mouse over the document you have edited and click the drop-down list control that appears. The document's hover menu will appear.

4. Click the Check In option. The Check In dialog box will open.

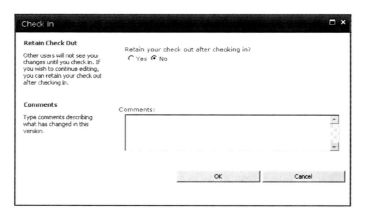

Figure 1: The Check In Dialog Box

5. If you want to keep the document checked out after checking in this version in, specify this in the Retain Check Out section.

6. Type any notes about this version of the document in the Comments field.

7. Click OK.

8. The document will be checked in.

The SharePoint Shepherd's Guide for End Users: 2010

Task: Check In a Library Item in Office 2010

Purpose: After you have completed your edits on a checked out document, you will need to check it back in to the document workspace so others can see your changes, as well as edit the document themselves.

Example: Once the document is edited by you, you can quickly check it in within Office 2010.

Steps:

1. Open an application in Microsoft Office. It can be Word, Excel, or PowerPoint.

2. Click the File tab and select Open from the menu. The Open window will appear.

3. Type the URL for the library you want to browse in the Location field. The Site Content page for your library will open.

4. Click the desired document, then click Open. The document will open in your Office application.

5. Click the File tab and select Info from the menu. The Info pane will appear.

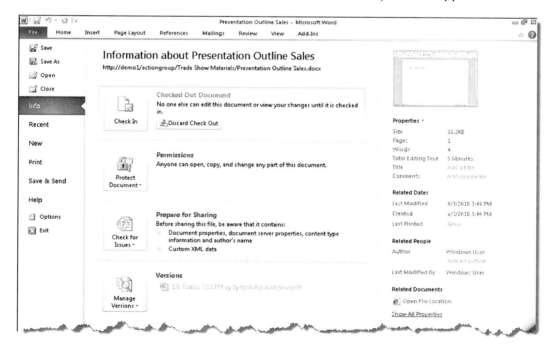

Figure 1: The Document Info Pane

6. Click the Check In icon. The Check In dialog box will appear.

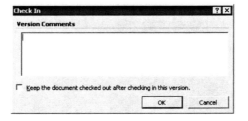

Figure 2: The Check In Dialog Box

7. Enter any notes in the Version Comments field.

8. Click OK. The document will be checked back in to the document workspace.

Task: Check In a Library Item with Office 2007

Purpose: After you have completed your edits on a checked out document, you will need to check it back in to the document workspace so others can see your changes, as well as edit the document themselves.

Example: Once the document is edited by you, you can quickly check it in within Office 2007.

Steps:

1. Open an application in Microsoft Office. It can be Word, Excel, or PowerPoint.

2. Click the Office jewel and select Open from the menu. The Open dialog box will appear.

3. Double-click the SharePoint Drafts folder in My Documents. The folder's content will appear.

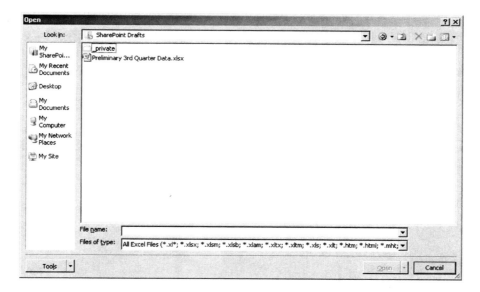

Figure 1: Opening the Draft Folder

4. Click on the desired document, then click Open. The document will open in your Office application.

5. When your edits are complete, click the Check In link in the Document Management pane. The Check In dialog box will appear.

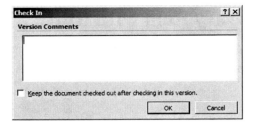

Figure 2: Checking In a Document

6.   Enter any notes in the Version Comments field.

7.   Click OK. The document will be checked back in its document library.

Task: Check In Documents in SharePoint Workspace

Purpose: After you have completed your edits on a checked out document, you will need to check it back in to the library so others can see your changes and/or edit the document themselves.

Example: Here's how to check in a document from within SharePoint Workplace.

Steps:

1. Start SharePoint Workspace 2010 by clicking the Start | All Programs | Microsoft Office | Microsoft SharePoint Workspace 2010 menu option. The Launchbar for SharePoint Workspace will open.

2. Double-click the library name that contains the document you want to edit. The main SharePoint Workspace window will open, displaying the contents of the library.

3. Select the document you want to check in.

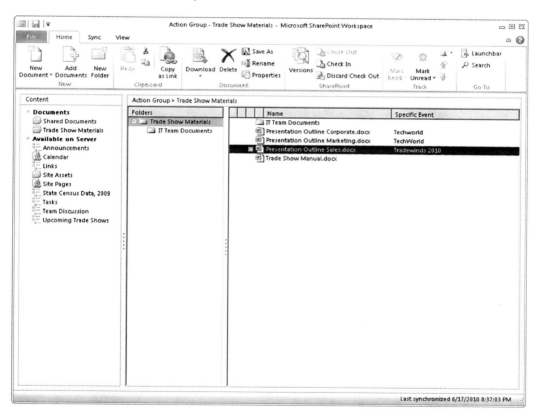

Figure 1: The Document Selected in SharePoint Workspace

4. Click the Check In button, or right-click the item and select Check In from the pop-up menu. The Check In dialog box will appear.

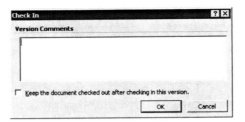

Figure 2: The Check In Dialog Box

5. Type any notes about this version of the document in the Comments field.

6. Click OK. The document will be checked in.

Task: Send a Copy of an Item to Another Library

Purpose: Many times you will have a single document that needs to be shared between libraries. You can use the Send To command to make a copy of a document in another library anywhere on your SharePoint site. This copy, also known as a Live Copy, is always linked to the original document. Thus, after making changes in the original, SharePoint will let you know there are copies of the document and give you the option of either updating the copies or breaking the link. Also, if you want to edit the copy, SharePoint will let you know it is a copy and give you the chance to edit the original instead.

Before beginning this process, navigate to the destination library and copy the URL, which is usually lengthy and hard to remember.

Steps:

1. Start Internet Explorer and type the URL for your organization's SharePoint server. The Start Page will open.

2. Navigate to the library in which you are interested. The library page will open.

3. Click the right side of an item you want to copy. The item's hover menu will appear.

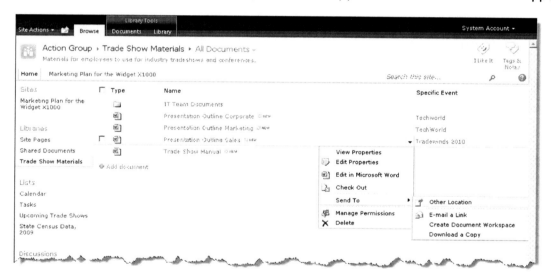

Figure 1: The Item Hover Menu

4. Select Send To. The Send To sub-menu will appear.

5. Select Other Location. The Copy dialog box will open.

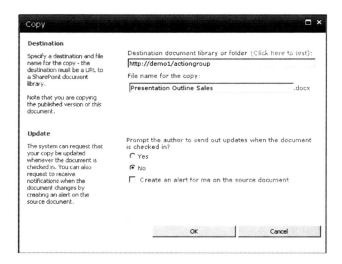

Figure 2: The Copy Dialog Box

6. Type or paste a valid URL for the destination library in the Destination document library or folder field.

7. Confirm or change the file's name in the File name for the copy field.

8. Click Yes in the Update section to prompt the file's author to let people know when the document is checked in to this library, to keep all copies of the document up to date.

9. Click OK. The Copy Progress dialog box will appear.

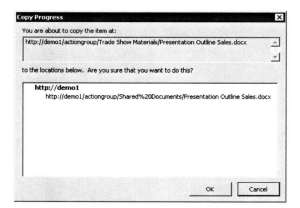

Figure 3: The Copy Progress Dialog Box

10. Click OK. The document will be copied and confirmed when finished.

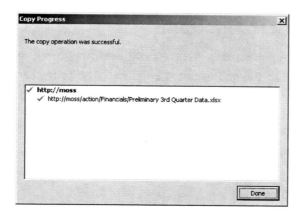

Figure 4: The Copy Progress Confirmation Dialog Box

11. Click Done. The Copy Progress dialog box will close.

Task: E-Mail a Link to the Item

Purpose: If you want to get many users involved in the editing/creation process for a document, an efficient way is to send a link to the document in an e-mail. Then they can click on the link and get right to work.

Example: One of your co-workers would like quick access to a document in the Trade Show Materials library. Sending a quick link is the fastest way.

Steps:

1. Start Internet Explorer and type the URL for your organization's SharePoint server. The Start Page will open.

2. Navigate to the library in which you are interested. The library page will open.

3. Click the right side of an item you want to send a link. The item's hover menu will appear.

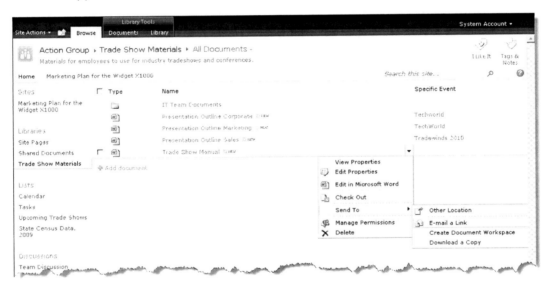

Figure 1: The Item's Context Menu

4. Select Send To. The Send To sub-menu will appear.

5. Select E-mail a Link. An Outlook message window will appear.

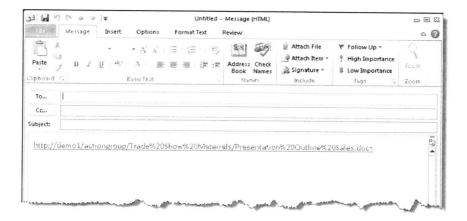

Figure 2: The Outlook Message Window with the Predetermined Link

NOTE: If Microsoft Outlook is not your default e-mail program, you will see a Compose E-mail window that contains a link to the document in the body of the e-mail.

6. Type e-mail address(es) in the To field.

7. Enter a subject in the Subject field.

8. Add a message in the body of the e-mail message.

9. Click Send. The message will be sent.

Task: Recovering Items from the Recycle Bin

Purpose: An important feature of SharePoint is the Recycle Bin. Items removed from a list are not deleted right away, but rather are sent to the Recycle Bin instead, in much the same fashion as your local Recycle Bin works on your Windows PC. Site administrators have an additional level of recycling, so even if you fair to recover an item in time, contact your SharePoint administrator. Odds are she may be able to recover the document.

Example: A document was mistakenly removed from the library, and must be recovered.

Steps:

1. Start Internet Explorer and type the URL for your organization's SharePoint server. The Start Page will open.

2. Navigate to the site from which you want to recover an item from the Recycle Bin. The site's home page will open.

3. Click the Recycle Bin link in the Quick Launch. The Recycle Bin page will open.

   NOTE: The Recycle Bin only displays the removed content for the site where it's located. So, you need to navigate to that site first to see the correct set of removed files.

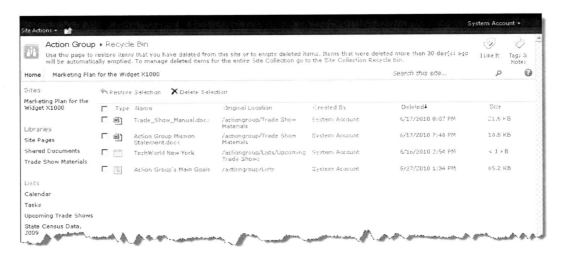

Figure 1 The Recycle Bin Page

4. Click the check boxes next to the items you want to restore to your site. The items are selected.

5. Click Restore Selection. A confirmation dialog box will open.

The SharePoint Shepherd's Guide for End Users: 2010

Figure 2: The Restore Selection Confirmation Dialog Box

6. Click OK. The selected items will be removed from the Recycle Bin and put back in their original location in the site.

7. If you want to clean out the Recycle Bin, click the check boxes next to the items you want to permanently delete (meaning you will not be able to recover them). The items are selected.

8. Click Delete Selection. A confirmation dialog box will open.

Figure 3: The Delete Selection Confirmation Dialog Box

9. Click OK. The items will be permanently deleted from the site.

NOTE: By default, all items in the Recycle Bin will be removed from your site after 30 days, to prevent storage problems on the SharePoint server. And the second level of recycling for administrators is also an option. Keep this timeline in mind if you ever need to recover a file.

Task: Edit Library Content Types

Purpose: SharePoint document libraries can contain multiple content types. You can set your library to do just that

Example: The Action Group team needs to build a library with multiple content types.

Steps:

1. Start Internet Explorer and type the URL for your organization's SharePoint server. The Start Page will open.

2. Navigate to the library in which you are interested. The document library page will open.

3. In the Library Tools tab, click the Library sub-tab. The Library Tools ribbon will open.

4. Click the Library Settings button. The Create View page will open.

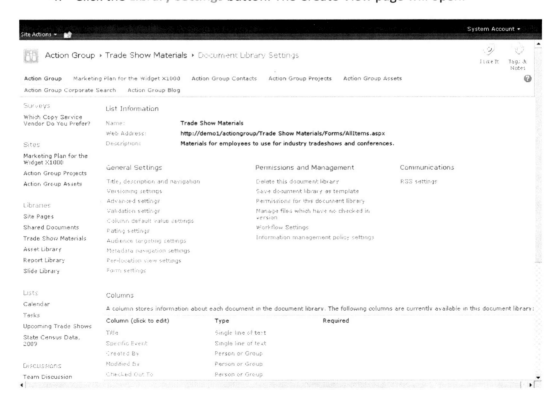

Figure 1: The Library Settings Page

5. Click Advanced Settings. The Advanced Settings page will open.

6. In the Content Types section, click Yes to allow multiple content types.

7. Click OK. The Advanced Settings page will open.

8. In the new Content Types section, click the Add from Existing Content Types link. The Select Content Types page.

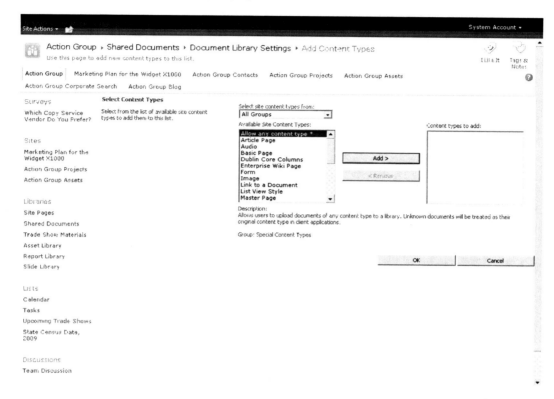

Figure 2: The Select Content Types Page

9. Select the content types you want to use, then click Add.

10. When complete, click OK. The content types will be added to the New button for the library.

Manage Business Data

SharePoint 2010 has a number of great new database templates that deliver the power of database management to an easy-to-use and flexible Web site.

In this section, you'll learn how to:

- **Create a Contacts Web Database**: The Contacts Web Database enables users to manage contact information about customers, vendors, and partners.

- **Add a Contact to the Contacts Web Database**: Start adding contacts to the Contacts Web database.

- **Edit a Contact in the Contacts Web Database**: Whenever a contact's information needs to be changed in a Contacts Web Database, you can quickly edit it.

- **Create a Projects Web Database**: The Projects Web Database enables users to create and manage ongoing projects.

- **Add New Users to the Projects Web Database**: Add new users to the Projects Web Database.

- **Add a New Project to the Projects Web Database**: After users have been added to the Projects Web Database, you can add a project to the Projects Web Database.

- **Create an Assets Web Database**: The Assets Web Database enables users to create and manage assets.

- **Add an Asset to the Assets Web Database**: To track the assets your team or company owns, you can easily add them to an Assets Web Database.

- **Retire an Asset from the Assets Web Database**: Once an asset is no longer used, you can formally retire it from an Assets Web Database.

Task: Create a Contacts Web Database

Purpose: One of the new site templates available in SharePoint 2010 is the Contacts Web Database, which enables users to manage contact information about customers, vendors, and partners.

Example: The Action Group wants to directly communicate with their customers, and have decided to build their own database to start tracking contact information.

Steps:

1. Start Internet Explorer and type the URL for your organization's SharePoint server. The Start Page will open.

2. Navigate to the site where you want to add a custom list. The site's home page will open.

3. Click the Site Actions menu and select More Options... The Create dialog box will open.

4. Click the Contacts Web Database icon. The Contacts Web Database information pane will appear.

5. Enter a title for the new database in the Title field. This will appear in any list of libraries in SharePoint.

6. Enter a short, descriptive URL in the URL name field.

7. Click the More Options button. The advanced Contacts Web Database dialog box will appear.

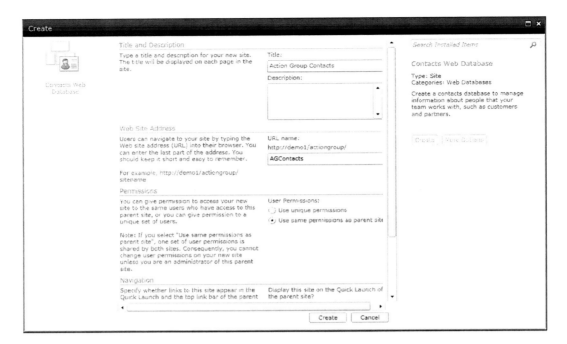

Figure 1: The Advanced Contacts Web Database Dialog Box

8. Enter any notes about the new database in the Description field.

9. Set the User Permissions field to Use same permissions as parent site.

10. If you want to have a link to the list in your site's Quick Launch, leave the Navigation option set to Yes. This will allow faster navigation by including a link to the database on the left column of most pages.

11. Set the Navigation Inheritance setting to Yes. This will keep the top link navigation bar the same as the parent site.

12. Click Create. The new database will be created and an introductory help video page will be displayed.

Figure 2: The Contacts Database Getting Started Page

Task: Add a Contact in the Contacts Web Database

Purpose: After a Contacts Web Database has been created, you can immediately start adding contacts to the database.

Example: Action Group contacts will be added to the Contacts Web Database.

Steps:

1. Start Internet Explorer and type the URL for your organization's SharePoint server. The Start Page will open.

2. Navigate to the contacts web database where you want to add a contact. The database's Getting Started page will open.

3. Click the Address Book tab. The Address Book page will open.

4. Click the Add New link. The Contact Details dialog box will appear.

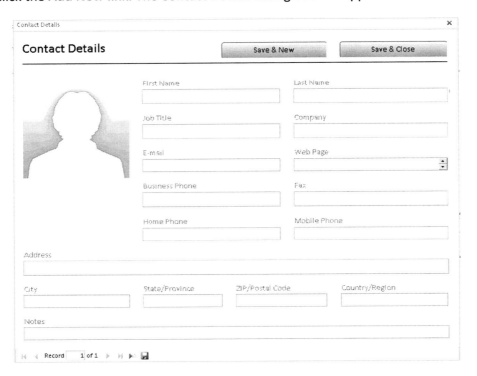

Figure 1: The Contact Details Dialog Box

5. Enter all of the relevant information in the appropriate fields. This information will populate the database.

6. Click Save & Close. The Contact Details dialog box will close and the contact will be added to the database.

Task: Edit a Contact in the Contacts Web Database

Purpose: Whenever a contact's information needs to be changed in a Contacts Web Database, you can quickly edit it.

Example: Corrections need to be made to the Action Group contacts database.

Steps:

1. Start Internet Explorer and type the URL for your organization's SharePoint server. The Start Page will open.

2. Navigate to the contacts web database where you want to edit a contact. The database's Getting Started page will open.

3. Click the Address Book tab. The Address Book page will open.

4. Click the link for the contact you want to edit. The contact's information will appear in the main pane.

5. Click the Edit Details link. The Contact Details dialog box will appear.

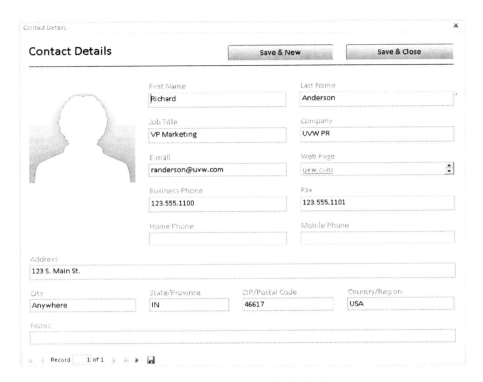

<figure>Figure 1: The Contact Details Dialog Box</figure>

6. Change the relevant information in the appropriate fields. This information will populate the database.

7. Click Save & Close. The Contact Details dialog box will close and the contact's new information will be added to the database.

Task: Create a Projects Web Database

Purpose: Another new site template available in SharePoint 2010 is the Projects Web Database, which enables users to create and manage ongoing projects.

Example: The Action Group has created its goals, and now needs to move forward with their projects. A project web database will help them achieve those ends.

Steps:

1. Start Internet Explorer and type the URL for your organization's SharePoint server. The Start Page will open.

2. Navigate to the site where you want to add a custom list. The site's home page will open.

3. Click the Site Actions menu and select More Options... The Create dialog box will open.

4. Click the Projects Web Database icon. The Projects Web Database information pane will appear.

5. Enter a title for the new database in the Title field. This will appear in any list of databases in SharePoint.

6. Enter a short, descriptive URL in the URL name field.

7. Click More Options. The advanced Create Projects Database dialog box will appear.

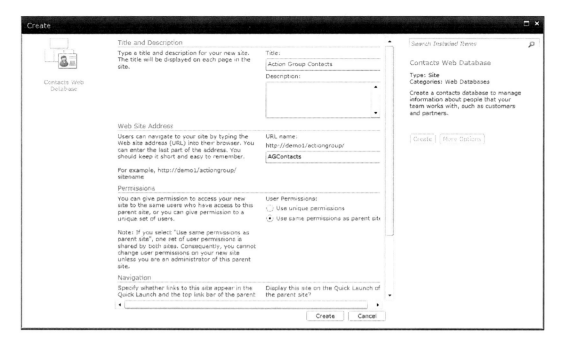

Figure 1: The Advanced Contacts Web Database Dialog Box

8.   Enter any notes about the new database in the Description field.

9.   Set the User Permissions to Use same permissions as parent site.

10. If you want to have a link to the list in your site's Quick Launch, leave the Navigation option set to Yes. This will allow faster navigation by including the database on the left column of most pages.

11. Set the Navigation Inheritance setting to Yes. This will keep the top link navigation bar the same as the parent site.

12. Click Create. The new database will be created and the Getting Started page will be displayed.

The SharePoint Shepherd's Guide for End Users: 2010

Task: Add New Users to the Projects Web Database

Purpose: Another new site template available in SharePoint 2010 is the Projects Web Database, which enables users to create and manage ongoing projects.

Example: The Action Group has created its goals, and now needs to move forward with their projects. A project web database will help them achieve those ends.

Steps:

1. Start Internet Explorer and type the URL for your organization's SharePoint server. The Start Page will open.

2. Navigate to the project database to which you want to add a user. The project database page will open.

3. Click the Users tab. The Users page will open.

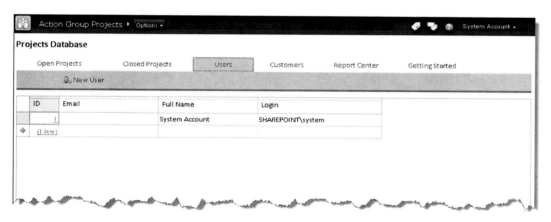

Figure 1: The Project Database Users Page

4. Click the New User link. The User Details dialog box will open.

Figure 2: The Project Database User Details Dialog Box

5. Complete the information for the fields and click Save & Close. The new user will be added to the database.

The SharePoint Shepherd's Guide for End Users: 2010

Task: Add a New Project to the Projects Web Database

Purpose: After users have been added to the Projects Web Database, you can add a project to the Projects Web Database.

Example: The Action Group will add one of their projects to the Projects Web Database.

Steps:

1. Start Internet Explorer and type the URL for your organization's SharePoint server. The Start Page will open.

2. Navigate to the projects web database where you want to add a project. The database's Getting Started page will open.

3. Click the Open Projects tab. The Open Projects page will open.

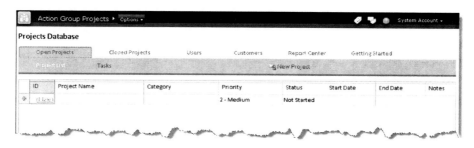

Figure 1: The Projects Database Open Projects Page

4. Click the New Project link. The Project Details dialog box will appear.

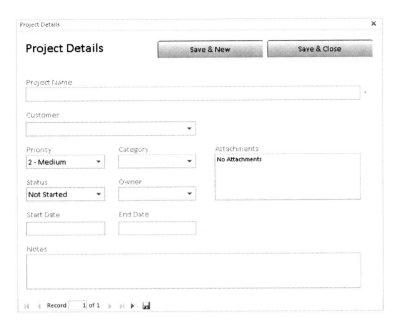

Figure 2: The Project Details Dialog Box

5. Enter a name for the project in the Project Name field.

6. Click the Customer drop-down list control. The Customer drop-down list will appear.

7. Click Edit List Items in the Customer drop-down list. The Customer Details dialog box will appear.

Figure 3: The Customer Details Dialog Box

8. Enter the information in the appropriate fields. The information will be added to the Customer database.

9. Click Save & Close. The Customer Details dialog box will close and the customer name will appear in the Customer drop-down list.

10. Select the customer in the Customer drop-down list.

11. Continue with adding information to the remaining fields.

12. Click Save & Close. The Project Details dialog box will close and the project will be added to the database. The new project will be listed on the projects database Open Projects page.

Task: Create an Assets Web Database

Purpose: Another new site template available in SharePoint 2010 is the Assets Web Database, which enables users to create and manage assets.

Example: The Action Group has created its goals, and now needs to move forward with identifying their assets. An assets web database will help them record and manage their company equipment.

Steps:

1. Start Internet Explorer and type the URL for your organization's SharePoint server. The Start Page will open.

2. Navigate to the site where you want to add an asset library. The site's home page will open.

3. Click the Site Actions menu and select More Options... The Create dialog box will open.

4. Click the Assets Web Database icon. The Assets Web Database information pane will appear.

5. Enter a title for the new asset library in the Title field. This will appear in any list of databases in SharePoint.

6. Enter a short, descriptive URL in the URL name field.

7. Click the More Options button. The advanced Create Assets Database dialog box will appear.

8. Enter any notes about the new database in the Description field.

9. Set the User Permissions to Use same permissions as parent site.

10. If you want to have a link to the list in your site's Quick Launch, leave the Navigation option set to Yes. This will allow faster navigation by including the database on the left column of most pages.

11. Set the Navigation Inheritance setting to Yes. This will keep the top link navigation bar the same as the parent site.

12. Click Create. The new database will be created and the Getting Started page will be displayed.

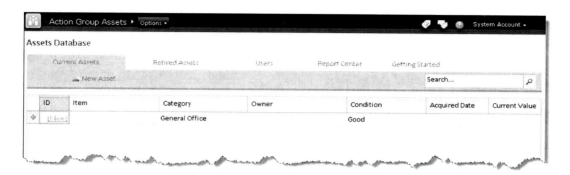

Figure 1: The Assets Database Current Assets Page

Task: Add an Asset to the Assets Web Database

Purpose: To track the assets your team or company owns, you can easily add them to an Assets Web Database.

Example: The Action Group will add their computer equipment to the Assets Web Database.

Steps:

1. Start Internet Explorer and type the URL for your organization's SharePoint server. The Start Page will open.

2. Navigate to the assets web database where you want to add an asset. The database's Getting Started page will open.

3. Click the Current Assets tab. The Current Assets page will open.

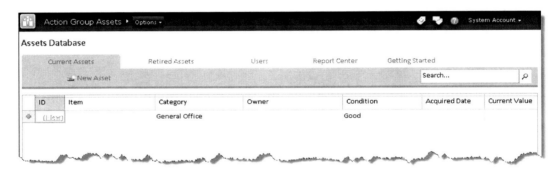

Figure 1: The Assets Database Current Assets Page

4. Click the New Asset link. The Asset Details dialog box will appear.

Figure 2: The Asset Details Dialog Box

5. Enter the information in the appropriate fields. The information will be added to the Asset database.

6. Click Save & Close. The Asset Details dialog box asset's information will be added to the database.

Task: Retire an Asset from the Assets Web Database

Purpose: Once an asset is no longer used, you can formally retire it from an Assets Web Database.

Example: The Action Group is removing some of their computer equipment, and will need to retire the assets from the Assets Web Database in order to keep track of the equipment for tax purposes.

Steps:

1. Start Internet Explorer and type the URL for your organization's SharePoint server. The Start Page will open.

2. Navigate to the assets web database where you want to retire an asset. The database's Getting Started page will open.

3. Click the Current Assets tab. The Current Assets page will open.

4. Click the ID link for the asset you want to retire. The Asset Details dialog box will appear.

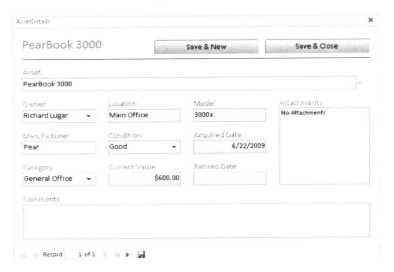

Figure 1: The Asset Details Dialog Box

5. Add a date to the Retired Date field. The information will be added to the Asset database.

6. Click Save & Close. The asset will now appear on the Retired Assets page in the Asset database.

SharePoint is very tightly integrated to the Microsoft Office applications including integration with Microsoft Outlook, which allows for much more efficient communications of SharePoint-hosted information. SharePoint will allow you to connect its document libraries, tasks lists and calendars directly to Outlook 2010 or 2007.

In this section, you'll learn how to:

- **Connect a SharePoint Resource to Outlook**: The basics of connecting from SharePoint to Outlook 2010 or 2007.

- **Share SharePoint Content with Outlook**: After a library or other SharePoint resource is connected to Outlook, you can use Outlook 2010 or 2007 to quickly share the contents of that resource with other users.

- **Connect to SharePoint from a Sharing Message**: Once a library or other SharePoint resource has been shared via an Outlook 2010 or 2007 message, the recipients can quickly connect when they open that message.

- **Edit Document Library Files in Outlook**: After you have connected to a document library in Outlook, you can access and edit the files in the library directly from Outlook 2010 or 2007, without connecting to the SharePoint server.

- **Remove a Connected Document from Outlook**: There may be instances where you won't need a copy of every document or file in the library. Here's how to remove offline copies of documents from Outlook 2010 or 2007.

- **View a SharePoint Calendar with Outlook**: Like document libraries or tasks lists, calendars can also be connected to and viewed in Outlook 2010 or 2007.

- **Edit a SharePoint Calendar in Outlook**: Any changes or additions you make to the copy of the SharePoint calendar in Outlook 2010 or 2007 will be reflected in the original calendar.

- **Create a Meeting Workspace with Outlook**: Just as you can create a document workspace in SharePoint with Office applications, you can create a Meeting Workspace in SharePoint with Outlook 2010 or 2007.

- **Remove a SharePoint Resource from Outlook**: Once you no longer need a connection to a SharePoint resource, you can remove it from Outlook 2010 or 2007 with ease.

Task: Connect a SharePoint Library to Outlook 2010

Purpose: SharePoint is very tightly integrated to the Microsoft Office applications. It also shares integration with Microsoft Outlook, which allows for much more efficient communications of SharePoint-related activities.

Example: You can't connect Outlook and SharePoint at the team site level. Only certain resources of a site, such as a document library, task list, or a calendar can be connected to Outlook. This will also allow easy offline editing of SharePoint items. Here's how to get that connection set up.

Steps:

1. Start Internet Explorer and type the URL for your organization's SharePoint server. The Start Page will open.

2. Navigate to the resource you want to connect to Outlook. The resource's page (in this case, a document library) will open.

3. In the Library Tools tab, click the Library sub-tab. The Library Tools ribbon will appear.

4. Click the Connect to Outlook button. A confirmation dialog box will open.

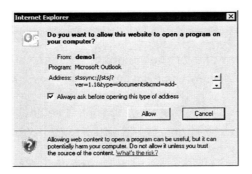

Figure 1: The Connect to Outlook Confirmation Dialog Box

5. Click Allow. A Connect to Outlook dialog box will open.

Figure 2: The Connect to Outlook Dialog Box

6. Click Yes. The library will appear in the SharePoint Lists section of the Outlook folder pane.

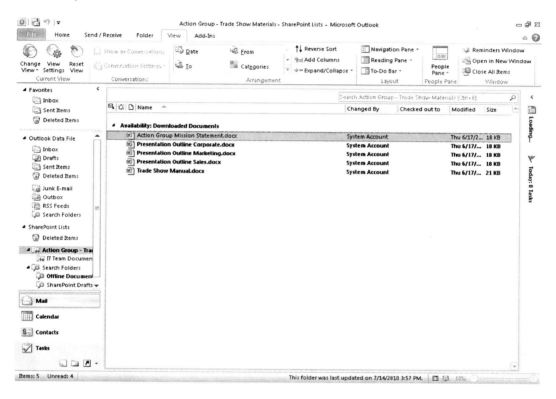

Figure 3: The Connected Library in Outlook

Task: Connect a SharePoint Library to Outlook 2007

Purpose: SharePoint is very tightly integrated to the Microsoft Office applications. It also shares integration with Microsoft Outlook, which allows for much more efficient communications of SharePoint-related activities.

Example: You can't connect Outlook and SharePoint at the team site level. Only certain resources of a site, such as a document library, task list, or a calendar can be connected to Outlook. This will also allow easy offline editing of SharePoint items. Here's how to get that connection set up.

Steps:

1. Start Internet Explorer and type the URL for your organization's SharePoint server. The Start Page will open.

2. Navigate to the resource you want to connect to Outlook. The resource's page (in this case, a document library) will open.

3. Click the Library sub-tab of the Library Tools tab. The Library Tools ribbon will appear.

4. Click the Connect to Outlook button. A confirmation dialog box will open.

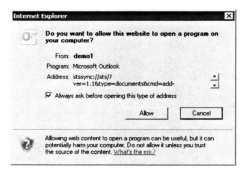

Figure 1: The Connect to Outlook Confirmation Dialog Box

5. Click Allow. Outlook will display its own confirmation dialog box for the library connection.

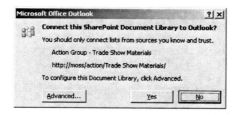

Figure 2: The Outlook Connection Confirmation Dialog Box

6. Click Yes. The library will appear in the Mail pane of Outlook.

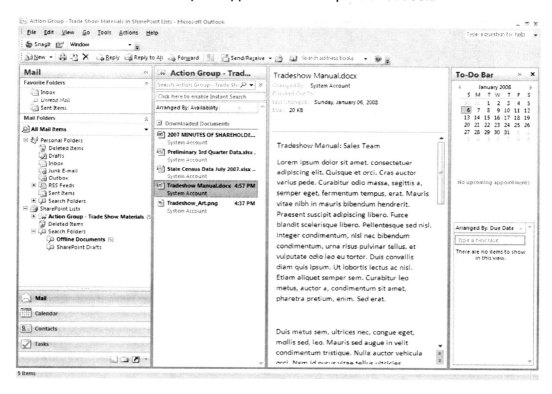

Figure 3: The Connected Library in Outlook

Task: Share SharePoint Content with Outlook 2010

Purpose: After a library or other SharePoint resource is connected to Outlook, you can use Outlook to quickly share the contents of that resource with other users. This is done by sending a message containing a special link that will automatically connect other users' Outlook installations to the SharePoint server.

Example: The Action Group wants to get the word out to employees about their Trade Show Materials library, and using Outlook to e-mail a link to the folder is the fastest way.

Steps:

1. In Outlook, navigate to the Mail column.

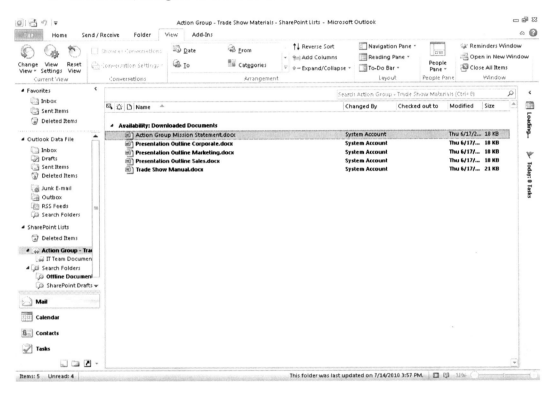

Figure 1: Outlook 2010

2. Right-click the folder for the SharePoint resource you want to share. The context menu will appear.

3. Select the Share menu, then Share this Folder. A message window will open with a predetermined subject detailing the contents of the library.

4. Enter an e-mail address in the To field.

5. Click Send. The message will be sent.

Task: Share Outlook Content with Outlook 2007

Purpose: After a library or other SharePoint resource is connected to Outlook, you can use Outlook to quickly share the contents of that resource with other users. This is done by sending a message containing a special link that will automatically connect other users' Outlook installations to the SharePoint server.

Example: The Action Group wants to get the word out to employees about their Trade Show Materials library, and using Outlook to e-mail a link to the folder is the fastest way.

Steps:

1. In Outlook, navigate to the Mail column.

2. Right-click the folder for the SharePoint resource you want to share. The context menu will appear.

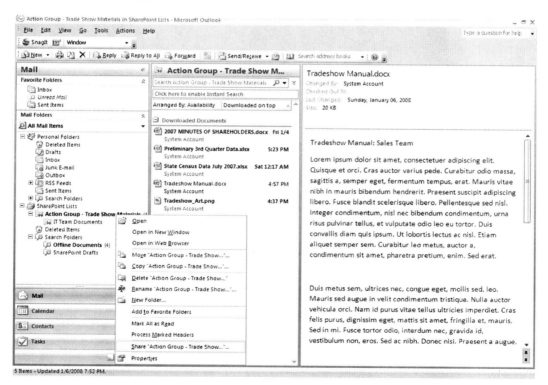

Figure 1: The Context Menu for the Resource to Share

3. Select the Share... option. A message window will open with a predetermined subject detailing the contents of the library.

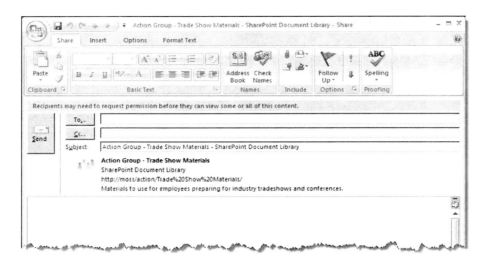

Figure 2: The Message Window with Predetermined Subject

4. Enter an e-mail address in the To field.

5. Click Send. The message will be sent.

Task: Connect to SharePoint from a Sharing Message in Outlook 2010

Purpose: Once a library or other SharePoint resource has been shared via an Outlook message, the recipients can quickly connect when they open that message.

Example: The Action Group has received the e-mail with the link to the Trade Show Materials library and now need to open it.

Steps:

1. In Outlook, navigate to the Inbox.

2. In the Inbox pane, double-click the message. The message window will appear.

3. In the Share ribbon, click the Connect to this Document Library button. A confirmation dialog box will open.

4. Click Yes. The library will appear in the Mail pane of Outlook.

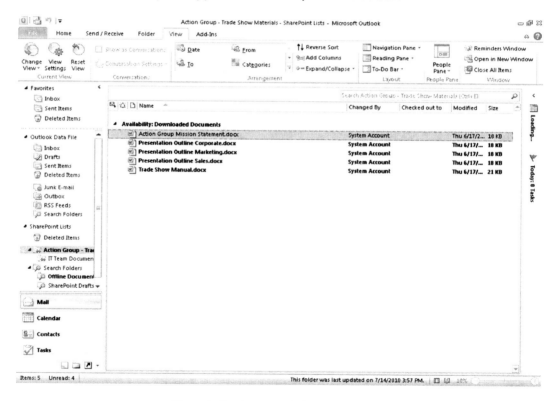

Figure 1: The Connected Library in Outlook

Task: Connect to SharePoint from a Sharing Message in Outlook 2007

Purpose: Once a library or other SharePoint resource has been shared via an Outlook message, the recipients can quickly connect when they open that message.

Example: The Action Group has received the e-mail with the link to the Trade Show Materials library and now need to open it.

Steps:

1. In Outlook, navigate to the Inbox.

2. In the Inbox pane, double-click the message. The message window will appear.

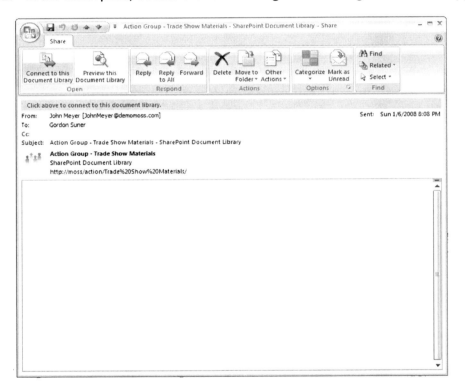

Figure 1: The Message Window

3. In the Share ribbon, click the Connect to this Document Library button. A confirmation dialog box will open.

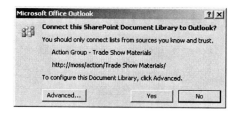

Figure 2: The Confirmation Dialog Box

4. Click Yes. The library will appear in the Mail pane in Outlook.

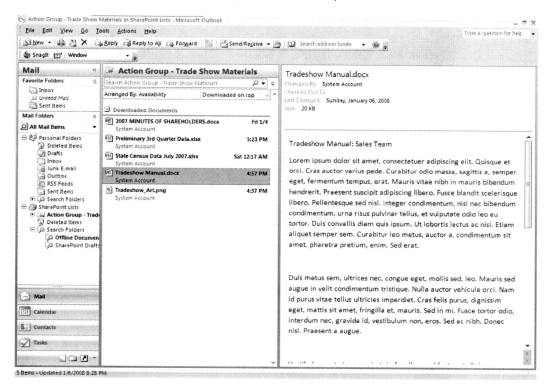

Figure 3: The Library in the Mail Pane in Outlook

Task: Edit Document Library Files in Outlook 2010

Purpose: After you have connected to a document library in Outlook, you can access and edit the files in the library directly from Outlook, without connecting to the SharePoint server.

Steps:

1. In Outlook, navigate to the Mail column.

2. Click the document library folder. The contents of the document library will appear in the library's pane.

3. Double-click a document in the library pane. The Opening File dialog box will open.

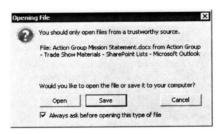

Figure 1: The Opening File Dialog Box

4. Click Open. The document will open in the appropriate application in read-only form.

Figure 2: The Document is Still in Read-Only Form

5. Click the Edit Document button just above the document. The Edit Offline dialog box will open.

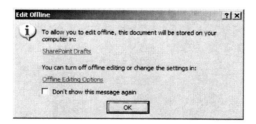

Figure 3: The Edit Offline Dialog Box

6. Click OK. The Edit Offline dialog box will close and the document will be stored in the SharePoint Drafts folder and can now be edited.

7. Edit and save the document.

8. Close the document. The Edit Offline dialog box will appear again if you are online.

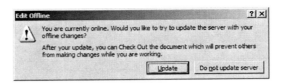

Figure 4: The Edit Offline Dialog Box

9. Click Update. The Edit Offline dialog box will close and the changes will be saved to the SharePoint document and reflected in the Outlook connection. If Outlook is offline, then any changes made to the document will be communicated back to the SharePoint library when Outlook is online again.

Task: Edit Document Library Files in Outlook 2007

Purpose: After you have connected to a document library in Outlook, you can access and edit the files in the library directly from Outlook, without connecting to the SharePoint server.

Steps:

1. In Outlook, navigate to the Mail pane.

2. Click the document library folder. The contents of the document library will appear in the library's pane.

3. Double-click a document in the library pane. The Opening File dialog box will open.

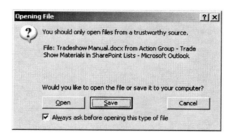

Figure 1: The Opening File Dialog Box

4. Click Open. The document will open in the appropriate application in read-only form.

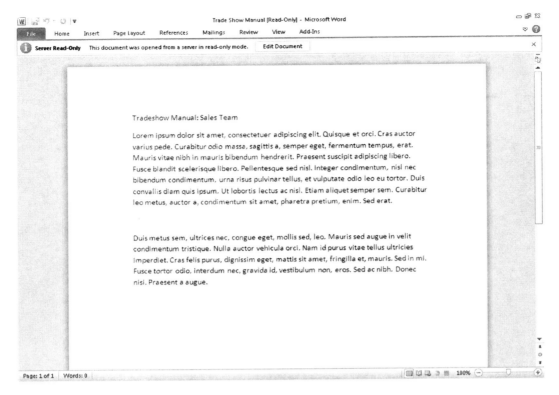

Figure 2: The Document Openin Read-Only Form

5. Click the Edit Document button just above the document. The Edit Offline dialog box will open.

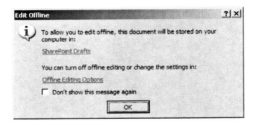

Figure 3: The Edit Offline Dialog Box

6. Click OK. The Edit Offline dialog box will close and the document will be stored in the SharePoint Drafts folder and can now be edited.

7. Edit and save the document.

8. Close the document. The Edit Offline dialog box will appear again if you are online.

Figure 4: The Edit Offline Dialog Box

9. Click Update. The Edit Offline dialog box will close and the changes will be saved to the SharePoint document and reflected in the Outlook connection. If Outlook is offline, then any changes made to the document will be communicated back to the SharePoint library when Outlook is online again.

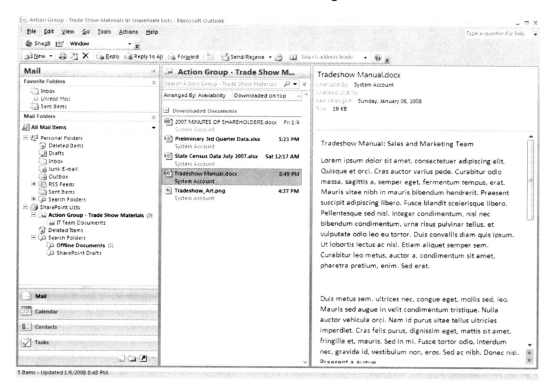

Figure 5: The Updated Document in Outlook

Task: Remove a Connected Document from Outlook 2010

Purpose: When you connect to a SharePoint document library, you get the whole contents of the library. There may be instances where you won't need a copy of every document or file in the library.

Example: Here's how to remove offline copies from Outlook. Note that this does not remove the original copy of the document from the SharePoint server.

Steps:

1. In Outlook, navigate to the Mail column.

2. Click the document library folder. The contents of the document library will appear in the library's pane.

3. Right click a document in the library pane. The context menu will appear.

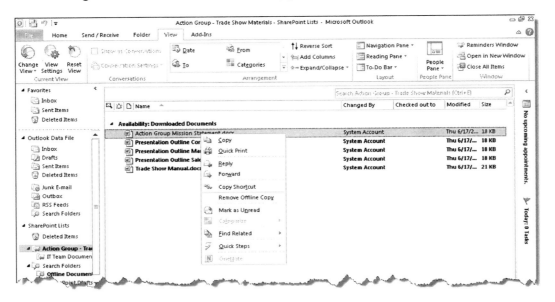

Figure 1: The Context Menu in the Library Pane

4. Select Remove Offline Copy. The document will now appear in the Available for Download section of the library pane.

NOTE: There may be other additional documents in the Available for Download section since the last time you connected to the library.

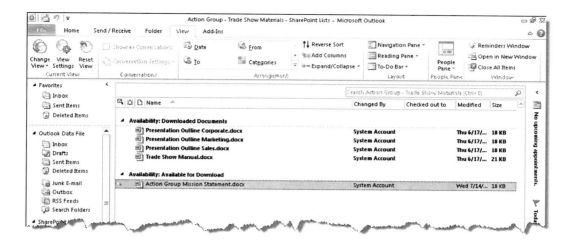

Figure 2: The Library Pane in Outlook

Task: Remove a Connected Document from Outlook 2007

Purpose: When you connect to a SharePoint document library, you get the whole contents of the library. There may be instances where you won't need a copy of every document or file in the library.

Example: Here's how to remove offline copies from Outlook. Note that this does not remove the original copy of the document from the SharePoint server.

Steps:

1. In Outlook, navigate to the Mail pane.

2. Click the document library folder. The contents of the document library will appear in the library's pane.

3. Right-click a document in the library pane. The context menu will appear.

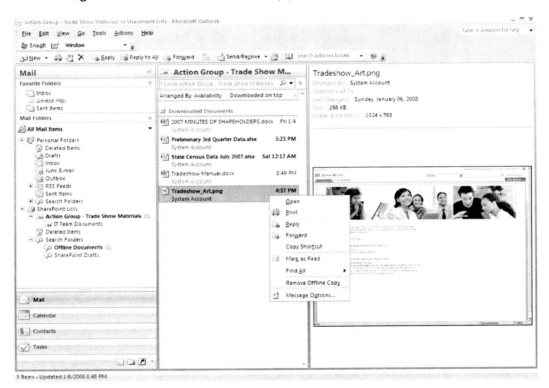

Figure 1: The Context Menu

4. Select Remove Offline Copy. The document will now appear in the Available for Download section of the library pane.

   NOTE: There may be other additional documents in the Available for Download section since the last time you connected to the library.

The SharePoint Shepherd's Guide for End Users: 2010

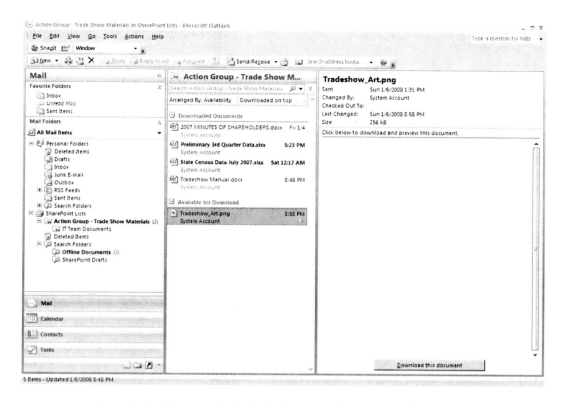

Figure 2: The File in the Available for Download Section of the Library Pane

Task: View a SharePoint Calendar with Outlook 2010

Purpose: Like document libraries or task lists, calendars can also be connected to and viewed in Outlook. Also, any changes or additions you make to the copy of the SharePoint calendar in Outlook will be reflected in the original calendar.

Example: The Action Group team members can connect to their SharePoint Calendars easily from Outlook.

Steps:

1. Start Internet Explorer and type the URL for your organization's SharePoint server. The Start Page will open.

2. Navigate to the resource you want to connect to Outlook. The resource's page (in this case, a calendar) will open.

3. In the Calendar Tools tab, click the Calendar sub-tab. The Calendar Tools ribbon will appear.

4. Click the Connect to Outlook button. A confirmation dialog box will open.

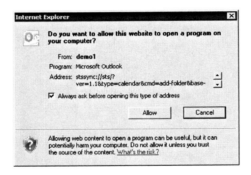

Figure 1: The Connect to Outlook Confirmation Dialog Box

5. Click Allow. A confirmation dialog box will appear.

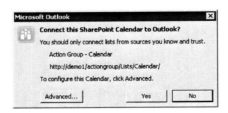

Figure 2: The Connect to Outlook Confirmation Dialog Box

NOTE: Clicking the Advanced button will display the SharePoint List Options dialog box, which will allow you to add more descriptive information, if needed.

6. Click Yes. The calendar will appear in the Calendar pane of Outlook.

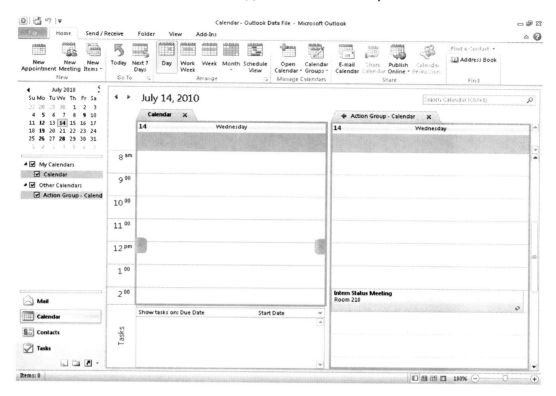

Figure 3: The Connected Calendar in Outlook

7. If you want to see both calendars at once to check for conflicts, click View in Overlay Mode button in the SharePoint calendar's tab. The calendars will be merged.

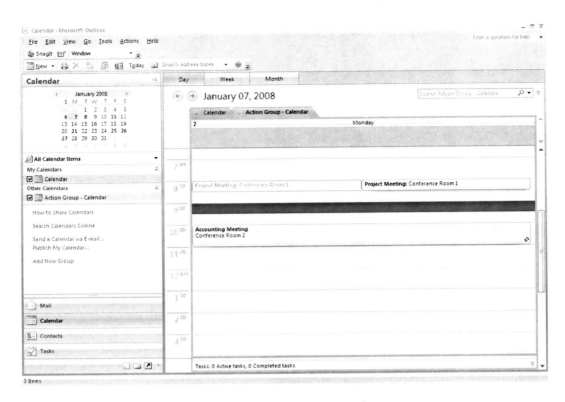

Figure 4: The View in Overlay Mode

8. To return to the default view, click the View in Side-by-Side mode button in either of the calendar tabs.

9. To view just the SharePoint calendar, click the Calendars check box under the My Calendars heading. The local calendar will close.

The SharePoint Shepherd's Guide for End Users: 2010

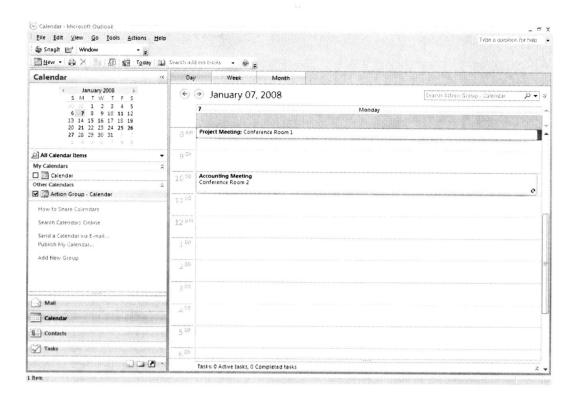

Figure 5: The Remote Calendar

Task: View a SharePoint Calendar with Outlook 2007

Purpose: Like document libraries or task lists, calendars can also be connected to and viewed in Outlook. Also, any changes or additions you make to the copy of the SharePoint calendar in Outlook will be reflected in the original calendar.

Example: The Action Group team members can connect to their SharePoint Calendars easily from Outlook.

Steps:

1. Start Internet Explorer and type the URL for your organization's SharePoint server. The Start Page will open.

2. Navigate to the resource you want to connect to Outlook. The resource's page (in this case, a document library) will open.

3. Click the Calendar sub-tab of the Calendar Tools tab. The Calendar Tools page will appear.

4. Click the Connect to Outlook button. A confirmation dialog box will open.

    NOTE: Clicking the Advanced button will display the SharePoint List Options dialog box, which will allow you to add more descriptive information, if needed.

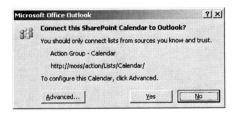

Figure 1: The Confirmation Dialog Box

5. Click Yes. The calendar will appear in the Calendar pane of Outlook.

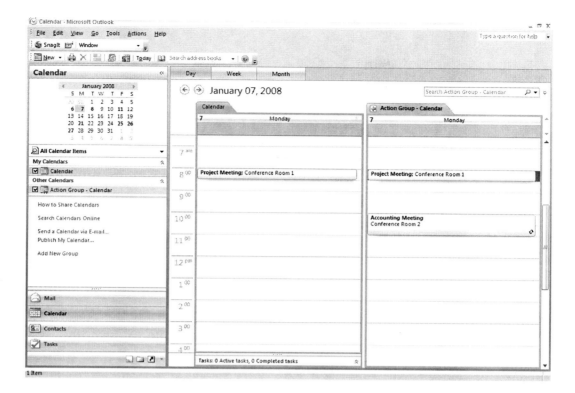

Figure 2: The Calendar in Outlook

6. If you want to see both calendars at once to check for conflicts, click the View in Overlay Mode button in the SharePoint calendar's tab. The calendars will be merged.

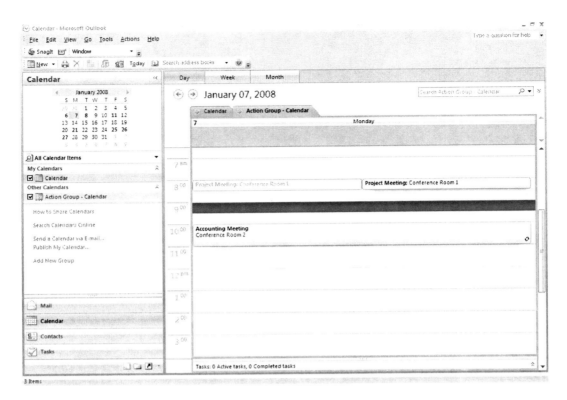

Figure 3: The Calendars in View in Overlay Mode

7. To return to the default view, click the View in Side-by-Side Mode button for either of the calendar tabs.

8. To view just the SharePoint calendar, click the Calendar check box under the My Calendars heading. The local calendar will close.

The SharePoint Shepherd's Guide for End Users: 2010

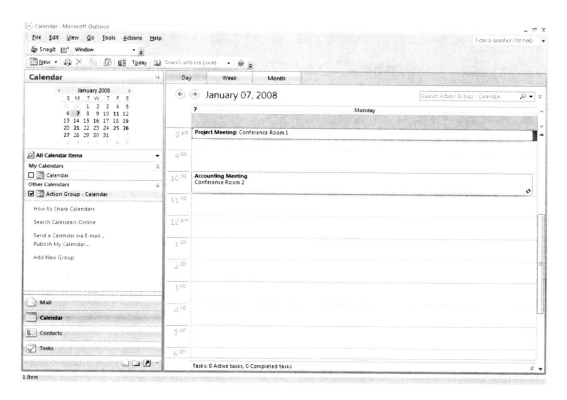

Figure 4: The Remote Calendar in Outlook

Task: Edit a SharePoint Calendar in Outlook 2010

Purpose: Any changes or additions you make to the copy of the SharePoint calendar in Outlook will be reflected in the original calendar.

Example: Action Group team members can copy personal calendar events to their SharePoint calendar, or vice versa, as well as make changes directly to the SharePoint calendar.

Steps:

1. Navigate to the Calendar pane in Outlook. The Calendar page will appear.

2. Click SharePoint Calendar check box to select it. The calendar will open.

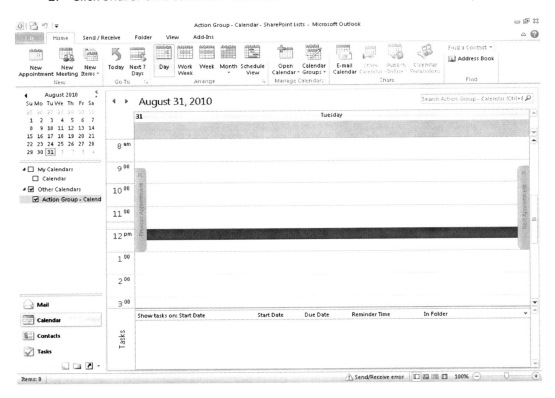

Figure 1: The Remote Calendars in Outlook

3. Click the New Appointment button. The Untitled Appointment dialog box will open.

The SharePoint Shepherd's Guide for End Users: 2010

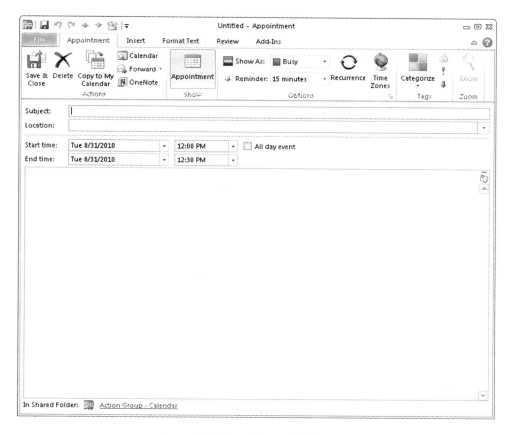

Figure 2: The Appointment Dialog Box.

4. Fill in the fields and click Save & Close. The event changes will appear on the SharePoint calendar.

Task: Edit a SharePoint Calendar in Outlook 2007

Purpose: Any changes or additions you make to the copy of the SharePoint calendar in Outlook will be reflected in the original calendar.

Example: Action Group team members can copy personal calendar events to their SharePoint calendar, or vice versa, as well as make changes directly to the SharePoint calendar.

Steps:

1. Navigate to the Calendar pane in Outlook. The Calendar page will appear.

2. Click the SharePoint calendar check box to select it. The calendar will open.

3. Click the View in Overlay Mode button on the left side of the SharePoint calendar tab. The calendar will display the Overlay Mode view.

4. Click the New button drop-down control, then click New Event. The Event window will open.

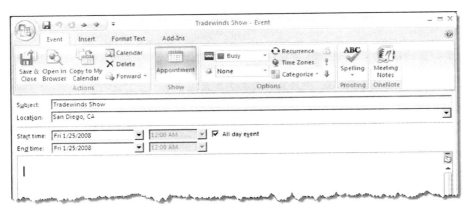

Figure 1: The Event Window

5. Fill in the event fields and click Save & Close. The event changes will appear on the SharePoint calendar.

The SharePoint Shepherd's Guide for End Users: 2010

Task: Create a Meeting Workspace with Outlook 2010

Purpose: Just as you can create a document workspace in SharePoint with Office applications, you can create a Meeting Workspace in SharePoint with Outlook 2010.

Example: The Action Group coordinator needs to get an appointment onto the SharePoint Calendar quickly.

Steps:

In Outlook, select the Home tab, then click New Items, Meeting. The Meeting window will open.

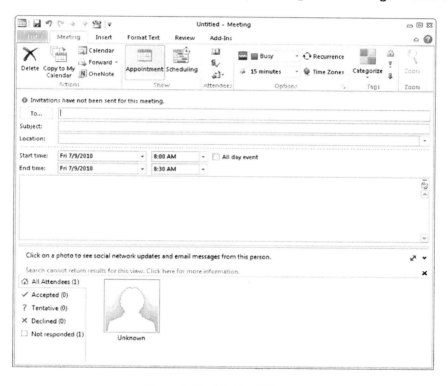

Figure 1: The Meeting Window

1. Set your appointment times and other parameters as you normally would in Outlook.

2. Add attendees' e-mail addresses in the To field.

3. Add a meeting title in the Subject field.

4. Add a place for the meeting in the Location field.

5. Click the Meeting Workspace icon in the Quick Access toolbar at the very top of the window. The Meeting Workspace pane will open.

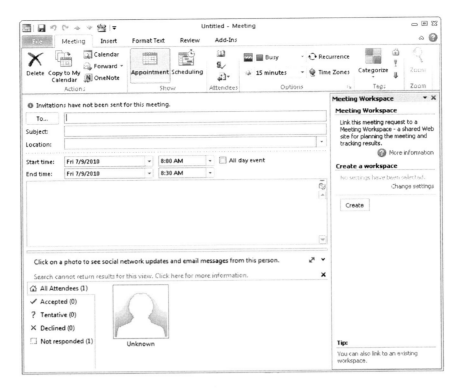

Figure 3: The Meeting Workspace Pane

6. Click the Change Settings link. The Meeting Workspace settings will appear.

7. Edit the settings and click OK. The Meeting Workspace pane will display the new settings.

8. Click Create. The meeting workspace will be created on the SharePoint server and linked in the meeting request message.

9. Click the Save button. The meeting request will be sent to the attendees.

Task: Create a Meeting Workspace with Outlook 2007

Purpose: Just as you can create a document workspace in SharePoint with Office applications, you can create a Meeting Workspace in SharePoint with Outlook.

Example: The Action Group coordinator needs to get an appointment onto the SharePoint Calendar quickly.

Steps:

1. In Outlook, click the File, New, Appointment menu option. The Appointment window will open.

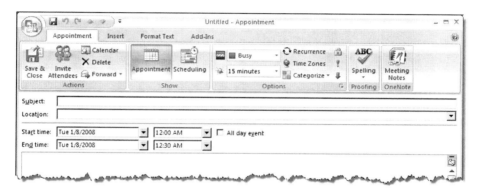

Figure 1: The Appointment Window

2. Set your appointment times and other parameters as you normally would in Outlook.

3. Click the Office jewel and select the Meeting Request option. The Meeting window will open.

   NOTE: You can also open the Meeting window by right-clicking a time in the Outlook calendar and selecting the Meeting Request option

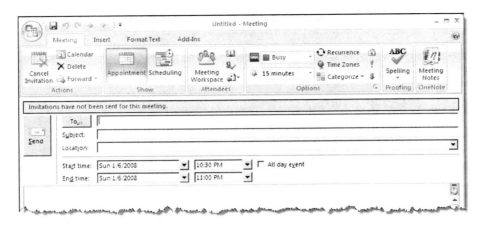

Figure 2: The Meeting Window

4. Add attendees' e-mail addresses in the To field.

5. Add a meeting title in the Subject field.

6. Add a place for the meeting in the Location field.

7. Click the Meeting Workspace button in the Attendees section of the Meeting ribbon. The Meeting Workspace pane will open.

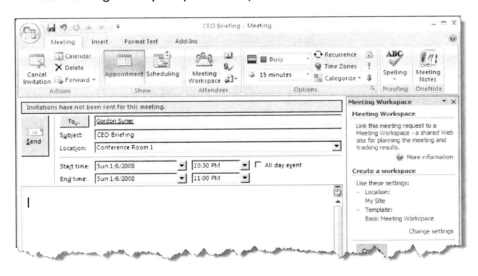

Figure 3: The Meeting Workspace Pane

8. Click the Change Settings link in the Meeting Workspace pane. The Meeting Workspace settings will appear.

The SharePoint Shepherd's Guide for End Users: 2010

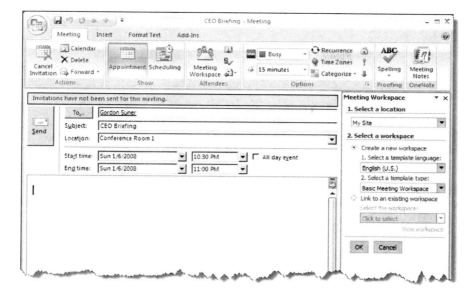

Figure 4: The Meeting Workspace Settings

9. Edit the settings and click OK. The Meeting Workspace pane will display the new settings.

10. Click Create. The meeting workspace will be created on the SharePoint server and linked in the meeting request message.

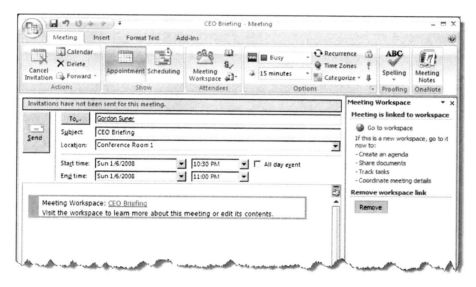

Figure 5: The Linked Meeting Workspace

11. Click Send. The meeting request will be sent to the attendees.

12. In the Appointment window, click Save & Close.

Task: Remove a SharePoint Resource from Outlook 2010

Purpose: Once you no longer need a connection to a SharePoint resource, such as a library, list, or document workspace, you can remove it from Outlook with ease. This disconnects Outlook from SharePoint for the specified resource.

Example: The Action Group coordinator no longer needs a connection to the SharePoint Calendar and will remove it.

Steps:

1. In Outlook, navigate to the pane containing the SharePoint resource you want to remove.

2. Right click the name of the resource. The context menu will appear.

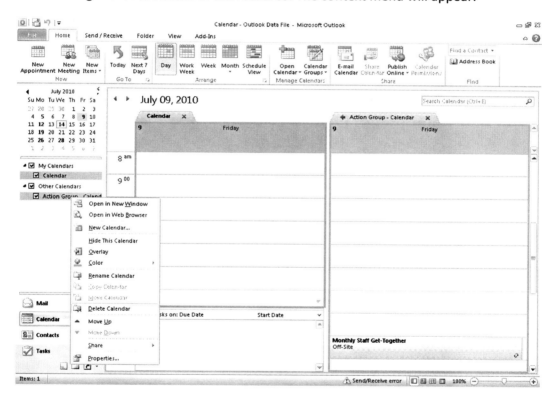

Figure 1: The Context Menu in Outlook

3. Select the Delete option. A confirmation dialog box will open.

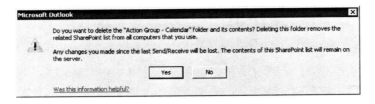

Figure 2: The Delete Confirmation Dialog Box

4. Click Yes. The resource will be removed from Outlook. It will still exist on the SharePoint server, but as a user, you will not be able to connect to the resource through Outlook until you create the link again.

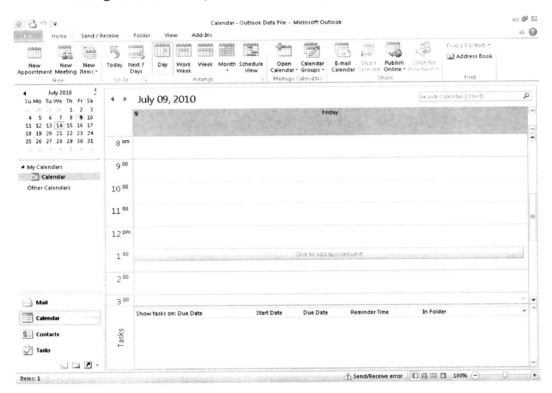

Figure 3: The Resource is Removed from the Left Navigation Menu

Task: Remove a SharePoint Resource from Outlook 2007

Purpose: Once you no longer need a connection to a SharePoint resource, such as a library, list, or document workspace, you can remove it from Outlook 2007 with ease. This disconnects Outlook from SharePoint for the specified resource.

Example: The Action Group coordinator no longer needs a connection to the SharePoint Calendar and will remove it.

Steps:

1. In Outlook, navigate to the pane containing the SharePoint resource you want to remove.

2. Right click the name of the resource. The context menu will appear.

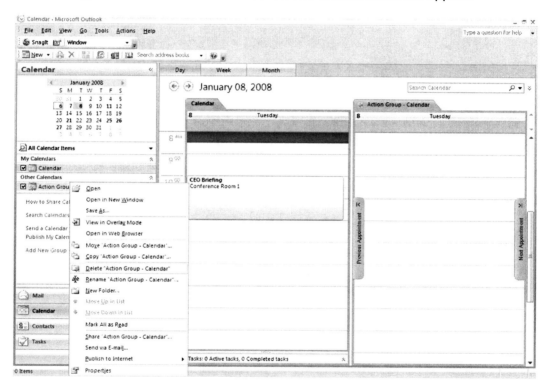

Figure 1: The Context Menu

3. Select the Delete option. A confirmation dialog box will open.

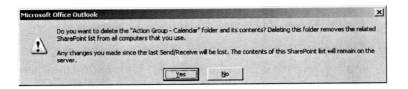

Figure 2: The Confirmation Dialog Box

4. Click Yes. The resource will be removed from Outlook. It will still exist on the SharePoint server, but as a user, you will not be able to connect to the resource through Outlook until you create the link again.

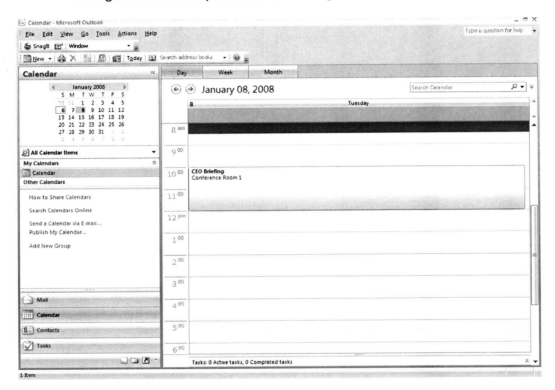

Figure 3: The Removed Resource in Outlook

Conduct Surveys

When you need to quickly gather data or opinions from a group, a fast way to accomplish this is to use a SharePoint survey. Surveys, which are specialized SharePoint tracking lists, are easy to make, easy to distribute, and easy to read.

In this section, you'll learn how to:

- Create a Survey: The basics of creating a survey.

- Preview Your Survey: Once a survey is created, testing it is a good idea.

- Enable Survey Branching: Branching is used when user's answer to a survey question will influence which questions are asked later in the survey. Branching is a vital component of effective survey design.

- Send a Survey Link: Like a document library or other SharePoint resource, it's often useful to send out a notice of a survey so users will be aware of it for participation.

- View Survey Results: Once a survey is completed, you can view the results in a comparative graphical form, or view the answers given by individual respondents.

- Compile Survey Results: When a survey with many questions and/or many respondents is completed, just viewing the results might not be enough. You may need to do some serious data tabulation and number crunching.

Task: Create a Survey

Purpose: When you need to quickly gather data or opinions from a group, a fast way to accomplish this is to use a SharePoint survey. Surveys, which are really specialized tracking lists, are easy to make, easy to distribute, and easy to read—complete with built-in analysis of the results.

Example: The Action Group can follow the steps in this task to get started with a multiple-choice survey.

Steps:

1. Start Internet Explorer and type the URL for your organization's SharePoint server. The Start Page will open.

2. Navigate to the site where you want to add a custom list. The site's home page will open.

3. Click the Site Actions menu and select More Options... The Create dialog box will open.

4. Scroll down and click the Survey icon. The Survey information pane will appear.

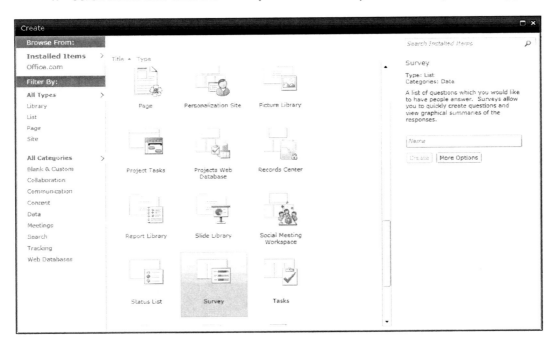

Figure 1: The Create Dialog Box

5. Enter a title for the new survey in the Name field. This will appear in any list of surveys in SharePoint.

6. Click More Options. The advanced create dialog box will appear.

7. Enter a summary of the survey in the Description field.

8. Click Yes to display the survey in the Quick Launch. This will keep a link present on the left side navigation menu.

9. Select the appropriate options in the Survey Options section. There are two options to select: you can choose whether you want user names to be displayed with each survey result, and if you want to allow users to submit multiple responses when filling out the survey.

10. Click Create. The New Question page will open.

System Account ▾

Action Group ▸ Which Copy Service Vendor Do You Prefer? ▸ Survey Settings ▸ New Question

Use this page to add a question to this survey.

I Like It   Tags & Notes

Home   Marketing Plan for the Widget X1000   Action Group Contacts   Action Group Projects   Action Group Assets

Surveys

Which Copy Service Vendor Do You Prefer?

Sites

Marketing Plan for the Widget X1000

Action Group Projects

Action Group Assets

Libraries

Site Pages

Shared Documents

Trade Show Materials

Lists

Calendar

Tasks

Upcoming Trade Shows

State Census Data, 2009

Discussions

Team Discussion

Recycle Bin

All Site Content

Question and Type

Type your question and select the type of answer.

Additional Question Settings

Specify detailed options for the type of answer you selected.

Branching Logic

Specify if branching is enabled for this question. Branching can be used to skip to a specific question based on the user response. A page break is automatically inserted after a branching enabled question. Learn about branching.

Column Validation

Question:

Type your question here...

The type of answer to this question is:

○ Single line of text
○ Multiple lines of text
● Choice (menu to choose from)
○ Rating Scale (a matrix of choices or a Likert scale)
○ Number (1, 1.0, 100)
○ Currency ($, ¥, €)
○ Date and Time
○ Lookup (information already on this site)
○ Yes/No (check box)
○ Person or Group
○ Page Separator (inserts a page break into your survey)
○ External Data
○ Managed Metadata

Require a response to this question:
○ Yes   ● No

Enforce unique values:
○ Yes   ● No

Type each choice on a separate line:

Enter Choice #1
Enter Choice #2
Enter Choice #3

Display choices using:
○ Drop-Down Menu
● Radio Buttons
○ Checkboxes (allow multiple selections)

Allow 'Fill-in' choices:
○ Yes   ● No

Default value:
● Choice   ○ Calculated Value

To define branching logic, add your questions and then, in the Survey Settings page, edit the questions to define the branching logic.

| Next Question | Finish | Cancel |

Figure 2: The New Question Page

11. Enter text for which you want to solicit user feedback in the Question field.

12. Select a type of answer. Based on your selection, the fields in the Additional Question Settings section will change.

13. Fill in the fields in the Additional Question Settings section.

14. If there is another question in the survey, click Next Question and repeat Steps 11-13. Otherwise, click Finish. The Survey Settings page will appear.

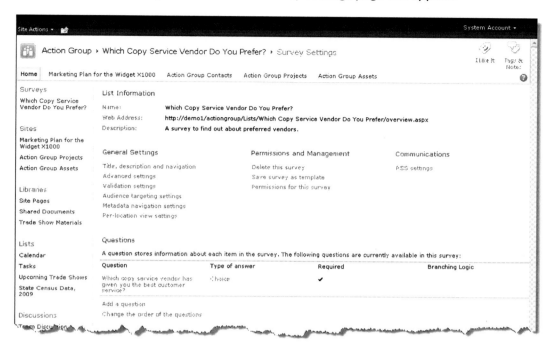

Figure 3: The Survey Settings Page

Task: Preview Your Survey

Purpose: Before opening a survey up it is a good idea to review the survey to ensure that it will meet your needs....

Example: These are the same steps that the Action Group survey respondents will use, so it makes for a good test for responding to a survey.

Steps:

1. Start Internet Explorer and type the URL for your organization's SharePoint server. The Start Page will open.

2. Navigate to the survey in which you are interested. The Survey Overview page will open.

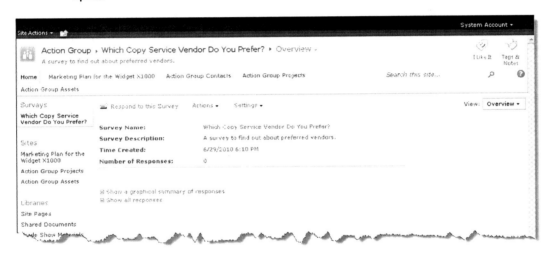

Figure 1: The Survey Overview Page

3. Click the Respond to this Survey link. The Survey – New Item dialog box will open.

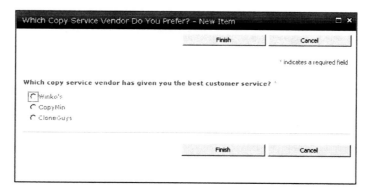

Figure 2: The Survey - New Item Dialog Box

4. Review the survey as a test to verify correctness. If all is in order, click the Cancel button on your browser so no results are actually saved.

5. To respond to the survey, answer all of the questions and click Finish. The answers will be recorded in the survey results.

Task: Enable Survey Branching

Purpose: When a survey is being created, not every question will be applicable to every respondent. For instance, if you want to poll users about their favorite candidate, and you've already asked their political party preference, you would want to narrow their choices to those candidates who are actually in that party. When a question asked depends on the answer of a previous question, this is known as branching.

Example: The survey for the copy vendors needs to be expanded, and the next question in the survey depends on the answer to the first.

Steps:

NOTE: If you are creating a new survey, follow all of the steps listed below. To modify an existing survey, navigate to the survey, and select the Survey Settings option on the Settings menu and begin with Step 15.

1. Start Internet Explorer and type the URL for your organization's SharePoint server. The Start Page will open.

2. Navigate to the site where you want to add a custom list. The site's home page will open.

3. Click the Site Actions menu and select More Options... The Create dialog box will open.

4. Scroll down and click the Survey icon. The Survey information pane will appear.

5. Enter a title for the new survey in the Name field. This will appear in any list of surveys in SharePoint.

6. Click More Options. The advanced create dialog box will appear.

7. Enter a summary of the survey in the Description field.

8. Click Yes to display the survey in the Quick Launch. This will keep a link present on the left side navigation menu.

9. Select the appropriate options in the Survey Options section. There are two options to select: you can choose whether you want user names to be displayed with each survey result, and if you want to allow users to submit multiple responses when filling out the survey.

10. Click Create. The New Question page will open.

---

11. Enter text for which you want to solicit user feedback in the Question field.

12. Select a type of answer. Based on your selection, the fields in the Additional Question Settings section will change.

13. Fill in the fields in the Additional Question Settings section.

14. If there is another question in the survey, click Next Question and repeat Steps 11-13. Otherwise, click Finish. The Survey Settings page will appear.

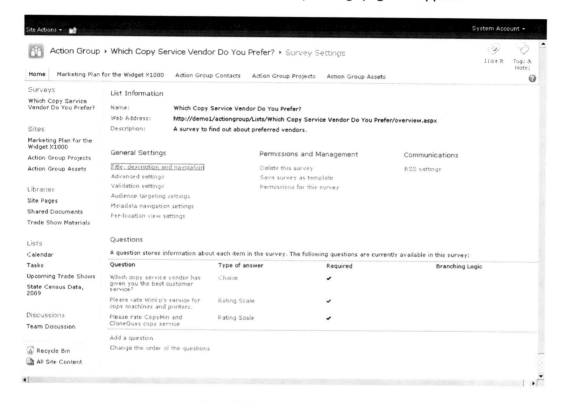

Figure 1: The Survey Settings Page

15. Click the link for the question with the answers that create a branch in the survey. The Edit Question page will open.

NOTE: Selecting the last question will only allow branching to a Content Type.

16. In the Branching Logic section, select the question that will appear after each individual answer is selected.

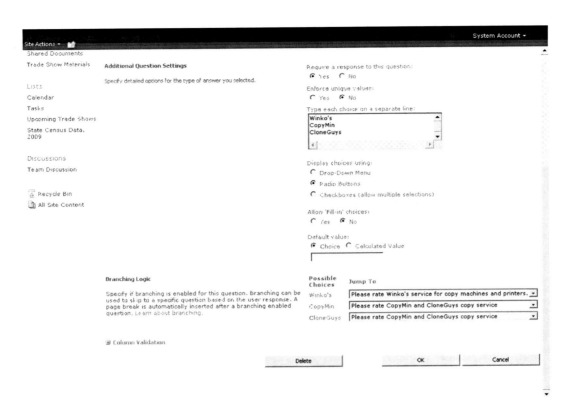

Figure 2: The Branching Logic Section on the Edit Question Page

17. When finished, click OK. The Survey Settings page will open and the survey will be ready for use.

Task: Send a Survey Link

Purpose: Like a document library or other SharePoint resource, it's often useful to send out a notice of a survey so users will be aware of it for participation.

Example: Now that the survey is completed, the team members need to be notified of its existence and encouraged to participate.

Steps:

1. Start Internet Explorer and type the URL for your organization's SharePoint server. The Start Page will open.

2. Navigate to the survey in which you are interested. The Survey page will open.

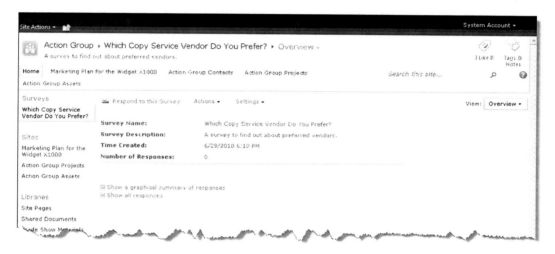

Figure 1: The Survey Overview Page

3. In the Address bar of your browser, select the entire address. Crtl + A is useful for this.

4. Press Ctrl + C to copy the URL.

5. Open a new message window in Microsoft Outlook.

6. Press Ctrl + V to paste the URL into the body of the message.

7. Complete the message and press Send. The survey link will be distributed.

Task: View Survey Results

Purpose: Once a survey is completed by one or more respondents, you can view the results in a comparative graphical form, or view the answers given by individual respondents.

Steps:

1. Start Internet Explorer and type the URL for your organization's SharePoint server. The Start Page will open.

2. Navigate to the survey in which you are interested. The Survey page will open.

3. Click the Show a graphical summary of responses link. The Graphical Summary page will open.

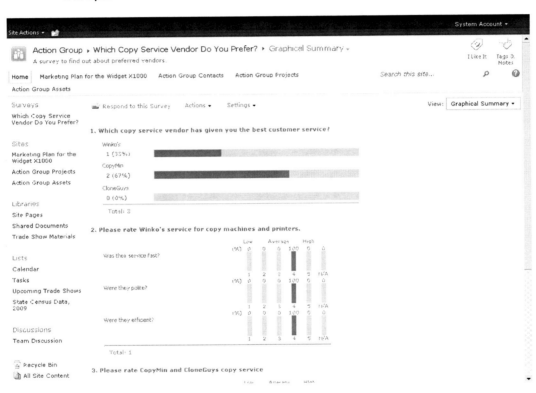

Figure 1: The Graphical Summary Page

4. Select the View menu on the upper right and click the Overview option. The Survey Overview page will open again.

5. Click the Show all responses link. The All Responses page will open.

Figure 2: The All Responses Page

6. Click any View Response link. The View Response page will open.

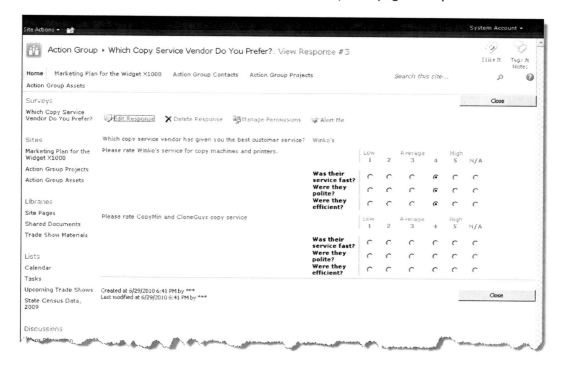

Figure 3: The View Response Page

7. When finished, click Close. You can now compile the survey, as demonstrated in the "Compile Survey Results" task.

Task: Compile Survey Results

Purpose: When a survey with many questions and/or many respondents is completed, just viewing the results might not be enough. You may need to do some serious data tabulation and number crunching. A perfect tool for that is Excel. Here's how to get the survey data compiled into Excel so you can work with it.

Steps:

1. Start Internet Explorer and type the URL for your organization's SharePoint server. The Start Page will open.

2. Navigate to the survey in which you are interested. The Survey page will open.

3. Click the Actions menu and select the Export to Spreadsheet option. The File Download dialog box will appear.

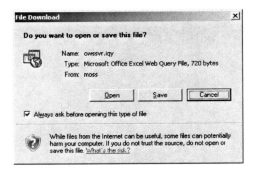

Figure 1: The File Download Dialog Box

4. Click Open. The file will download and Excel will open.

   NOTE: If a warning dialog box appears identifying a potential security concern, click Enable if you were the one who initiated the export from SharePoint.

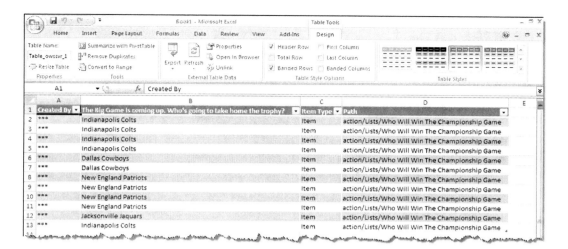

Figure 2: The Survey in Excel

5. Edit the spreadsheet as you normally would, using the table tools.

Create and Customize a My Site

One of the more compelling features of SharePoint is its capability to create personal web pages for users, known as My Sites. These sites give users a place to express themselves more creatively, share interests and hobbies, and generally make the work environment a more pleasant place. Not every SharePoint installation will have My Sites. This functionality has to be activated by the SharePoint administrator. But if your SharePoint implementation has My Sites, it's an easy way to put yourself on the Internet. My Sites, if activated, are ready to go for every user. To create a new My Site, all you need to do is click the My Site link, and SharePoint will automatically create the site for you.

In this section, you'll learn how to:

- **Create a My Site**: The basics of creating a My Site.

- **Edit a My Site Profile**: The first thing a user should do is edit their profile to start building their My Site.

- **Add Colleagues to a My Site**: SharePoint offers a way to link to and track colleague information.

- **Configure a Newsfeed on Your My Site**: RSS is a way to automatically pick up the latest bits of news or updated content from any Web site with an RSS feed. Adding RSS content to a My Site is very simple.

- **Tag SharePoint Content**: One of the great new features of SharePoint is the capability to tag any SharePoint page you find as a favorite, thus allowing you to find it again

- **Tag External Content**: Another nifty feature of SharePoint is the capability to tag any Internet page

- **Edit Public and Private Views**: While everything on the My Site home page is visible to the general public visiting your site, this is not the case for the My Profile page.

- **Apply a Theme to My Site**: You're not just one of the crowd. Be bold. Be different. Use another theme for your My Site.

- **Add a Web Part to My Site**: You can add new Web Parts to your site and even position them where you want.

- **Add a Silverlight Web Part to My Site**: One of the coolest Web Parts available to SharePoint 2010 users is the multimedia Silverlight web part.

- **Add a My Links Web Part to My Site**: You can add the My Links feature to your My Site as a web part in SharePoint 2010.

- **Target a Web Part Audience**: Any Web parts can be configured to appear for just certain groups or users.

- **Remove a Web Part from My Site**: You may not want to use all of the web parts that are initially created for your My Site.

- **Create a My Site Blog**: SharePoint includes a blog management system to get you started on a blog right away.

- **Add a New Page to My Site**: Not only can you customize pages within My Site, you can also add new pages.

Task: Create a My Site

Purpose: One of the more compelling features of SharePoint is its capability to create personal web sites for users, known as My Sites. These sites give users a place to express themselves more creatively, share interests and hobbies, and generally make the work environment a more personal place. Not every SharePoint installation will have My Sites. This functionality has to be activated by the SharePoint administrator. But if your SharePoint implementation has My Sites, it's an easy way to create a personal space on the Intranet.

Example: One of the Action Group team members wants to start a My Site within his organization's SharePoint implementation.

Steps:

1. Start Internet Explorer and type the URL for your organization's SharePoint server. The Start Page will open.

2. Click the user menu in the upper-right corner of any SharePoint page and select the My Site option. If this is the first time this option is selected, the My Site for your user account will be automatically created and then displayed.

   NOTE: If you don't see the My Site option, contact your system administrator to have them activate the function for your user account.

Figure 1: The My Site Page

3. Click the My Content link on the top navigation bar. If this is the first time this option is selected, the My Content page for your user account will be automatically created and then displayed.

Figure 2: The My Content Page

4. Click the My Profile link on the top navigation bar. The My Profile page will open.

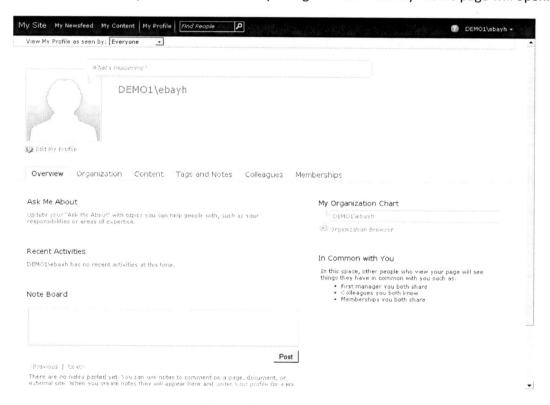

Figure 3: The My Profile Page

Task: Edit Your My Site Profile

Purpose: The core of personal information in the My Site is found in the My Profile page.

Example: The first thing the Action Group team member will do is edit the profile to start building their My Site.

Steps:

1. Start Internet Explorer and type the URL for your organization's SharePoint server. The Start Page will open.

2. Click the user menu in the upper-right corner of any SharePoint page and select the My Site option. The My Site What's New page will open.

3. Click the My Profile link. The My Profile page will open.

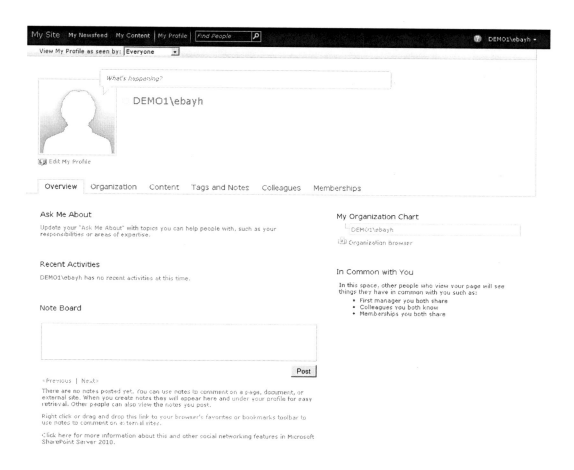

Figure 1: The My Profile Page

4. Click the Edit My Profile link. The Edit Profile page will open with the Editing Tools ribbon.

Figure 2: The Editing Tools ribbon on the Edit Profile Page

5. Fill in the relevant fields as needed, leaving all Show To settings as is. See "Edit Public and Private Views" for information on changing the Show To settings.

6. To add a picture to the site, click the Choose Picture button. The Upload Picture dialog box will appear.

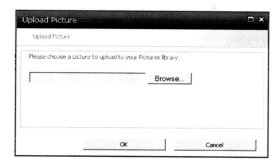

Figure 3: The Upload Picture Dialog Box

7. Click the Browse button. The Choose File to Upload dialog box will open.

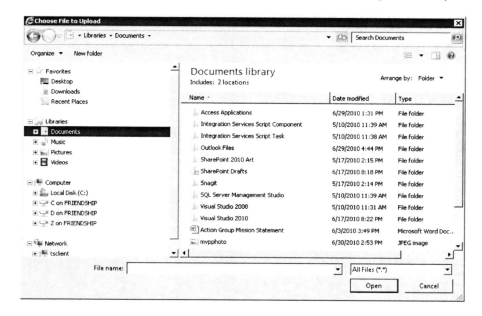

Figure 4: The Choose File to Upload Dialog Box

8. Navigate to the photo file you want to use and click Open. The file name and path will appear in the Upload Picture dialog box.

9. Click OK. The photo will be uploaded.

Figure 5: The Edit Profile Page

10. Click the Save and Close link. The My Profile page will open.

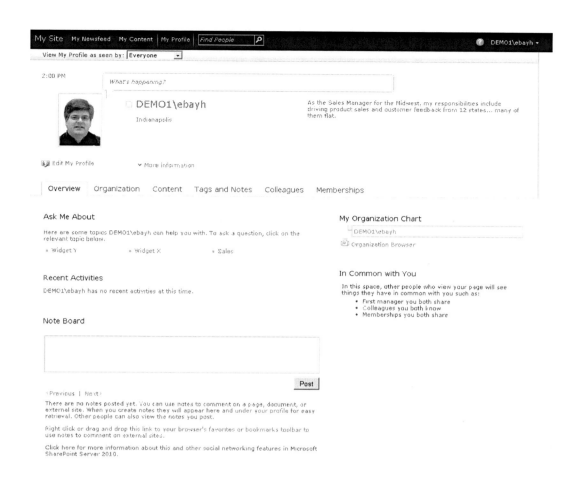

Figure 6: The Updated My Profile Page

Task: Add Colleagues to Your My Site

Purpose: In any business, you will have people you work with on a regular basis. These colleagues will be a big part of your work environment, and as such, they should be a part of your My Site. SharePoint offers a way to link to and track colleague information.

Example: The Action Group team member now will add colleagues to his My Site.

Steps:

1. Start Internet Explorer and type the URL for your organization's SharePoint server. The Start Page will open.

2. Click the user menu in the upper-right corner of any SharePoint page and select the My Site option. The My Site What's New page will open.

3. Click the My Profile link. The My Profile page will open.

4. Click the Colleagues tab. The Colleagues page will open.

Figure 1: The Colleagues Page

5. Click the Add Colleagues link. The Add Colleagues dialog box will open.

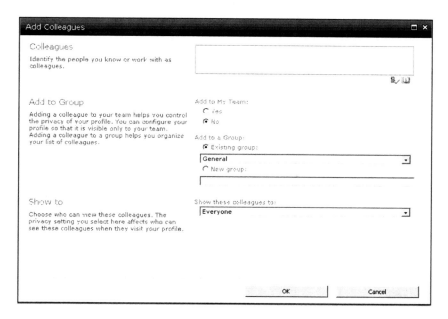

Figure 2: The Add Colleagues Dialog Box

6. Enter colleagues in the Colleagues field.

7. Click the Check Names icon to confirm the colleagues as fellow users on your SharePoint system.

8. Set the appropriate Add to Group and Show to settings and click OK. The user(s) will be added to the Colleagues page.

NOTE: If you communicate with certain people by e-mail or instant messaging quite a bit, SharePoint will note those communications and ask you if you want to add additional colleagues when you close the Add Colleagues dialog box. You should take advantage of this feature, since it allows for faster networking with minimal effort.

Task: Configure a Newsfeed on Your My Site

Purpose: As part of the social media tools in SharePoint 2010, users can define what news and information from the rest of their team can appear on their own My Site page.

Example: The Action Group team member would like to configure some newsfeeds for topics that interest him.

Steps:

1. Start Internet Explorer and type the URL for your organization's SharePoint server. The Start Page will open.

2. Click the user menu in the upper-right corner of any SharePoint page and select My Site. The My Site What's New page will open.

3. Click Newsfeed Settings. The Edit Profile page will open to the Newsfeed Settings section.

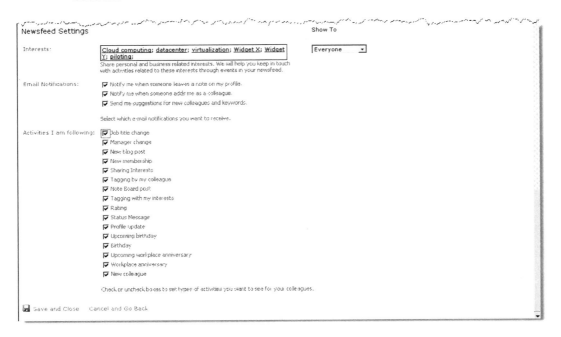

Figure 1: The Newsfeed Settings on the Edit Profile Page

4. Check or uncheck the options for activities you want to see from your colleagues.

5. Edit Interests to match your current interests.

6. Click Save and Close. The newsfeed will display on the My Newsfeed page when activity occurs.

The SharePoint Shepherd's Guide for End Users: 2010

Task: Tag SharePoint Content

Purpose: One of the great new features of SharePoint is the capability to tag any SharePoint page you find as a favorite, thus allowing you to find it again and, more importantly, letting others see projects and documents that you're working on.

Example: The Action Group team member is tagging SharePoint content that interests him.

Steps:

1. Start Internet Explorer and type the URL for your organization's SharePoint server. Visit any page on the SharePoint site.

2. When you find a page that interests you, click the I Like It icon. The page will be tagged, and the Tags & Notes icon will change color to indicate its tagged status.

Figure 1: A Tagged Page

3. To manage tags for a page, click the Tags & Notes icon for a tagged page. The Tags dialog box will open.

Figure 2: The Tags Dialog Box

4. Add tags, separated by commas or semicolons, to the My Tags field. As you type, suggested keywords may appear that you can click if appropriate.

5. Click Save. The page will be tagged with the new tags.

6. Click the Note Board tab. The Note Board page will appear.

7. Add notes about the page in the main field.

8. Click Post. The notes will be assigned to this page.

9. Click the Close control. The Tags dialog box will close.

Task: Tag External Content

Purpose: Another nifty feature of SharePoint is the capability to tag any Internet page, letting others in the organization see things in which you found valuable.

Example: The Action Group team member is tagging SharePoint content that interests him.

Steps:

1. Start Internet Explorer and type the URL for your organization's SharePoint server. The Start Page will open.

2. Click the user menu in the upper-right corner of any SharePoint page and select the My Site option. The My Site What's New page will open.

3. Click the My Profile link. The My Profile page will open.

4. Right-click the Right click or drag and drop this link to your browser's favorites or bookmarks toolbar to use notes to comment on external sites link The context menu will appear.

5. Select the Add to Favorites option. The Add a Favorite dialog box will open.

Figure 1: The Add a Favorite Dialog Box

6. Select the Favorites Bar option in the Create in field, then click Add. The favorite will appear in the browser's Favorites Bar.

   NOTE: You may receive an Overwrite dialog box if the favorite already exists.

7. Navigate to any page of interest. This can be any Internet page.

8. Click the Tags & Note Board favorite. The Tags & Note Board page will appear in a separate window.

9. Add tags, separated by commas or semicolons, to the My Tags field. As you type, suggested keywords may appear that you can click if appropriate.

10. Click Save. The page will be tagged with the new tags.

11. Click the Note Board tab. The Note Board page will appear.

12. Add notes about the page in the main field.

13. Click Post. The notes will be assigned to this page.

14. Close the window displaying the Tags and Note Board page and navigate to another page and continue your Internet session.

Task: Edit Public and Private Views

Purpose: While everything on the My Profile page is generally visible to those visiting your site, you may want to modify these settings, given that some of the information displayed may not be for public consumption.

Example: The Action Group team member has decided to keep some of his information private.

Steps:

1. Start Internet Explorer and type the URL for your organization's SharePoint server. The Start Page will open.

2. Click the user menu in the upper-right corner of any SharePoint page and select the My Site option. The My Site What's New page will open.

3. Click the My Profile link. The My Profile page will open.

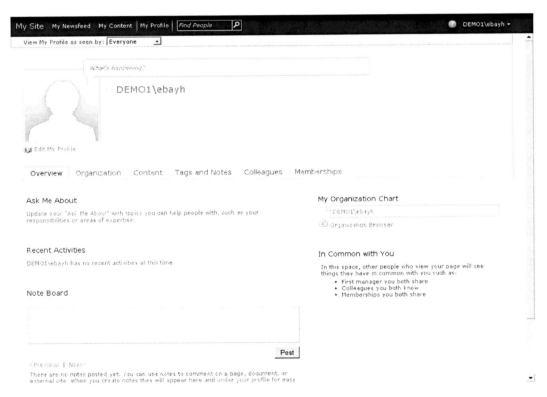

Figure 1: The My Profile Page

4. Click the Edit My Profile link. The Edit Profile page will open.

5. For information you want displayed for yourself only, select the Only Me option in the appropriate Show To field.

6. Select the My Manager option in the Show To field for information you want only your boss to view.

7. Continue setting Show To options as desired.

8. Click the Save and Close link. The My Profile page will appear.

9. Select the My Team option in the As Seen By drop down control near the top of the page. The page will display only the options you chose to be visible to the team.

Task: Apply a Theme to My Site

Purpose: The default theme for My Site matches the same yellow and blue soft tones found in the rest of SharePoint. But you're not just one of the crowd. You need to be able to apply your corporate brand to your site.

Example: The Action Group team member would like to use another theme for his My Site.

Steps:

1. Start Internet Explorer and type the URL for your organization's SharePoint server. The Start Page will open.

2. Click the user menu in the upper-right corner of any SharePoint page and select the My Site option. The My Site What's New page will open.

3. Click the My Content link. The My Content page will open.

4. Click the Site Actions menu and select Site Settings. The Site Settings page will open.

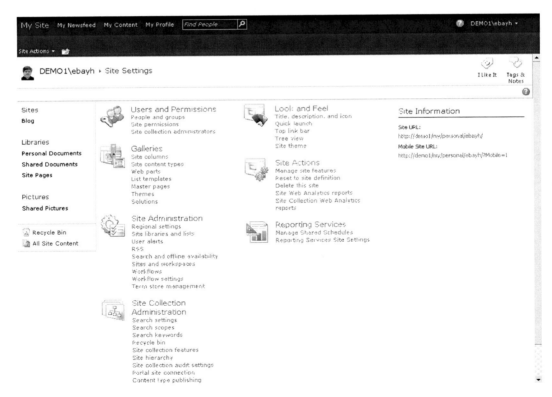

Figure 1: The Site Settings Page

5. In the Look and Feel section, click the Site Theme link. The Site Theme page will open.

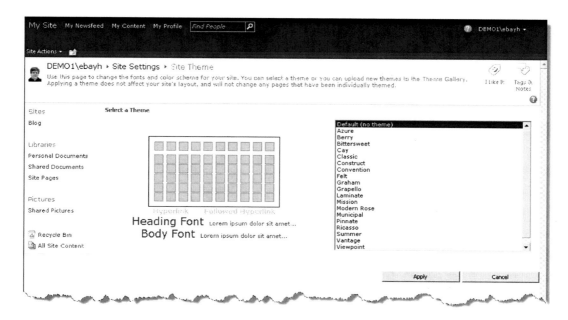

Figure 2: The Site Theme Page

6. Click any of the listed themes. The preview will change to reflect the theme's look.

7. When you have decided on a theme, click Apply. The Site Settings page will open, with the new theme applied.

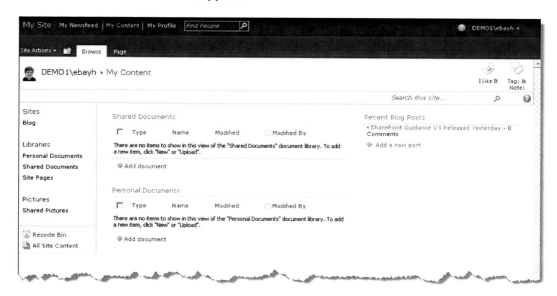

Figure 3: The Selected Classic Theme on the Site Settings Page

Task: Add a Web Part to My Site

Purpose: My Sites come with a number of tools, known as Web Parts, already pre-defined, such as the RSS feed and the calendar. These are not your only options for your My Site. You can add new Web Parts to your site and even position them where you want.

Example: The Action Group team member would like to add a tag cloud to the My Content page.

Steps:

1. Start Internet Explorer and type the URL for your organization's SharePoint server. The Start Page will open.

2. Click the user menu in the upper-right corner of any SharePoint page and select the My Site option. The My Site What's New page will open.

3. Click the My Content link. The My Content page will open.

4. Click the Page tab and select the Edit Page button. The My Content Page will open in Edit Mode.

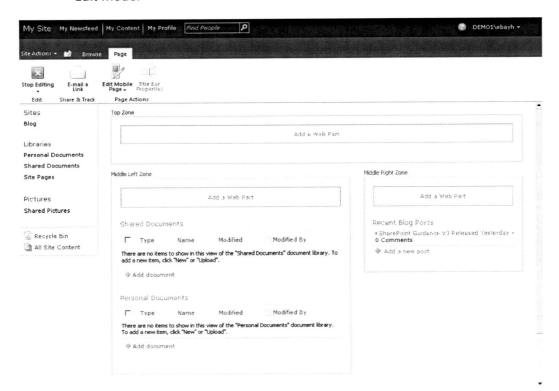

Figure 1: The My Content Page in Edit Mode

5. Select a zone and click Add a Web Part. The Add Web Parts header will open.

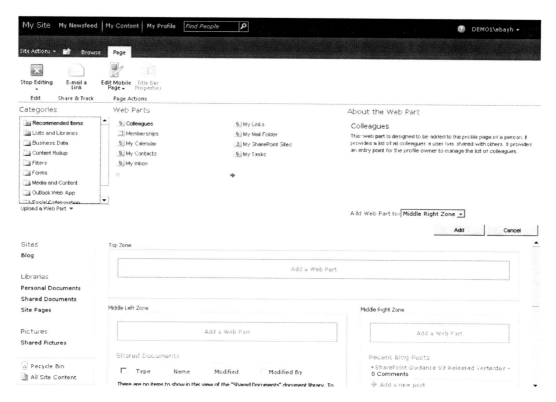

Figure 2: The Add Web Parts Header on the My Content Page in Edit Mode

6. Click the Social Collaboration option, then click the Tag Cloud Web Part. The Web Part will be selected.

7. Click Add. The Add Web Parts header will close and the new Web Part will appear in the selected zone.

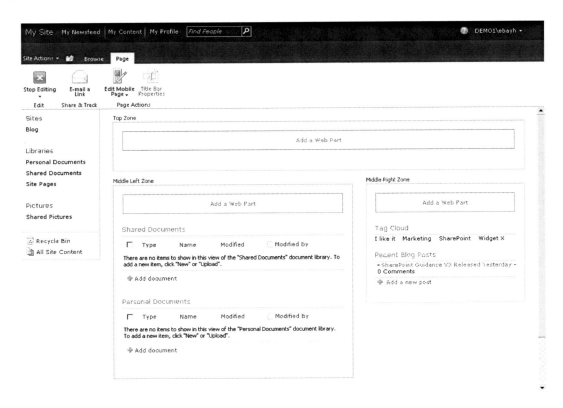

Figure 3: The New Web Part on the My Content Page in Edit Mode

8. Click the Stop Editing button. The My Content page will be displayed in normal mode.

Figure 4: The New Web Part on the My Content Page in Normal Mode

Task: Add a Silverlight Web Part to My Site

Purpose: One of the coolest Web Parts available to SharePoint 2010 users is the multimedia Silverlight web part. If you have a web part package uploaded to a library on your SharePoint site, you can quickly add it to any page.

Example: The Action Group team member would like to add a Silverlight web part to the My Content page.

Steps:

1. Start Internet Explorer and type the URL for your organization's SharePoint server. The Start Page will open.

2. Click the user menu in the upper-right corner of any SharePoint page and select the My Site option. The My Site What's New page will open.

3. Click the My Content link. The My Content page will open.

4. Click the Page tab and select the Edit Page button. The My Content page will open in Edit Mode.

5. Select a zone and click Add a Web Part. The Add Web Parts header will open.

6. Click Media and Content category and then the Silverlight Web Part. The Web Part will be selected.

7. Click Add. The Silverlight Web Part dialog box will open.

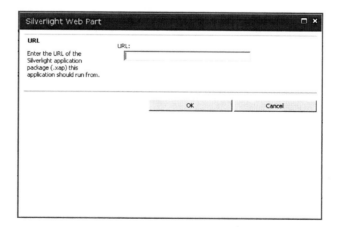

Figure 1: The Silverlight Web Part Dialog Box

8. Enter the URL to your Silverlight application package in the URL field.

NOTE: The URL will be the link to the application package in a library on your site.

9. Click OK. The Silverlight Web Part dialog box will close and the new Web Part will appear in the selected zone.

10. Click the Stop Editing link. The My Content page will be displayed in normal mode.

Task: Add a My Links Web Part to My Site

Purpose: In SharePoint 2007, the My Links control was commonly available in a drop-down box at the top right of SharePoint page. While it seems that this control has been removed from SharePoint 2010, it can quickly be added as a web part.

Example: The Action Group team member would like to add My Links to the My Content page.

Steps:

1. Start Internet Explorer and type the URL for your organization's SharePoint server. The Start Page will open.

2. Click the user menu in the upper-right corner of any SharePoint page and select the My Site option. The My Site What's New page will open.

3. Click the My Content link. The My Content page will open.

4. Click the Page tab and select the Edit Page button. The My Content page will open in Edit Mode.

5. Select a zone and click Add a Web Part. The Add Web Parts header will open.

6. Click the My Links Web Part. The Web Part will be selected.

7. Click Add. The Add Web Parts header will close and the new Web Part will appear in the selected zone.

8. Click the Stop Editing link. The My Content page will be displayed in normal mode.

Figure 1: The My Links Web Part on the My Content Page in Normal Mode

Task: Target a Web Part Audience

Purpose: Any Web parts can be configured to appear for just certain groups or users. To do so, you first must enable audience targeting in the Web Part.

Example: The Action Group would like to adjust some of the site's Web Parts to appear just when certain user groups peruse the site.

Steps:

1. Start Internet Explorer and type the URL for your organization's SharePoint server. The Start Page will open.

2. Navigate to the Web Part you want to target on the site. Select Edit Web Part from the drop down control to the right of the Web Part title. The Edit Web Part pane will appear.

Figure 2: The Edit Web Part Pane

3. Click the Advanced expand control. The Advanced settings will appear.

Figure 3: The Advanced Settings in the Edit Web Part Pane

4. Type in the name of any group or compiled audience you want to view the web part in the Target Audiences field and click on the Check Names icon, . If the group is part of the authenticated network, their name will be underlined, which means they are authorized. If a group is not recognized, a red squiggly line will appear. You will need to correct the group name.

5. Click OK. The Web Part will be edited to appear only for the specified groups.

Task: Remove a Web Part from My Site

Purpose: You may not want to use all of the Web Parts that are initially created for your My Site. The "Get Started" Web Part is usually a very good candidate for removal after you have finished all of its steps.

Example: Deleting a web part is different from simply closing a web part. Closing merely removes it from view, while deleting a web part removes it entirely. Removing Web Parts is a very quick operation.

Steps:

1. Start Internet Explorer and type the URL for your organization's SharePoint server. The Start Page will open.

2. Click the user menu in the upper-right corner of any SharePoint page and select the My Site option. The My Site What's New page will open.

3. Click the My Content link. The My Content page will open.

4. Click the Page tab and select the Edit Page button. The My Content page will open in Edit Mode.

5. Select the drop down control to the right of the Web Part title and click the edit menu for the Web Part you want to remove. The Web Part menu will appear.

Figure 1: The Web Part Menu

6. Select Delete. A confirmation dialog box will open.

Figure 2: The Delete Web Part Dialog Box

7. Click OK. The Web Part will be removed from the page.

8. Click the Stop Editing button. The page will be displayed in normal mode and the web part will be removed.

Task: Add a New Page to My Site

Purpose: Not only can you customize pages within My Site, you can also add new pages.

Example: The Action Group team member would like to add a new page to his My Site.

Steps:

1. Start Internet Explorer and type the URL for your organization's SharePoint server. The Start Page will open.

2. Click the user menu in the upper-right corner of any SharePoint page and select the My Site option. The My Site What's New page will open.

3. Click the My Content link. The My Content page will open.

4. Click the Site Pages link in the Quick Launch. The user will be prompted to allow SharePoint to create a default Assets Library and Site Pages library if one has not already been created.

5. Agree to the prompts, if presented. The All Pages page will open.

Figure 1: The All Pages Page

6. Click the Add new page link. The New Page dialog box will open.

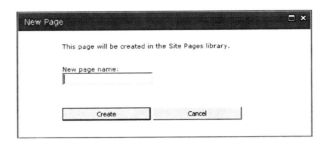

Figure 2: The New Page Dialog Box

7. Enter a title for the page in the New page name field.

8. Click Create. A new blank page will open in Editing Tools mode.

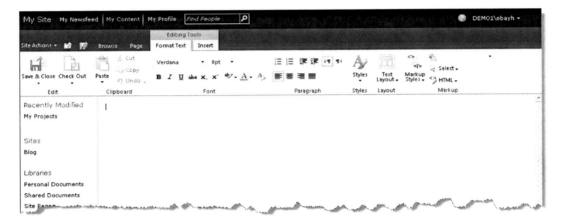

Figure 3: The New Page in Editing Tools Mode

9. Enter the text for the new page, formatting it as desired.

10. Click the Save & Close button. The page will now appear in Browse mode.

The SharePoint Shepherd's Guide for End Users: 2010

Figure 4: The New Page in Browse Mode

NOTE: Once a new page is created, you can add various Web Parts as detailed in "Add a Web Part to My Site."

Task: Upload a Document to My Site

Purpose: As with any business oriented site in SharePoint, you can also upload existing documents from your local PC to My Site.

Example: The Action Group team member would like to upload a document to the Personal Documents library of his My Site.

Steps:

1. Start Internet Explorer and type the URL for your organization's SharePoint server. The Start Page will open.

2. Click the user menu in the upper-right corner of any SharePoint page and select the My Site option. The My Site What's New page will open.

3. Click the My Content link. The My Content page will open.

4. Click the Add document link in the Personal Documents section. The Personal Documents - Upload Document dialog box will open.

    NOTE: You can upload more than one file by clicking the Upload Multiple Files link.

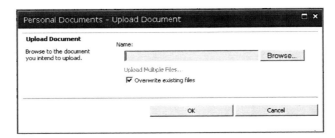

Figure 1: The Personal Documents - Upload Document Dialog Box

5. Click the Browse button. The Choose File to Upload dialog box will open.

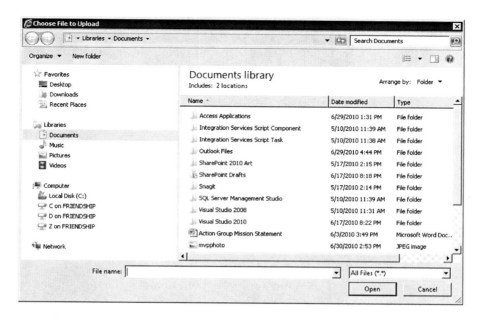

Figure 2: The Choose File to Upload Dialog Box

6. Select a file and click Open. The file and its file path will appear in the Name field.

7. Click OK. The file will be uploaded and will appear in the Personal Documents section of the My Content Page.

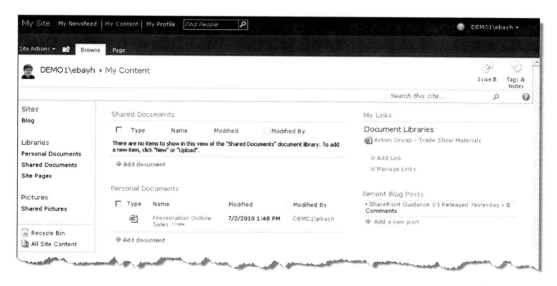

Figure 3: The Uploaded Document on the My Content Page

SharePoint primarily deals with two kinds of sites. The first type is the collaborative site, which has been discussed through much of this manual. The second type, which will be addressed in this section, is the publishing site. A publishing site contains content intended not to be created but rather shared as is. It can be your team's web presence, or a collection of documents and tools for fellow users to read and use.

In this section, you'll learn how to:

- **Create a Site for Published Content**: The basics of creating a publishing site.

- **Create a Content Page**: Once a publishing site is created, users can start creating the content for the site.

- **Edit a Page Content Live**: Any time you need to make changes on your pages, you can quickly enter edit mode to implement the changes with ease.

- **Spell Check Page Content**: One of the handier tools in the page content editor is the spell checker. It might seem obvious, but web editor spell checkers are not as robust as one would think ... until now.

- **Add an Image to a Content Page**: Images are sometimes the best thing about a web page. Add your images easily in SharePoint.

- **Add Publishing Approvers**: Within a Publishing Web site, all pages must be approved for publication every time they are changed or added to the site. This is known as a workflow.

- **Submit Page for Publishing Approval**: Since publishing sites are more static and represent you or your business, you should not just create the site on your own and publish it as is.

- **Approve Content for Publication**: If you are designated as a content approver, here's how to edit and formally approve the document.

- **Change Page Schedule/Expiration Date**: Times, you will have a page that only needs to be up for a limited amount of time. Perhaps for a sale, or a contest.

- **Manually Start a Workflow for a Page**: At any time, a site administrator can tag a page for improvement using the workflow process.

- **Create a Custom Permission Level:** Whenever you create a site, you may need to grant permission levels for users that don't match existing types of permissions. In SharePoint, you can create a brand-new permission level to meet your needs

Task: Create a Site for Published Content

Purpose: SharePoint primarily deals with two kinds of sites. The first type is the collaborative site, which has been discussed through much of this manual. The second type, which has not been as fully addressed, is the publishing site.

Example: A publishing site contains content to be shared as is, and not worked on collaboratively. It can be your team's web presence, or a collection of documents and tools for fellow users to read and use. The Action Group SharePoint administrator will need to create the Publishing Portal.

Steps:

1. In Windows, start the SharePoint 2010 Central Administration application. The SharePoint 2010 Central Administration home page will open.

   NOTE: This task must be done by the farm administrator, who will access to central administration.

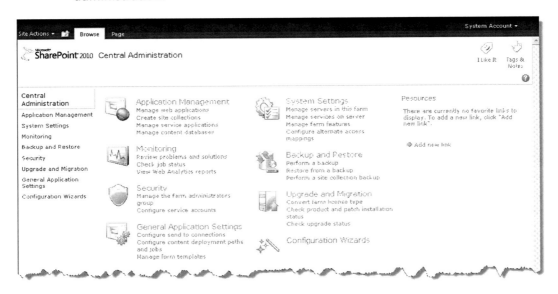

Figure 1: The SharePoint 2010 Central Administration Home Page

2. Click the Create site collections link in the Application Management section. The Create Site Collection page will appear.

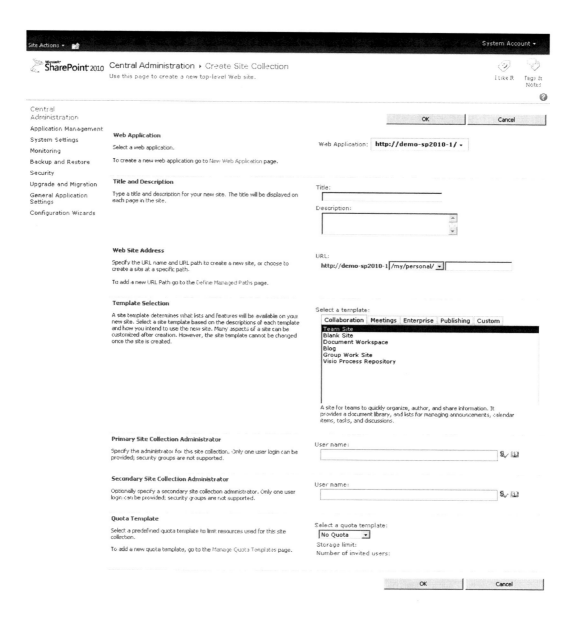

Figure 2: The Create Site Collection Page

3. Type a title for your site in the Title field. The title of your site should be descriptive and can be up to about 50 letters before becoming intrusive. It will appear on the top of your new site.

4. Type a description for your site in the Description field. The description is like a sub-title that will be displayed on some of the pages. It should further clarify the title so that anyone can understand the site's purpose.

5. Select the /sites/ option in the first URL field.

NOTE: Publishing sites do not have to be created in /sites/.

6. Type a short, descriptive name for your team in the URL field. This will become part of the full Web Site Address for your new Publishing site. Some features don't work with long URLs so keeping the names in the URL short but descriptive is recommended.

7. Click on the Publishing tab in the Template Selection section and select Publishing Portal.

   NOTE: Your organization may have its own publishing template.

8. In the Primary Site Collection Administrator field, enter the user assigned to administrate the new site collection.

9. In the Secondary Site Collection Administrator field, enter another user assigned to administrate the new site collection, if any.

10. Click OK. The Processing screen will briefly appear, followed by the Top-Level Site Successfully Created page.

11. Click the link to the new site. The home page for the Publishing site will open.

Home

Press Releases

Enable anonymous access
Anonymous access allows users to view the pages on this site without logging in. This is useful when creating internet facing sites or sites where you want everyone to have access to read the content without editing.

Manage navigation
Change the navigation links in this site.

Go to master page gallery
Change the page layouts and master page of this site collection.

Manage site content and structure
Reorganize content and structure in this site collection.

Set up multilingual support
Use the variations feature to manage multi-lingual sites and pages.

Add users to the Approvers and Members groups
Users in the Approvers group can publish pages, images, and documents in this site. Users in the Members group can create and edit pages, and they can upload images and documents, but they cannot publish the pages, images, or documents. Workflow is enabled in the Pages library, and content approval is enabled in the Documents and Images libraries.

Figure 3: The New Publishing Site's Home Page

Task: Create a Content Page

Purpose: Once a publishing site is created, authorized users can set about creating the content for the site. This is initially accomplished by creating individual pages for your publishing site.

Example: The new Action Group public site needs new content pages.

Steps:

1. Start Internet Explorer and type the URL for your organization's SharePoint server. The Start Page will open.

2. Navigate to the publishing site. The publishing site's home page will open.

3. Click the Site Actions menu and select New Page. The New Page dialog box will open.

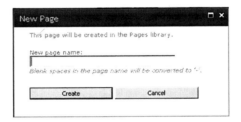

Figure 1: The New Page Dialog Box

4. Enter a name for the new page in the New page name field. This is used as the listing for this page throughout SharePoint.

5. Click Create. The new page with the Editing Tools ribbon will appear.

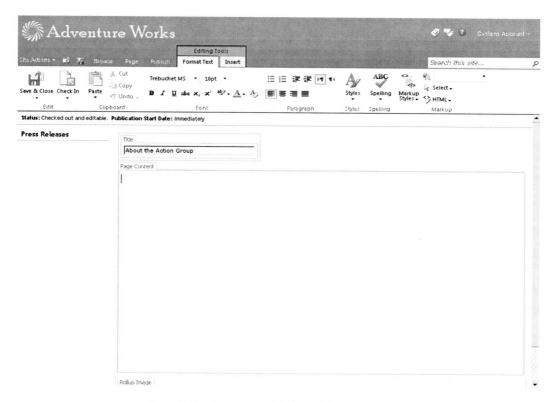

Figure 2: The New Page with the Editing Tools Ribbon

6. Click the Page tab. The Page ribbon will appear.

7. Click the Page Layout button. A list of possible layouts for the page will appear.

8. Select the layout option you want to use. The layout of the page will be adjusted.

9. Enter the content on the page, using the available tools to format the text.

10. Click the Check In button. The Check In dialog box will appear.

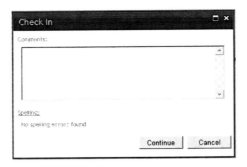

Figure 3: The Check In Dialog Box

11. Enter any comments you might have for this version of the page and click Continue. The page will be checked in and viewable to just the users with the appropriate permission.

12. Click the Publish tab. The Publish ribbon will appear.

13. Click Publish. The page will be now viewable to all users.

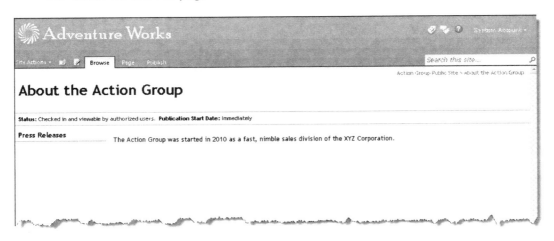

Figure 4: The New Page

Task: Edit Page Content In Place

Purpose: Any time you need to make changes on your pages, you can quickly enter Edit Mode to implement the changes with ease. This will work regardless of the page layout you've chosen to use for your page.

Example: As the About Us page receives more content, it will be added to the page.

Steps:

1. Start Internet Explorer and navigate to the page you want to edit. The page will open.

2. Click the Edit Page icon. The Editing Tools ribbon will appear.

   NOTE: If the system administrator has deactivated the Edit Page button, click the Site Actions menu and select Edit Page.

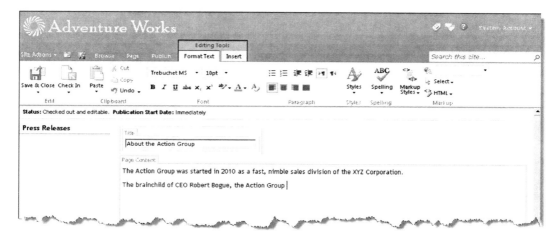

Figure 1: The Editing Tools Ribbon

3. Edit the document as needed.

4. When finished, click the Check In button. The Check In dialog box will appear.

5. Enter any comments you might have for this version of the page and click Continue. The page will be checked in and viewable to just the users with the appropriate permission.

6. Click the Publish tab. The Publish ribbon will appear.

7. Click Publish. The page will be now viewable to all users.

Task: Create a Content Page in Word

Purpose: Once a publishing site is created, authorized users can set about creating the content for the site, even in Word.

Example: The new Action Group public site needs new content pages and will put them together in Word.

Steps:

1. In Microsoft Word, create a web document.

2. Click the File tab. The File pane will appear.

3. Click Save As. The Save As dialog box will open.

4. Click the SharePoint Sites link. The SharePoint Sites location will open.

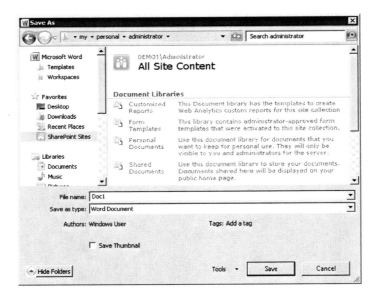

Figure 1: The New Page Dialog Box

5. Navigate to the site where you want the page to be.

6. Set the Save as type field to Web Page.

7. Click Save. The page will be saved to the SharePoint site.

Task: Spell Check Page Content

Purpose: One of the handier tools in the page content editor is the spell checker. It might seem obvious, but web editor spell checkers are not as robust as one would think … until now.

Example: The About Us page will need to be spell checked.

Steps:

1. Start Internet Explorer and navigate to the page you want to edit. The page will open.

2. Click the Page tab then the Edit Page button. The Editing Tools ribbon will appear.

   NOTE: If the system administrator has deactivated the Edit Page button, click the Site Actions menu and select Edit Page.

3. Edit the document as needed.

4. Click the Spelling icon. The Spell Check dialog box will appear, notifying you of any spelling errors.

Figure 1: The Spell Check Dialog Box

5. Click OK. The Spell Check dialog box will close, and the spelling errors will be highlighted on the page.

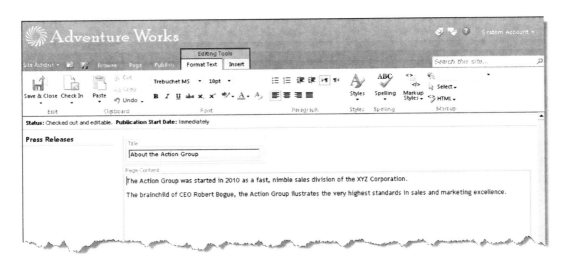

Figure 2: The Highlighted Spelling Errors on the Page.

6. Click on each error to see potential suggestions. You can select a suggested spelling or choose to ignore the word.

7. When the errors are corrected, click the Check In button. The Check In dialog box will appear.

8. Enter any comments you might have for this version of the page and click Continue. The page will be checked in and viewable to all users with the appropriate permission.

Task: Add an Image to a Content Page

Purpose: Images are sometimes the best thing about a web page. Add your images easily in SharePoint.

Example: The About Us page can have an image added to it for visual candy.

Steps:

1. Start Internet Explorer and navigate to the page you want to edit. The page will open.

2. Click the Edit Page icon. The Editing Tools ribbon will be displayed.

3. In the Editing Tools tab, click the Insert sub-tab. The Editing Tools Insert ribbon will appear.

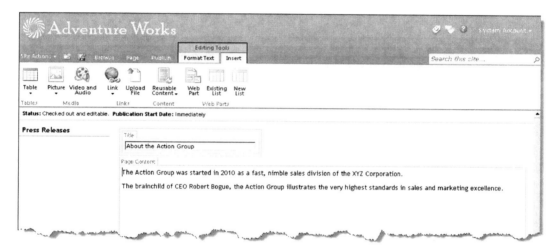

Figure 1: The Editing Tools Insert Ribbon

4. Click the Picture button. The Upload Picture dialog box will open.

5. Click the Browse button. The Choose File to Upload dialog box will appear.

6. Select a file and click Open. The file and its file path will appear in the Name field.

7. Select the Site Collection Images option in the Upload to field.

8. Click OK. The Site Collection Images dialog box will appear.

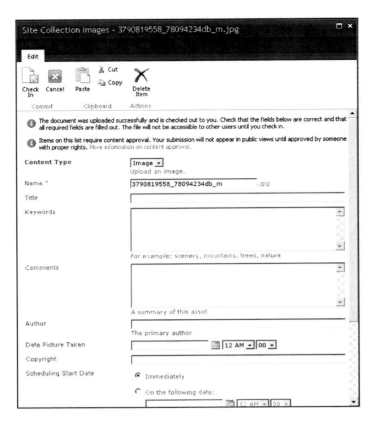

Figure 2: The Site Collection Images Dialog Box

9. Add any pertinent information and click Save. The Site Collection Images dialog box will close.

10. In the Insert ribbon, click the Picture button. The Select an Asset dialog box will appear.

The SharePoint Shepherd's Guide for End Users: 2010

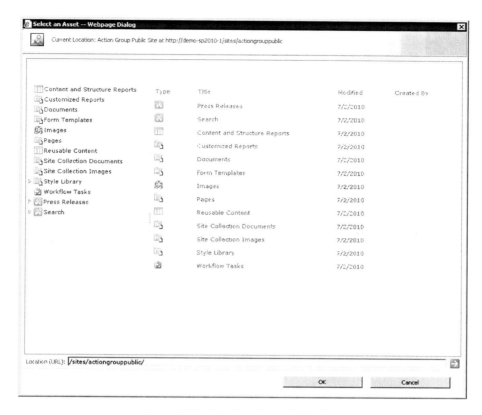

Figure 3: The Select an Asset Dialog Box

11. Click Site Collection Images in the left pane. The contents of that library will be displayed.

12. Select the image you want to add to your page in the right pane and click OK. The image will appear on your page at the insertion point.

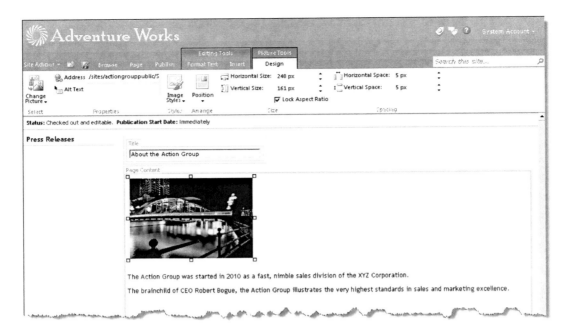

Figure 4: The Inserted Image

13. Click the Position button's menu control and select Right option in the menu's Float section. The image will shift to the right side of the page with the text wrapping around it.

14. Click the Check In button. The Check In dialog box will appear.

15. Enter any comments you might have for this version of the page and click Continue. The page will be checked in and viewable to all users with the appropriate permission.

Figure 5: The Updated Page with Inserted Image

Task: Add Publishing Approvers

Purpose: Within a Publishing Web site, all pages must be approved for publication every time they are changed or added to the site. This is known as a workflow—a process through which only specified designers and approvers can formally edit and approve pages for publication. Before such a workflow can be utilized, however, approvers and designers must be specified.

Example: The new Action Group Public Site needs to have approvers and designers assigned so that the publishing workflow can begin.

Steps:

1. Start Internet Explorer and type the URL for your organization's SharePoint server. The Start Page will open.

2. Navigate to the publishing site. The publishing site's home page will open.

3. Click the Site Actions menu and select Site Settings. The Site Settings page will open.

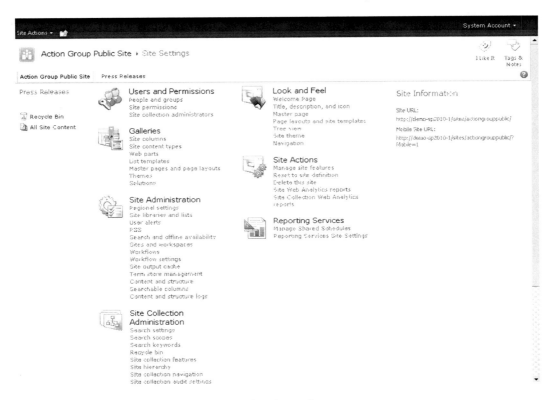

Figure 1: The Site Settings Page

4. Click the Site permissions link in the Users and Permissions section. The Permission Tools ribbon will open on the Permissions page.

The SharePoint Shepherd's Guide for End Users: 2010

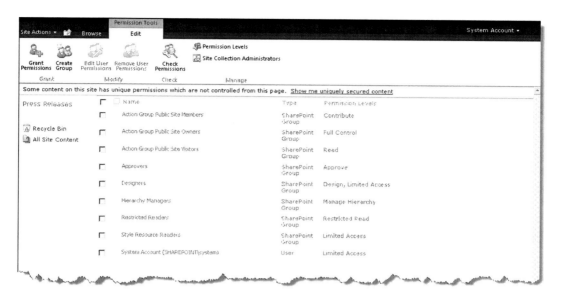

Figure 2: The Permission Tools Ribbon on the Permissions Page

5. Click the Approvers link. The People and Groups – Approvers page will appear.

6. Click the New link. The Grant Permissions dialog box will open.

7. Type in the name of the user in the Users/Groups field and click on the Check Names icon, &. If the user is part of the authenticated network, their name will be underlined, which means they are authorized. If a user is not recognized, a red squiggly line will appear. You will need to correct the user name.

8. Add additional names, separating the names with semicolons.

9. Click OK. The Grant Permissions dialog box will close and the user will appear in the group list on the People and Groups – Approvers page.

10. Click the Designers link in the Quick Launch and repeat steps 6-9 to add users to the Designers group.

11. Click the site's link at the top of the page to return to the site's home page.

Task: Submit Page for Publishing Approval

Purpose: After a page has been completely revised to everyone's satisfaction, it will need to be approved for publication.

Example: The Action Group About Us page is ready to be formally published, but must first be submitted for approval.

Steps:

1. Start Internet Explorer and navigate to the page you want to edit. The page will open.

2. Click the Edit button. The Editing Tools ribbon will be displayed on the page.

3. Edit the document as needed.

4. When finished, click the Check In button. The Check In dialog box will appear.

5. Enter any comments you might have for this version of the page and click Continue. The page will be checked in and viewable to all users with the appropriate permission.

6. Click the Publish tab. The Publish ribbon will appear.

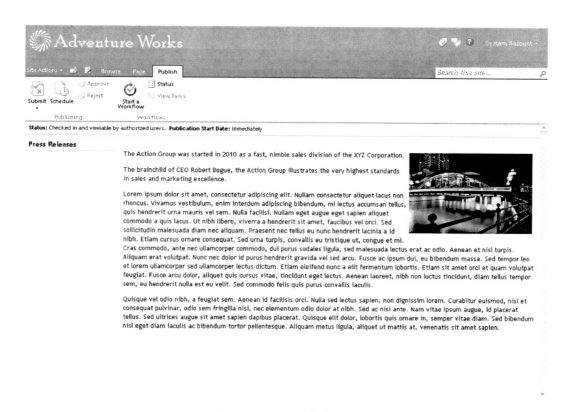

Figure 1: The Publish Ribbon

7. Click the Submit button. The Start "Page Approval" page will appear.

Figure 2: The Start "Page Approval" Page

8. Fill in the pertinent information for the approval workflow. Pay particular attention to the Due Date and Duration fields.

9. Type in the name of any users you want to follow along in the approval process in the CC field and click on the Check Names icon, 🖧✓. If the user is part of the authenticated network, their name will be underlined, which means they are authorized. If a user is not recognized, a red squiggly line will appear. You will need to correct the user name.

10. Click Start. The workflow will be started and the page will move to Waiting for Approval status.

Task: Approve Content for Publication

Purpose: If you have an important page that needs approval prior to publication, you can send the page through the workflow process. This will allow other users to examine the content and make necessary changes before the content goes live. If you are a part of the approval group of users, here's how to edit and formally approve the document.

Example: The About Us page has been submitted for Approval and will need to be approved for publication.

Steps:

1. Start Internet Explorer and type the URL for your organization's SharePoint server. The Start Page will open.

2. Navigate to the publishing site. The publishing site's home page will open.

3. Navigate to the page you want to approve. The page will open.

4. Click the Publish tab. The Publish ribbon will appear.

5. If the page is satisfactory, click the Approve button. The Approve dialog box will appear.

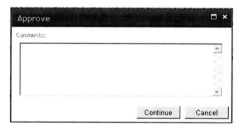

Figure 1: The Approve Dialog Box

6. Enter any pertinent information in the Comments field.

   NOTE: If you are in a Publishing Site with Workflow, you will be asked to complete additional steps to complete the publishing action.

7. Click Continue. The page will be approved and published.

Exception: If the Approve button is disabled, you may be trying to approve your own changes or your do not have specific permission to change content within this particular workflow. Have another authorized user approve your changes, or check the permissions settings to ensure you have the appropriate access rights.

Task: Change Page Schedule/Expiration Date

Purpose: At times, you will have a page that only needs to be up for a limited amount of time. Perhaps for a sale, or a contest. Regardless, you can set a page's schedule to start and end its publishing status with ease.

Example: The Action Group has a contest page that only needs to run for three months, so it will be scheduled to expire.

Steps:

1. Start Internet Explorer and type the URL for your organization's SharePoint server. The Start Page will open.

2. Navigate to the publishing site. The publishing site's home page will open.

3. Navigate to the page you want to schedule. The page will open.

4. Click the Publish tab. The Publish ribbon will appear.

5. Click the Schedule button. The Schedule Page dialog box will appear.

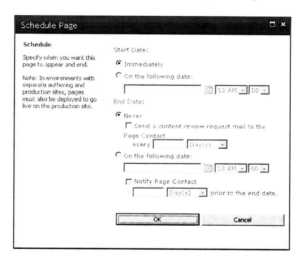

Figure 1: The Schedule Page Dialog Box

6. Set the Start and End Dates for the page.

7. Click OK. Schedule Page dialog box will close and the page will need to be submitted for approval and approved.

Exception: If the Schedule button is disabled, you may be trying to approve your own changes or your do not have specific permission to change content within this particular workflow. Have another authorized user approve your changes, or check the permissions settings to ensure you have the appropriate access rights.

Task: Manually Start a Workflow for Publication

Purpose: All Web sites need nearly constant revision in order to maintain accuracy and freshness. At any time, a site administrator can tag a page for improvement using the workflow process.

Example: The Action Group site is undergoing review, and some pages need to be selected for revision and approval.

Steps:

1. Start Internet Explorer and type the URL for your organization's SharePoint server. The Start Page will open.

2. Navigate to the publishing site. The publishing site's home page will open.

3. Navigate to the page that needs a workflow started.

4. If the editing tools are not available, click the Site Actions menu and select Edit Page. The editing tools ribbon will be displayed.

5. Click the Publish tab. The Publish ribbon will be displayed.

6. Click the Start a Workflow button. The Workflows page will open.

   NOTE: Workflows for sites must be set up by the system administrator or anyone with design rights. If you do not have any workflows available, contact the administrator and discuss what workflow templates you would like to have activated.

Figure 1: The Workflows Page

7. Click the Page Approval template link. The Start "Page Approval" page will open.

8. Fill in the pertinent information. Pay particular attention to the Due Date and Duration fields.

9. Type in the name of any users you want to follow along in the approval process in the CC field and click on the Check Names icon, &. If the user is part of the authenticated network, their name will be underlined, which means they are authorized. If a user is not recognized, a red squiggly line will appear. You will need to correct the user name.

10. Click Start. The workflow will be started and the page will move to Waiting for Approval status.

Exception: If the page does not change to Waiting for Approval status , it may need to be refreshed, so the cache for the page and the page's status will be in sync. Press Ctrl+F5 in your browser to update the status of the page.

Task: Create a Custom Permission Level

Purpose: Whenever you create a site, you may need to grant permission levels for users that don't match existing types of permissions. In SharePoint, you can create a brand-new permission level to meet your needs. This allows you to control which specific rights you assign to users and groups.

Example: The Action Group wants to create a permission level for registered guests to its public site.

Steps:

1. Start Internet Explorer and type the URL for your organization's SharePoint server. The Start Page will open.

2. Navigate to the site that needs a new permission level.

   NOTE: For sites that inherit permissions from the parent, navigate to the parent site.

3. Select the Site Actions menu and select Site Settings. The Site Settings page will open.

4. Click the Site permissions link. The Permission Tools ribbon on the Permissions page will open.

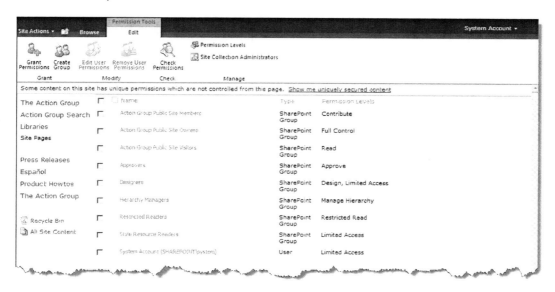

Figure 1: The Permission Tools Ribbon on the Permissions Page

5. Click the Permission Levels button. The Permission Levels page will open.

Figure 2: The Permission Levels Page

6. Click the Add a Permission Level link. The Add a Permission Level page will appear.

Figure 3: The Add a Permission Level Page

7. Add a Name and Description for the new permission level.

8. Select the permission options that you want to use.

9. Click Create. The new permission level will be created.

Site owners have more responsibilities and more capabilities than SharePoint site authors. Owners can create whole sites, and modify existing sites at a deeper level.

In this section, you'll learn how to:

- **Change a Site Theme**: As the owner of a site, you have the ability to make broad changes to the look and feel of your site.

- **Create a Site Theme from PowerPoint**: If you have a PowerPoint theme that might look good on your Web site for consistency's sake, you can use it.

- **Change a Site Logo**: When SharePoint builds a site from a template, it includes many placeholders, such as images and logos, to mark the general feel of a site.

- **Change a Site Master Page**: SharePoint site templates include a number of master page settings, which define the basic layout options for the site.

- **Add Cascading Style Sheets**: If you don't prefer what SharePoint has to offer in terms of style libraries, you can attach your own CSS document to customize the site.

- **Organize Pages in a Web Site**: As you edit a Web site, you may discover that you will need to re-organize your site to create a better flow of information and traffic.

- **Save a Site as a Template**: Once you have a site created to your specifications, you can save the site as a template to use for future site projects.

- **Upload a Site Solution**: Whenever you need to use a site template from another SharePoint instance, you can upload it to your SharePoint site collection.

- **Allow Users to Create Different Subsites**: SharePoint will, by default, limit access in a publishing site to two site templates.

- **Create a Subsite**: If you have the appropriate permissions, you can create a new sub-site fairly easily in SharePoint

- **Create a Wiki Page Home Page**: One of the very interesting features in SharePoint 2010 is the capability to create a wiki page and have it become your site's home page.

- **Edit a Wiki Page Home Page**: If you decide to use a wiki page in your SharePoint site, either as a home page or as some other utility, editing it will be a very straightforward process.

- **Customize Site Navigation**: Make things very clear to site visitors, you need to make sure your navigation tools are laid out properly.

- **Implement and Configure the Content Query Web Part**: All SharePoint Sites come with a number of tools, to assist users, such as the Content Query Web Part.

- **Implement and Configure the Content Query Web Part Using Custom Properties**: Many SharePoint developers have created customized versions of Content Query Web Parts that can be easily plugged in to an existing SharePoint site.

- **Implement and Configure the Summary Links Web Part**: Another useful Web Part is the Summary Links Web Part, which lets you manually add links to articles and pages on your site as well as to other sites.

Task: Change a Site Theme

Purpose: The default themes offered by SharePoint are perfectly fine for a basic Web site, but like everything else in life, they can be improved upon. As the owner of a site, you have the ability to make broad changes to the look and feel of your site.

Example: The Action Group site is getting ready for final publication, and it's time to make design changes that will better reflect the identity of the team.

Steps:

1. Start Internet Explorer and type the URL for your organization's SharePoint server. The Start Page will open.

2. Navigate to the publishing site. The publishing site's home page will open.

3. Click the Site Actions menu and select Site Settings. The Site Settings page will open.

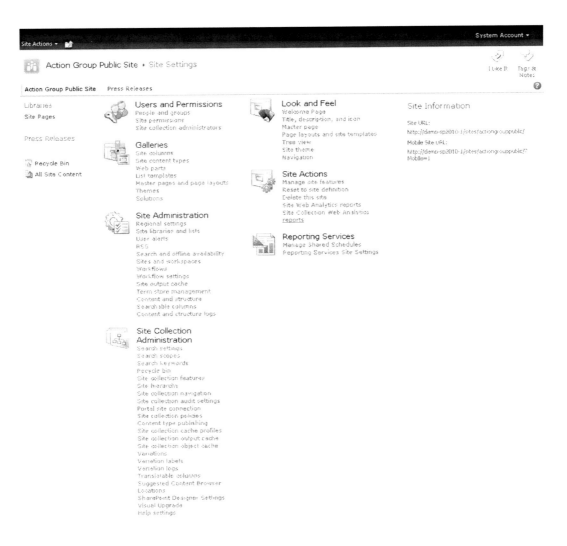

Figure 1: The Site Settings Page

4. Click the Site theme link in the Look and Feel section. The Site Theme page will open.

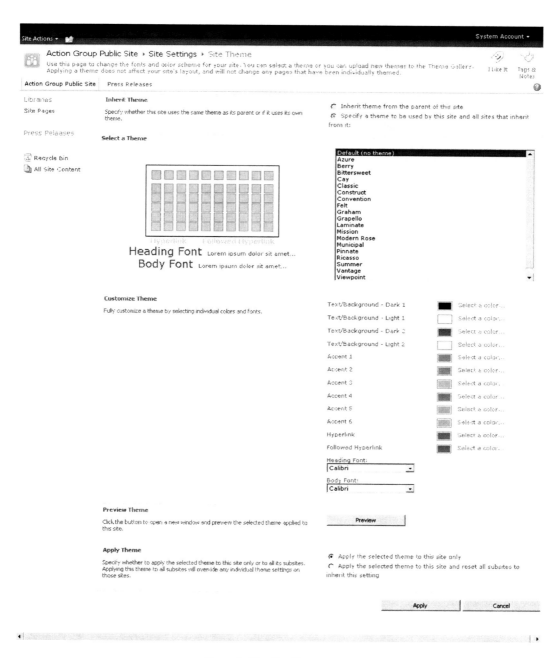

Figure 2: The Site Theme Page

5. Click any of the listed themes. The preview will change to reflect the theme's look.

6. When you have decided on a theme, click Apply. The Site Settings page will open, with the new theme applied.

Figure 3: The New Theme on the Home Page

Task: Create a Site Theme in PowerPoint

Purpose: Site themes for SharePoint can be done quite easily if you know a little shortcut: instead of hiring a graphic designer, you can set up a theme in PowerPoint and then use that for the SharePoint theme.

Example: The Action Group will create a corporate "GreyMan" theme for their site.

Steps:

1. Start Microsoft PowerPoint. A blank presentation will open.

2. Use the Colors, Fonts, and Effects menus to get create a theme you would like for the SharePoint site. The initial slide will take on the appearance of the theme.

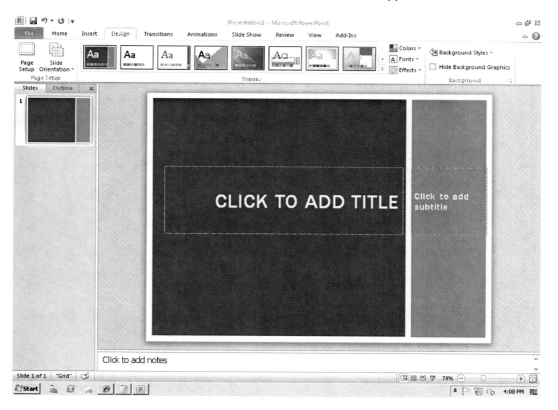

Figure 1: A PowerPoint Theme in Progress

3. Click the All Themes drop-down control. The All Themes menu will open.

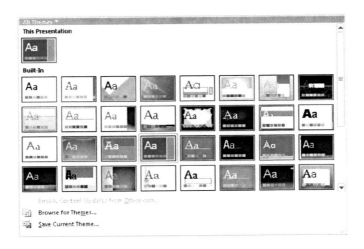

Figure 2: The All Themes Menu

4. Click Save Current Theme. The Save Current Theme dialog box will open.

5. Navigate to the folder you want to save the PowerPoint theme file, name the file, and click Save. The theme will be saved in the specified location.

Task: Apply a Site Theme from PowerPoint

Purpose: As the owner of a site, you have the ability to make broad changes to the look and feel of your site. If you have a PowerPoint theme that might look good on your Web site for consistency's sake, you can use it. You can create themes from a PowerPoint file by saving it as a theme once you have the design and colors set.

Example: The Action Group will use their corporate "GreyMan" theme for their site.

Steps:

1. Start Internet Explorer and type the URL for your organization's SharePoint server. The Start Page will open.

2. Navigate to the publishing site. The publishing site's home page will open.

3. Click the Site Actions menu and select Site Settings. The Site Settings page will open.

4. In the Look and Feel section, click the Site theme link. The Site Theme page will open.

5. Click the Theme Gallery link in the introduction section. The Theme Gallery will appear.

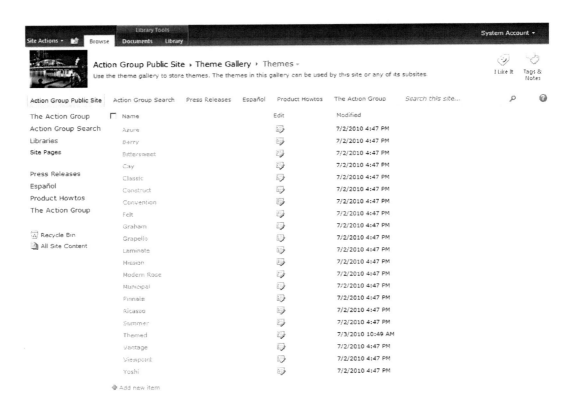

Figure 1: The Theme Gallery

6. Click the Add new item link. The Upload Document dialog box will appear.

7. Click Browse. The Choose File to Upload dialog box will open.

8. Navigate to the PowerPoint theme file you want to use and click Open. The file will appear in the Name field.

9. Click OK. The Theme Gallery dialog box will appear.

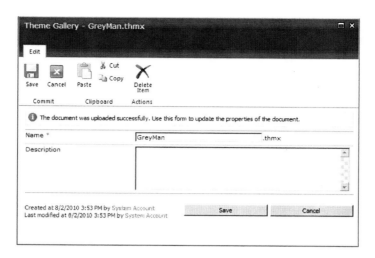

Figure 2: The Theme Gallery Dialog Box

10. Add a Description to the theme and click Save. The theme will appear in the Theme Gallery.

11. Click the Site Actions menu and select Site Settings. The Site Settings page will open.

12. In the Look and Feel section, click the Site theme link. The Site Theme page will open.

13. Click the new theme. The preview will change to reflect the theme's look.

14. Click Apply. The Site Settings page will open, with the new theme applied.

Figure 3: The New Theme on the Home Page

Task: Change a Site Logo

Purpose: When SharePoint builds a site from a template, it includes many placeholders, such as images and logos, to mark the general feel of a site. Eventually, though, these will need to be changed to match your own corporate feel.

Example: The Action Group logo will need to be added to the site's pages.

Steps:

1. Start Internet Explorer and type the URL for your organization's SharePoint server. The Start Page will open.

2. Navigate to the publishing site. The publishing site's home page will open.

3. Click the Site Actions menu and select Site Settings. The Site Settings page will open.

4. Click the Title, description, and icon link in the Look and Feel section. The Title, Description, and Icon page will open.

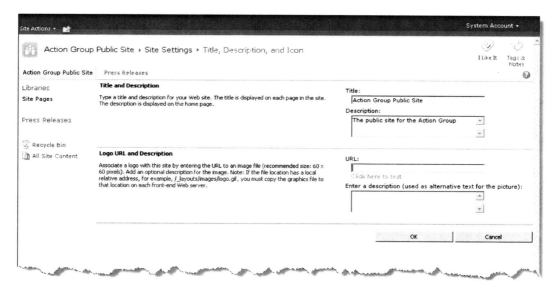

Figure 1: The Title, Description, and Icon Page

5. Enter the URL of the image you want to use for the site logo in the URL field.

6. Click the Click here to test link. If the image URL is correct, a browser will appear with the logo displayed.

7. Enter text about the image in the Enter a description field.

8. Click OK. The Site Settings page will open, with the new logo applied.

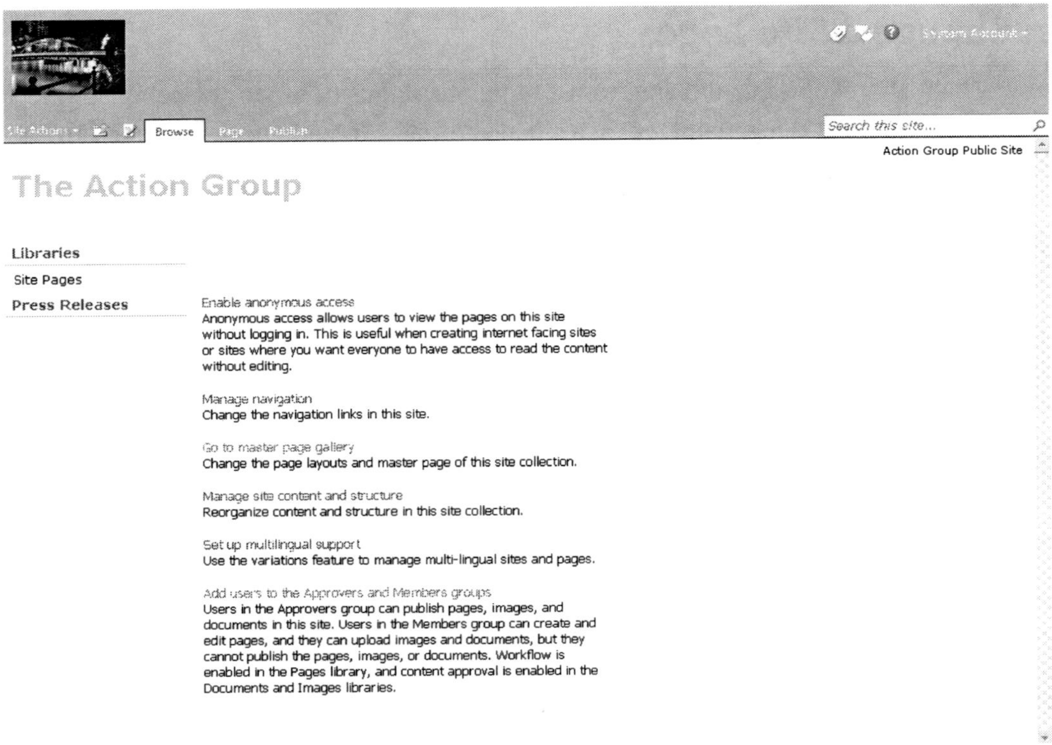
Browse
Search this site...
Action Group Public Site
The Action Group
Libraries
Site Pages
Press Releases
Enable anonymous access
Anonymous access allows users to view the pages on this site without logging in. This is useful when creating internet facing sites or sites where you want everyone to have access to read the content without editing.
Manage navigation
Change the navigation links in this site.
Go to master page gallery
Change the page layouts and master page of this site collection.
Manage site content and structure
Reorganize content and structure in this site collection.
Set up multilingual support
Use the variations feature to manage multi-lingual sites and pages.
Add users to the Approvers and Members groups
Users in the Approvers group can publish pages, images, and documents in this site. Users in the Members group can create and edit pages, and they can upload images and documents, but they cannot publish the pages, images, or documents. Workflow is enabled in the Pages library, and content approval is enabled in the Documents and Images libraries.

Figure 2: The New Logo Applied to the Home Page

Task: Change a Site Master Page

Purpose: SharePoint site templates include a number of master page settings, which define the basic layout options for the site.

Example: The Action Group site will try a different master page layout for its site, changing from the default SharePoint master page to the Night and Day master page to the.

Steps:

1. Start Internet Explorer and type the URL for your organization's SharePoint server. The Start Page will open.

2. Navigate to the publishing site. The publishing site's home page will open.

3. Click the Site Actions menu and select Site Settings. The Site Settings page will open.

4. Click the Master page link in the Look and Feel section. The Site Master Page Settings page will open.

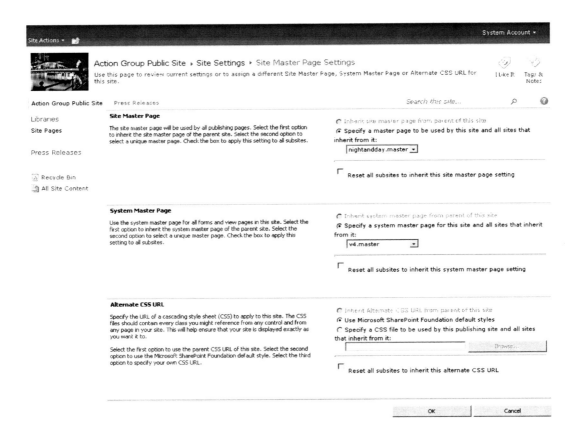

Figure 1: The Site Master Page Settings Page

5. Confirm the Specify a master page to be used by the site and all sites that inherit from it option is selected.

6. Select the v4.master option in the drop down control.

7. Click the Reset all subsites to inherit this site master page setting checkbox.

8. Click OK. The Site Settings page will open.

Figure 2: The New Master Page Setting Applied to the Home Page

Task: Add Cascading Style Sheets

Purpose: Of course, there are uncountable creative ways to create a Web site—beyond the themes and master pages provided by SharePoint. These aspects of a Web site can be controlled by Cascading Style Sheets (CSS). CSS define the look and feel of all parts of a Web site: fonts, link colors, etc. If you don't prefer what SharePoint has to offer in terms of style libraries, you can attach your own CSS document to customize the site.

Example: The Action Group site will use a different CSS to determine the look and feel of its site.

Steps:

1. Start Internet Explorer and type the URL for your organization's SharePoint server. The Start Page will open.

2. Navigate to the publishing site. The publishing site's home page will open.

Home

Press Releases

Enable anonymous access
Anonymous access allows users to view the pages on this site without logging in. This is useful when creating internet facing sites or sites where you want everyone to have access to read the content without editing.

Manage navigation
Change the navigation links in this site.

Go to master page gallery
Change the page layouts and master page of this site collection.

Manage site content and structure
Reorganize content and structure in this site collection.

Set up multilingual support
Use the variations feature to manage multi-lingual sites and pages.

Add users to the Approvers and Members groups
Users in the Approvers group can publish pages, images, and documents in this site. Users in the Members group can create and edit pages, and they can upload images and documents, but they cannot publish the pages, images, or documents. Workflow is enabled in the Pages library, and content approval is enabled in the Documents and Images libraries.

Figure 1: The Publishing Site's Home Page

3. Click the Site Actions menu and select Site Settings. The Site Settings page will open.

4. In the Look and Feel section, click the Master page link. The Site Master Page Settings page will open.

5. In the Alternate CSS URL section, click the Specify a CSS file to be used by this publishing site and all sites that inherit from it option.

6. Add the URL for the CSS file you would like to use, using the Browse button to find the file.

7. Click the Reset all subsites to inherit this alternate CSS URL checkbox.

8. Click OK. The Site Settings page will open with the new CSS settings applied.

Task: Organize Pages in a Web Site

Purpose: As you edit a Web site, you may discover that you will need to re-organize your site to create a better flow of information and traffic.

Example: The Action Group has set up its pages in the Pages section, and needs to move them to another sub site.

Steps:

1. Start Internet Explorer and type the URL for your organization's SharePoint server. The Start Page will open.

2. Navigate to the publishing site. The publishing site's home page will open.

3. Click the Site Actions menu and select the Manage Content and Structure option. The Site Content and Structure page will open.

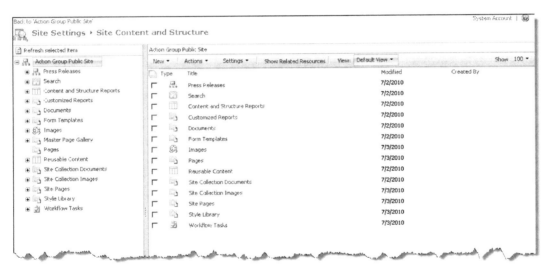

Figure 1: The Site Content and Structure Page

4. In the navigation pane, click the Pages folder. The contents will be displayed in the contents pane.

5. Select the checkboxes for the files you would like to move.

6. Click the Move option in the Actions menu. The Move dialog box will appear.

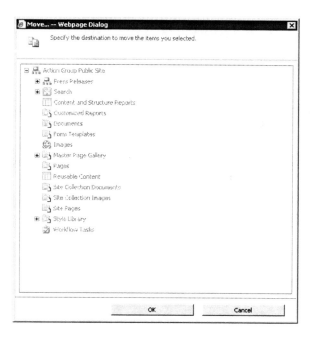

Figure 2: The Move Dialog Box

7. Click the folder for the sub site to which you want to move the files.

8. Click OK. The Move dialog box will close and the files will be moved to the new folder.

Task: Upload a User Solution to the Site Collection Solution Gallery

Purpose: Whenever you need to use a site template from another SharePoint instance, you can upload it to your SharePoint site collection. In SharePoint 2010, however, a new site template is referred to as a solution.

Example: Another team in the XYZ Corporation wants to use the team template created by the Action Group to build their own site, but they are using their own SharePoint installation and therefore need to upload the file.

Steps:

1. Start Internet Explorer and type the URL for your organization's SharePoint server. The Start Page will open.

2. Navigate to the main site from which the new site will be added. The site's home page will open.

3. Click the Site Actions menu and select Site Settings. The Site Settings page will open.

4. In the Galleries section, click the Solutions link. The Solutions page will open.

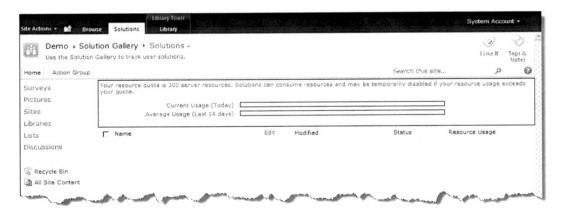

Figure 1: The Solutions Page

5. Click the Solutions tab. The Solutions ribbon will appear.

6. Click the Upload Solution button. The Solution Gallery – Upload Solution dialog box will appear.

The SharePoint Shepherd's Guide for End Users: 2010

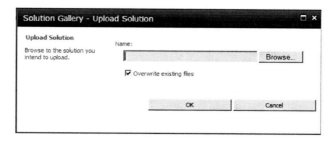

Figure 2: The Solution Gallery – Upload Solution Dialog Box

7. Click Browse. The Choose File to Upload dialog box will open.

8. Navigate to the solution file you want to use and click Open. The file will appear in the Name field.

9. Click OK. The new solution will be uploaded. Once the solution is activated, it will be available for use.

Task: Allow Users to Create Different Subsites

Purpose: At any point, site owners and authorized users can create subsites within a publishing site. However, SharePoint will, by default, limit access in a publishing site to two site templates. In the spirit of full control, you can change this so that the site templates you want can be created – and the ones you do not want are excluded.

Example: The Action Group would like to create a new Basic Search Center subsite on its public site, but needs to have it made available.

Steps:

1. Start Internet Explorer and type the URL for your organization's SharePoint server. The Start Page will open.

2. Navigate to the publishing site. The publishing site's home page will open.

3. Click the Site Actions menu and select Site Settings. The Site Settings page will open.

4. In the Look and Feel section, click the Page layouts and site templates link. The Page Layout and Site Template Settings page will open.

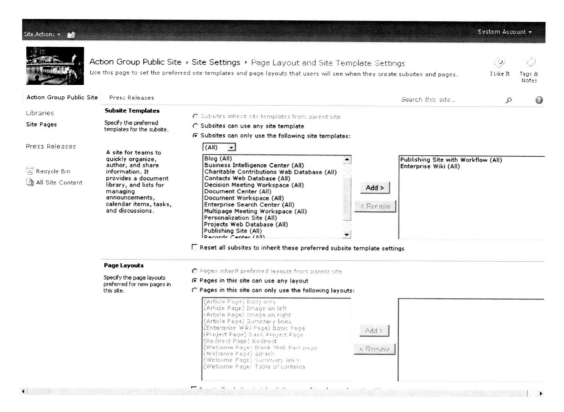

Figure 1: The Page Layout and Site Template Settings Page

5. In the Subsite Templates section, select Basic Search Center (All) and click Add.

6. Click OK. The Site Settings page will open and the template will be available when you add a subsite, as reviewed in the "Create a Subsite" task.

Task: Create a Sub-site

Purpose: If you have the appropriate permissions, you can create a new sub-site fairly easily in SharePoint. You might create a sub-site to gather a collection of content into a single area, or when you want to provide some separation from the existing content.

Example: The Action Group will add a Basic Search sub-site to its public site.

Steps:

1. Start Internet Explorer and type the URL for your organization's SharePoint server. The Start Page will open.

2. Click the Site Actions menu and select New Site. The Create site dialog box will open. If you do not see the New Site option, you do not have the proper authorization. Please contact your administrator.

3. Click the Basic Search Center icon. The Basic Search Center information will appear in the right pane.

4. Type a title for your site in the Title field. The title of your site should be descriptive and can be up to about 50 letters before becoming intrusive.

5. Type a short, descriptive name for your team in the URL Name field. This will become part of the full Web Site Address for your new subsite.

6. To add more settings for the site, click More Options. The advanced Create Basic Search Center dialog box will appear.

7. Type a description for your site in the Description field. The description is like a sub-title that will be displayed on some of the pages. It should further clarify the title so that anyone can understand the site's purpose.

8. In the User Permissions field, select the Use same permissions as parent site option. You can change to unique permissions later as shown in "Assign Users to a Group."

9. In the Use the iop link bar from the parent site field, select the Yes option.

10. Click Create. The Processing screen will briefly appear, followed by the new Basic Search Center page.

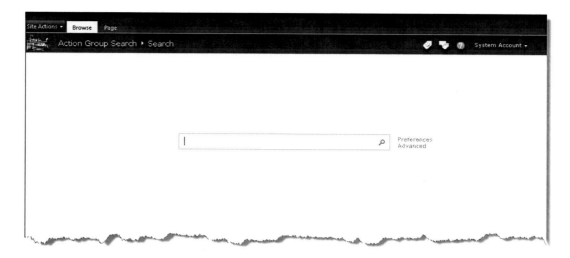

Figure 1: The New Basic Search Center Page

Task: Create a Wiki Page Home Page

Purpose: One of the very interesting features in SharePoint 2010 is the capability to create a wiki page and have it become your site's home page.

Example: The Action Group will try a wiki page as its public site's home page to increase the ease of content generation from the team.

Steps:

1. Start Internet Explorer and type the URL for your organization's SharePoint server. The Start Page will open.

2. Navigate to the publishing site. The publishing site's home page will open.

3. Click the Site Actions menu and select Site Settings. The Site Settings page will open.

4. In the Site Actions section, click the Manage site features link. The Features page will open.

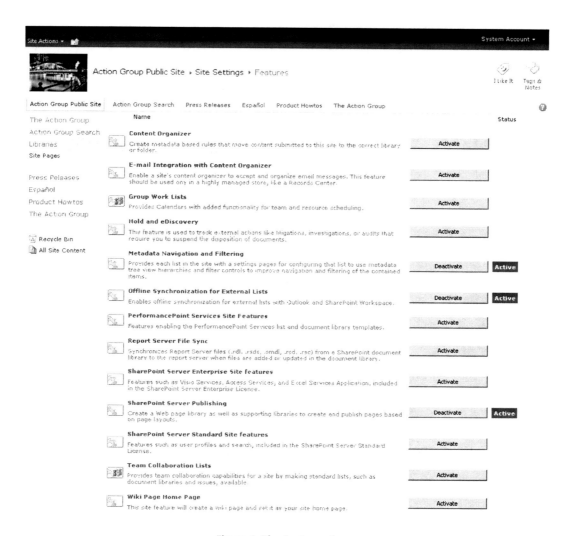

Figure 1: The Features Page

5. Click the Activate button for the Wiki Page Home Page feature. The feature will become active.

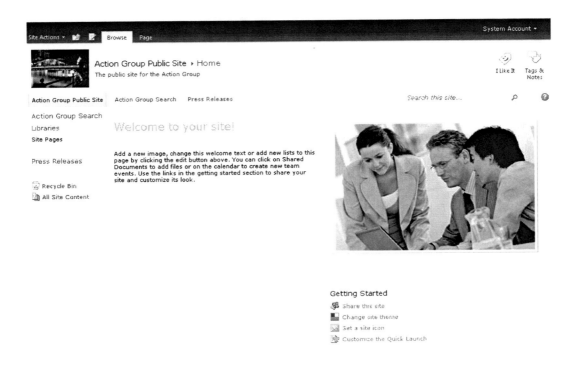

Figure 2: The New Wiki Home Page

NOTE: If you want to return to the original home page, simple Deactivate the Wiki Page Home Page setting in the Site Features page.

Task: Edit a Wiki Page Home Page

Purpose: If you decide to use a wiki page in your SharePoint site, either as a home page or as some other utility, editing it will be a very straightforward process. There is no approval workflow associated with wiki pages, so publishing can be a much faster process.

Example: The Action Group needs to edit its new wiki home page.

Steps:

1. Start Internet Explorer and navigate to the page you want to edit. The page will open.

2. Click the Site Actions menu and select Edit Page. The Editing Tools ribbon will be displayed in edit mode.

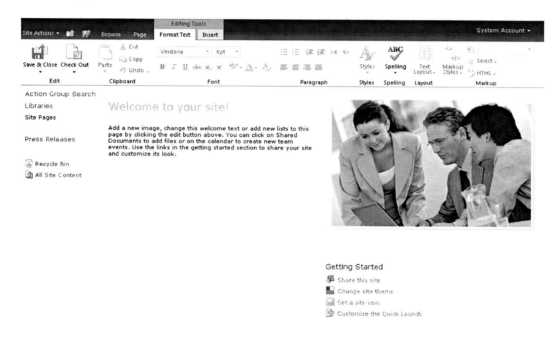

Figure 1: The Editing Tools Ribbon on the Wiki Home Page in Edit Mode

3. Edit the document as needed.

4. When finished, click the Save & Close button. The changes will immediately be saved and published, without the need for a formal approval process.

Figure 2: The Updated Wiki Home Page

Task: Customize Publishing Site Navigation

Purpose: To make things very clear to site visitors, you need to make sure your navigation tools are laid out properly.

Example: The Action Group site needs its navigation toolbar properly configured.

Steps:

1. Start Internet Explorer and type the URL for your organization's SharePoint server. The Start Page will open.

2. Navigate to the publishing site. The publishing site's home page will open.

3. Click the Site Actions menu and select Site Settings. The Site Settings page will open.

4. In the Look and Feel section, click the Navigation link. The Navigation Settings page will open.

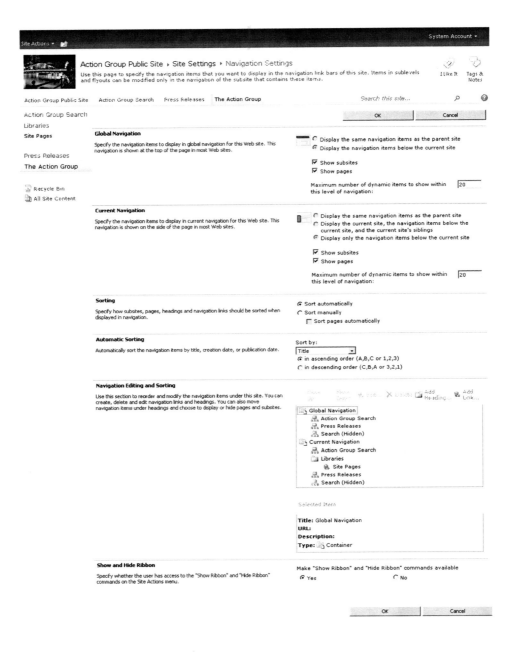

Figure 1: The Navigation Settings Page

5. In the Sorting section, select the Sort manually option.

6. In the Navigation Editing and Sorting section, select the Current Navigation folder then click Add Link. The Navigation Link dialog box will open.

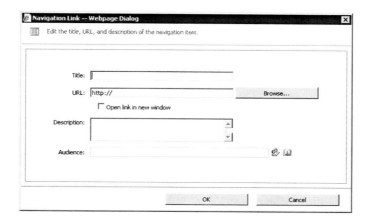

Figure 2: The Navigation Link Dialog Box

7. Add the pertinent information, using the Browser button to find the correct URL.

8. Click OK. The new link will be visible in the Navigation Editing and Sorting section.

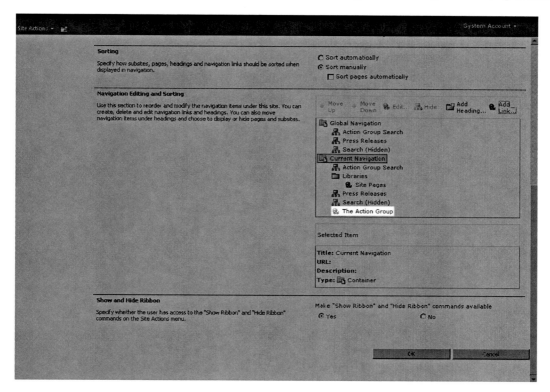

Figure 3: The New Navigation Link

9. Click the new link to select it, then click Move Up until the menu item is listed in the order you desire.

10. Click OK. The Site Settings page will open and the new link will be visible in the site's navigation menu.

Task: Implement and Configure the Content Query Web Part

Purpose: All SharePoint Sites come with a number of tools, known as Web Parts, already pre-defined, such as the RSS feed and the calendar. The more useful of these is the Content Query Web Part, which allows you to roll up content from other parts of your Web site onto another page. If you want to accomplish more advanced customization, visit the "Customizing the Content Query Web Part in SharePoint" white paper at http://msdn.microsoft.com/en-us/library/ff380147.aspx.

Example: The Action Group site will add a content query Web Part for its Press Releases subsite.

Steps:

1. Start Internet Explorer and type the URL for your organization's SharePoint server. The Start Page will open.

2. Navigate to the site where you want to add the Content Query Web Part.

3. Click the Page tab and select the Edit button. The Page ribbon will appear and the page will open in Edit Mode.

Figure 1: The Page Ribbon and Page in Edit Mode

4. Select a zone and click Add a Web Part. The Add Web Parts header will open.

5. Select the Content Rollup folder and then click the Content Query Web Part. The Web Part will be selected.

6. Click Add. The Add Web Parts header will close and the new Web Part will appear in the selected zone.

7. Click the open the tool pane link. The tool pane for the Content Query Web Part will appear.

Figure 2: The Content Query Web Part Tool Pane

8. Click the Query expand control to expand the section, then click the Show items from the following site and all subsites option.

9. Enter the URL for the Press Releases site in the adjacent URL field.

10. Continue to fill out the remainder of the Content Query tool pane as desired.

11. Click OK. The Content Query Web Part Tool Pane will close and the new Web Part will be visible on the page.

NOTE: Follow the site approval steps to save and publish the modified page.

Task: Export a Custom Query Web Part

Purpose: After it's been customized to your specifications, any Content Query Web Part can be exported for use in another site.

Example: The Action Group site will export a custom content query Web Part, to be shared with another site in the company.

Steps:

1. Start Internet Explorer and type the URL for your organization's SharePoint server. The Start Page will open.

2. Navigate to the site to from which you want to export the Content Query Web Part.

3. Click the Page tab and select the Edit Page button. The Page ribbon will appear and the page will open in Edit Mode.

4. Click the drop-down control for the custom Content Query Web Part and click the Export option. The File Download dialog box will open.

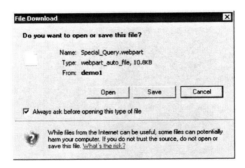

Figure 1: The File Download Dialog Box

5. Click Save. The Save As dialog box will open.

6. Name and navigate to the folder in which you want to save the Web Part, clicking Save. The Web Part will be saved.

Task: Implement and Configure Custom Content Query Web Parts

Purpose: The Content Query Web Part is very useful, especially since you can import a custom query web part from another site.

Example: The Action Group site will add a custom content query Web Part, recently developed by an in-house developer in another division.

Steps:

1. Start Internet Explorer and type the URL for your organization's SharePoint server. The Start Page will open.

2. Navigate to the site to add the Content Query Web Part.

3. Click the Page tab and select the Edit Page button. The Page ribbon will appear and the page will open in Edit Mode.

4. Select a zone and click Add a Web Part. The Add Web Parts header will open.

5. Click the Upload a Web Part control. The control will expand to an upload field.

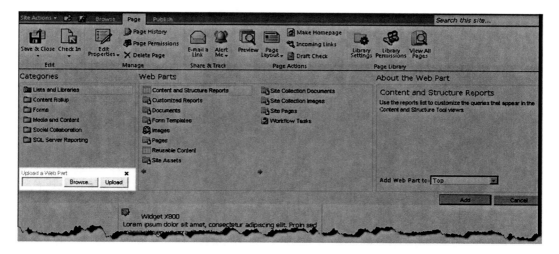

Figure 1: The Upload a Web Part Control

6. Click Browse. The Choose File to Upload dialog box will open.

7. Navigate to the Web Part you want to upload and click Open. The file path and name of the folder will appear in the field.

8. Click Upload. The Web Part will be uploaded.

9. Click Imported Web Parts folder and then the new Web Part. The Web Part will be selected.

10. Click Add. The Add Web Parts header will close and the new Web Part will appear in the selected zone.

Task: Implement and Configure the Summary Links Web Part

Purpose: Another useful Web Part is the Summary Links Web Part, which lets you manually add links to articles and pages on your site as well as to other sites. This is done to provide additional resources for the information on the page.

Example: The Action Group site will add a Summary Links Web Part to its home page.

Steps:

1. Start Internet Explorer and type the URL for your organization's SharePoint server. The Start Page will open.

2. Navigate to the site to add the Content Query Web Part.

3. Click the Page tab and select the Edit button. The Page ribbon will appear and the page will open in Edit Mode.

4. Select a zone and click Add a Web Part. The Add Web Parts header will open.

5. Click Content Rollup folder and then the Summary Links Web Part. The Web Part will be selected.

6. Click Add. The Add Web Parts header will close and the Summary Links Web Part will appear in the selected zone.

7. To add a new summary link, click New Link at the top of the Summary Links Web Part. The New Link dialog box will open.

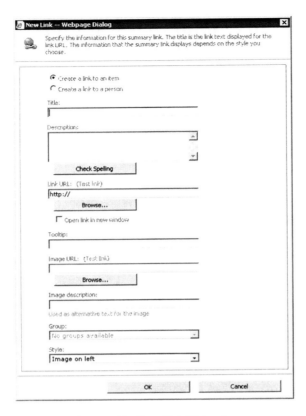

Figure 1: The New Link Dialog Box

8. Add the pertinent information about the link. You can add as much or as little information as needed.

9. Click OK. The new summary link will be added to the page.

Site Collection Owners will have the ability to manage entire collections of sites, which gives them the responsibility to maintain consistency in style as well as site collection efficiency.

In this section, you'll learn how to:

- **Enable Output Cache**: To counter the time it takes to query a database, and to effectively speed up the time pages are served, Site Collection owners can implement caching.

- **Configure Site Collection Default Profiles**: Once output caching is implemented on a site, the Site Collection owner can specify which profiles will apply to which kinds of site visitors.

- **Configure Output Cache Profiles**: SharePoint provides you with a few preconfigured output cache profiles to apply to your site. Each of these profiles can be tweaked to match your exact needs.

- **Add an Output Cache Profile**: Sometimes a Site Collection owner might need to create a new output cache from scratch.

- **Override the Configured Output Cache Profile**: You can set SharePoint to allow site administrators and designers to configure cache settings for individual pages.

- **Configure the Object Cache**: Object caching is another way to improve page rendering in SharePoint.

- **Flush Disk-based and Object Caches**: If you have made significant changes to the cache settings on your site or you suspect that the cache is invalid, it might be a good idea to purge the object and disk-based caches for your server.

- **Enable and Configure Cross-List Query Cache**: The cross-list query caching improves query performance, but only if the content of your lists or libraries is relatively unchanging.

- **Install a Sandbox Solution**: Sandbox solutions are designed for situations where the developer of a solution isn't trusted by the central administration or the solution pertains only to a single site collection.

- **Deactivate a Sandbox Solution**: Sandbox solutions can use up a certain number of server resources and thus need to be managed accordingly.

Task: Enable Output Cache

Purpose: Whenever a user requests a page from a Web site, the request has to go through a variety of steps before the page is actually transmitted back to the user's browser. In the case of SharePoint pages, a big piece of time can be taken up by the process of checking the content database. To counter this, and to effectively speed up the time pages are served, Site Collection owners can implement caching.

Example: The Action Group site needs to have its performance increased. The Site Collection owner will enable the output cache for the site.

Steps:

1. Start Internet Explorer and type the URL for your organization's SharePoint server. The Start Page will open.

2. Navigate to the publishing site. The publishing site's home page will open.

3. Click the Site Actions menu and select Site Settings. The Site Settings page will open.

4. In the Site Collection Administration section, click the Site collection output cache link. The Output Cache Settings page will open.

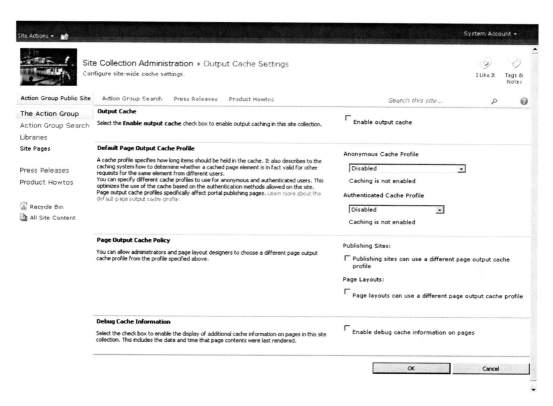

Figure 1: The Output Cache Settings Page

5. In the Output Cache section, select the Enable output cache checkbox.

6. Click OK. The Site Settings page will open.

NOTE: To disable the output cache, repeat these steps and de-select the Enable output cache checkbox.

Task: Configure Site Collection Default Cache Profiles

Purpose: Once output caching is implemented on a site, the Site Collection owner can specify which profiles will apply to which kinds of site visitors.

Example: The Action Group site cache settings will need different cache settings for anonymous (unauthenticated) users and authenticated users.

Steps:

1. Start Internet Explorer and type the URL for your organization's SharePoint server. The Start Page will open.

2. Navigate to the publishing site. The publishing site's home page will open.

3. Click the Site Actions menu and select Site Settings. The Site Settings page will open.

4. In the Site Collection Administration section, click the Site collection output cache link. The Output Cache Settings page will open.

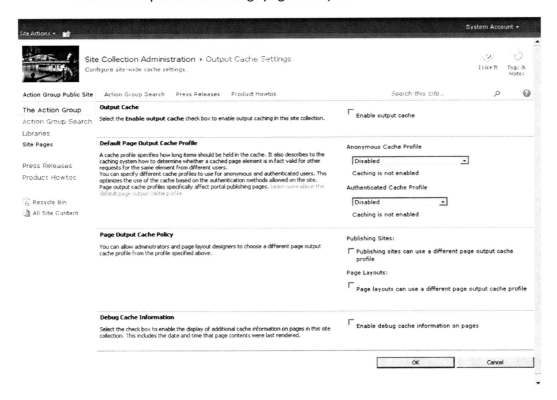

Figure 1: The Output Cache Settings Page

5. In the Default Page Output Cache Profile section, set the Anonymous Cache Profile field to the Public Internet (Purely Anonymous) option. The site will be optimized

---

The SharePoint Shepherd's Guide for End Users: 2010

for public Internet facing sites or areas that are meant to serve the same content to all users.

6. In the Default Page Output Cache Profile section, set the Authenticated Cache Profile field to the Extranet (Published Site) option. The site will be optimized for a public extranet site with the following characteristics: authoring does not take place on the tier; only major versions of pages are deployed to the tier; and users can not customize Web Parts on a page in the tier.

7. Click OK. The Site Settings page will open.

Task: Configure Output Cache Profiles

Purpose: SharePoint provides you with a few preconfigured output cache profiles to apply to your site. Each of these profiles can be tweaked to match your exact needs.

Example: The Action Group site cache setting for anonymous users needs its cache duration increased from 180 seconds to 360 seconds.

Steps:

1. Start Internet Explorer and type the URL for your organization's SharePoint server. The Start Page will open.

2. Navigate to the publishing site. The publishing site's home page will open.

3. Click the Site Actions menu and select Site Settings. The Site Settings page will open.

4. In the Site Collection Administration section, click the Site collection cache profiles link. The Cache Profiles page will open.

Figure 1: The Cache Profiles Page

5. Click the Public Internet (Purely Anonymous) link. The Cache Profiles dialog box will open.

The SharePoint Shepherd's Guide for End Users: 2010

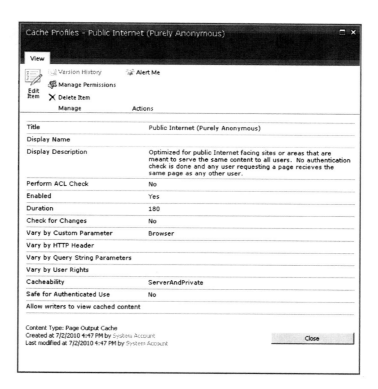

Figure 2: The Cache Profiles Dialog Box

6. Click the Edit Item button. The Cache Profiles dialog box will change to edit mode.

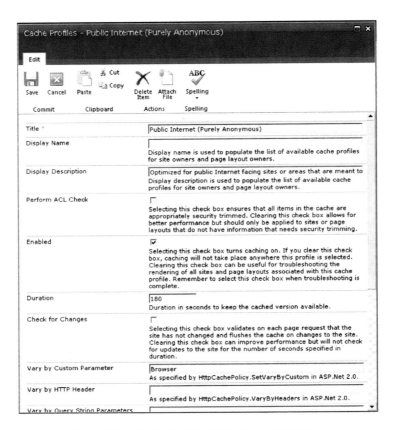

Figure 3: The Cache Profiles Dialog Box in Edit Mode

7. Change the Duration field to 360.

8. Click Save. The Cache Profiles dialog box will close.

Task: Add an Output Cache Profile

Purpose: SharePoint provides you with a few preconfigured output cache profiles to apply to your site. Sometimes, however, a Site Collection owner might need to create a new output cache from scratch.

Example: The Action Group site needs a cache setting for site developers to optimize the performance for these users.

Steps:

1. Start Internet Explorer and type the URL for your organization's SharePoint server. The Start Page will open.

2. Navigate to the publishing site. The publishing site's home page will open.

3. Click the Site Actions menu and select Site Settings. The Site Settings page will open.

4. In the Site Collection Administration section, click the Site collection cache profiles link. The Cache Profiles page will open.

5. Click the Add new item link. The Cache Profiles – New Item dialog box will open.

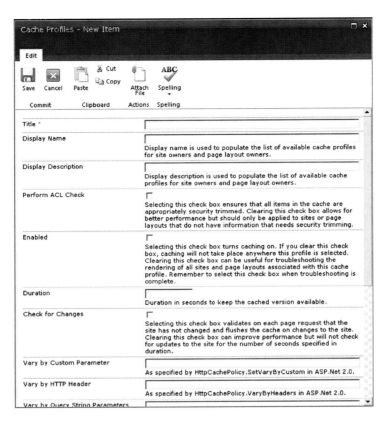

Figure 1: The Cache Profiles – New Item Dialog Box

6. Add the settings in the Cache Profiles – New Items dialog box as needed.

7. Click Save. The Cache Profiles dialog box will close and the new cache profile will be added to Cache Profiles Page.

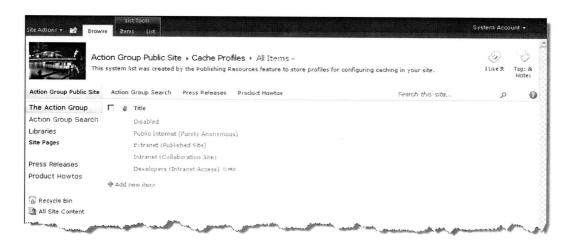

Figure 2: The New Cache Profile on the Cache Profiles Page

Task: Override the Configured Output Cache Profile

Purpose: Not every page in a site will need output cache settings applied. You can set SharePoint to allow site administrators and designers to configure cache settings for individual pages.

Example: The Action Group site cache settings will be set by the Site Collection owner to allow cache settings to be configured by page.

Steps:

1. Start Internet Explorer and type the URL for your organization's SharePoint server. The Start Page will open.

2. Navigate to the publishing site. The publishing site's home page will open.

3. Click the Site Actions menu and select Site Settings. The Site Settings page will open.

4. In the Site Collection Administration section, click the Site collection output cache link. The Output Cache Settings page will open.

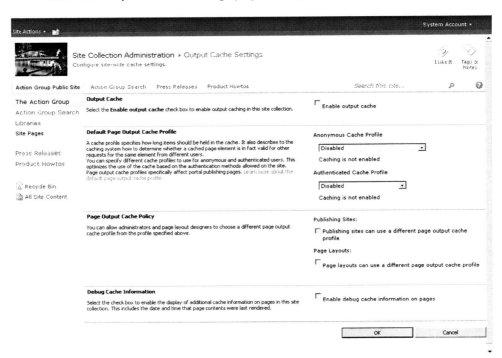

Figure 1: The Output Cache Settings Page

5. In the Page Output Cache Policy section, click the Page layouts can use a different page output cache profile checkbox.

6. Click OK. The Site Settings page will open.

Task: Configure the Object Cache

Purpose: Object caching is another way to improve page rendering in SharePoint. Caching for page items is fast and it eliminates the need to retrieve data from the database each time a page is rendered.

Example: The Action Group object cache size will be increased to improve performance on the site's pages.

Steps:

1. Start Internet Explorer and type the URL for your organization's SharePoint server. The Start Page will open.

2. Navigate to the publishing site. The publishing site's home page will open.

3. Click the Site Actions menu and select Site Settings. The Site Settings page will open.

4. In the Site Collection Administration section, click the Site collection object cache link. The Object Cache Settings page will open.

Figure 1: The Object Cache Settings Page

5. In the Object Cache Size section, set the Max. Cache Size (MB) field to 200.

---

6. Click OK. The Site Settings page will open.

Task: Flush Disk-Based and Object Caches

Purpose: If you have made significant changes to the cache settings on your site or you suspect that the cache is invalid, it might be a good idea to purge the object and disk-based caches for your server. SharePoint enables you to do this for one server, or all servers in the SharePoint server farm.

Example: The Action Group Site Collection owner will flush the disk-based and object caches for the individual Action Group public site's server.

Steps:

1. Start Internet Explorer and type the URL for your organization's SharePoint server. The Start Page will open.

2. Navigate to the publishing site. The publishing site's home page will open.

3. Click the Site Actions menu and select Site Settings. The Site Settings page will open.

4. In the Site Collection Administration section, click the Site collection object cache link. The Object Cache Settings page will open.

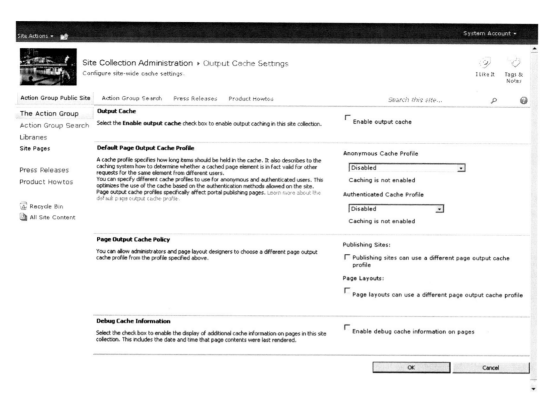

Figure 1: The Output Cache Settings Page

5. In the Object Cache Reset section, click the Object Cache Flush checkbox.

6. Click OK. The object and disk-based caches for the server will immediately be flushed and the Site Settings page will open.

Task: Enable and Configure Cross-List Query Cache

Purpose: The cross-list query caching improves query performance, but only if the content of your lists or libraries is relatively unchanging. You can change your query cache settings to reflect the dynamic nature of your content.

Example: The Action Group Site Collection owner will set the query cache option to a longer cache because the site's content does not change often.

Steps:

1. Start Internet Explorer and type the URL for your organization's SharePoint server. The Start Page will open.

2. Navigate to the publishing site. The publishing site's home page will open.

3. Click the Site Actions menu and select Site Settings. The Site Settings page will open.

4. In the Site Collection Administration section, click the Site collection object cache link. The Object Cache Settings page will open.

Figure 1: The Object Cache Settings Page

5. In the Cross List Query Cache section, click the Check the server for changes every time a cross list query runs option if your content changes often. Otherwise, click the Use the cached result of a cross list query for this many seconds option.

6. Click OK. The Site Settings page will open.

Task: Install and Activate a Sandbox Solution

Purpose: In prior versions of SharePoint, deploying a new Web Part or other dynamic tool on a SharePoint site, whether deploying it on a virtual system or creating an entirely new site collection, would involve the farm administrator and thus create a bottleneck, since farm administrators have other things to manage, too. Sandbox solutions can be used where the developer of a solution isn't a trusted resource for central administration or the solution pertains only to a single site collection.

Example: The XYZ Corporation would like to deploy a test site before implementing it in a production environment.

Steps:

1. Start Internet Explorer and type the URL for your organization's SharePoint server. The Start Page will open.

2. Navigate to the main site from which the new site will be added. The site's home page will open.

3. Click the Site Actions menu and select Site Settings. The Site Settings page will open.

4. Click the Solutions link in the Galleries section. The Solutions page will open.

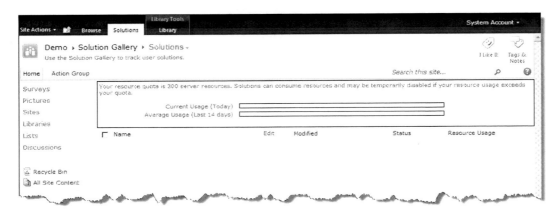

Figure 1: The Solutions Page

5. Click the Solutions tab. The Solutions ribbon will appear.

6. Click the Upload Solution button. The Solution Gallery – Upload Solution dialog box will appear.

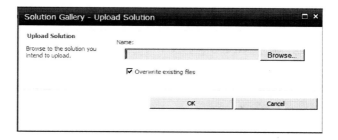

Figure 2: The Solution Gallery – Upload Solution Dialog Box

7. Click Browse. The Choose File to Upload dialog box will open.

8. Navigate to the sandbox solution file you want to use and click Open. The file will appear in the Name field.

9. Click OK. The new template will be uploaded and appear in the Solutions gallery.

10. Click the solution item to select it. A confirmation dialog box will open.

11. Click the Activate button. The solution will be activated.

Task: Deactivate a Sandbox Solution

Purpose: Sandbox solutions can use up a certain number of server resources and thus need to be managed accordingly. When a solution meets its quota, the solution will be stopped until the farm administrator can extend the quota. At that point, or before, you may want to deactivate the solution when its testing is complete.

Example: The sandboxed solution has completed its test run, and can be deactivated.

Steps:

1. Start Internet Explorer and type the URL for your organization's SharePoint server. The Start Page will open.

2. Navigate to the main site from which the new sandbox site will be deactivated. The site's home page will open.

3. Click the Site Actions menu and select Site Settings. The Site Settings page will open.

4. In the Galleries section, click the Solutions link. The Solutions page will open.

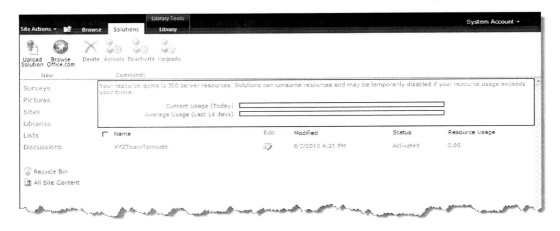

Figure 1: The Solutions Page

5. Click the solution item to select it.

6. Click the Deactivate button. After confirming the action, the sandbox solution will be deactivated.

Appendix A: Site Definitions

Purpose: There are many different kinds of sites that can be created in SharePoint. You have seen some in action throughout the tasks in this book. In this Appendix, all of the site definitions will be reviewed and displayed, to make your choices easier when it's time to create your own site.

The site definitions available on the SharePoint Create Site dialog box are:

- Blank & Custom Sites

  - Blank Site

  - Personalization Site

- Collaboration Sites

  - Team Site

  - Document Workspace

  - Group Work Site

  - Business Intelligence Center

- Content Sites

  - My Site Host

  - Document Workspace

  - Blog

  - Document Center

  - Visio Process Repository

- Data Site

  - Records Center

- Meetings Sites

  - Basic Meeting Workspace

  - Blank Meeting Workspace

  - Decision Meeting Workspace

- o Social Meeting Workspace

- o Multipage Meeting Workspace

- Search Site

  - o Basic Search Center

  - o Enterprise Search Center

  - o FAST Search Center

- Web Databases

  - o Assets Web Database

  - o Charitable Contributions Web Database

  - o Contacts Web Database

  - o Issues Web Database

  - o Projects Web Database

- Publishing Sites

  - o Publishing Site with Workflow

  - o Publishing Site

  - o Publishing Portal

  - o Enterprise Wiki

Blank and Custom Sites
The two sites in this category are designed to get you started with the bare minimum SharePoint sites.

Blank Site
This is a blank site for you to customize based on your requirements. No lists or libraries are created; the user adds what they need from scratch.

Figure 1: Blank Site

Personalization Site

A personalization site is for delivering personalized views, data, and navigation from this site collection into My Site. It includes personalization specific web parts and navigation that is optimized for My Site sites.

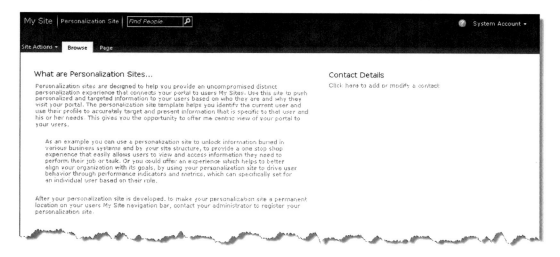

Figure 2: Personalization Site

Collaboration Sites

The three sites in this category all have the same basic purpose: to allow you and your co-workers to share and collaborate on documents to get work done more efficiently.

Team Site

A team site is a site for teams to quickly organize, author, and share information. It provides a document library, and lists for managing announcements, calendar items, tasks, and discussions.

The Team Site creates default instances of these lists and libraries:

- Shared Documents (Document Library)

- Site Assets

- Site Pages

- Announcements

- Calendar

- Links

- Tasks

- Team Discussion

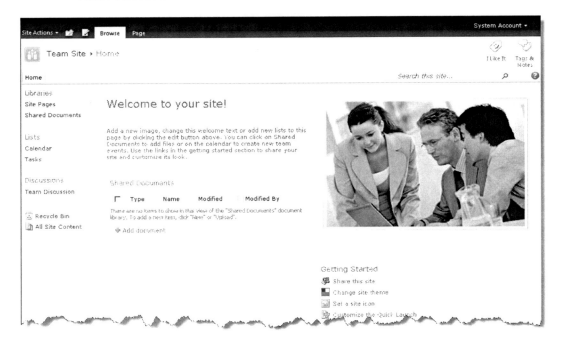

Figure 3: Team Site

Document Workspace

A document workspace is a site for colleagues to work together on a document. It provides a Shared Documents document library for storing the primary document and supporting files, a Tasks list for assigning to-do items, and a Links list for resources related to the document. The document workspace also includes these lists:

- Announcements

- Calendar

- Team Discussion

The SharePoint Shepherd's Guide for End Users: 2010

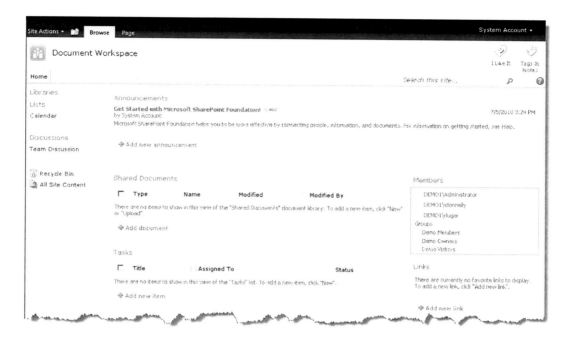

Figure 4: Document Workspace

Group Work Site

A Group Work Site provides a groupware solution that enables teams to create, organize, and share information quickly and easily. It includes Group Calendar, Circulation, Phone-Call Memo, the Document Library, and the other basic lists included in the Team Site. In addition, the Resources list and Whereabouts list are also included when a Group Work Site is created.

Figure 5: Group Work Site

Business Intelligence Center

The Business intelligence Center site helps you organize that data in a useful way and present that data as meaningful information. It uses business intelligence tools such as scorecards, dashboards, data connections, status lists, and status indicators to convey the information you need.

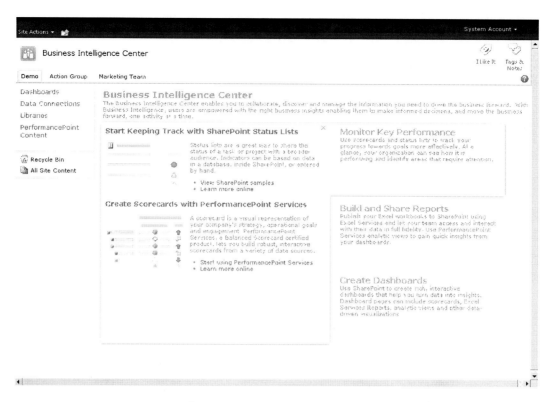

Figure 6: Business Intelligence Center

Content Sites

Content sites are specialized SharePoint sites designed to provide visitors with content in a well-presented, efficient manner.

My Site Host

My Sites give users a place to express themselves more creatively, share interests and hobbies, and generally make the work environment a more personal place.

Figure 7: The My Site Page

Document Workspace

A document workspace, as noted earlier, is a site for colleagues to work together on a document. It provides a document library for storing the primary document and supporting files, a Tasks list for assigning to-do items, and a Links list for resources related to the document in addition to the Announcements list, Calendar, and Team Discussion board.

Blog

This is a site for a person or team to post ideas, observations, and expertise that site visitors can comment on.

The lists and libraries created in a Blog site are:

- Photos (Photo library)

- Categories

- Comments

- Links

- Posts

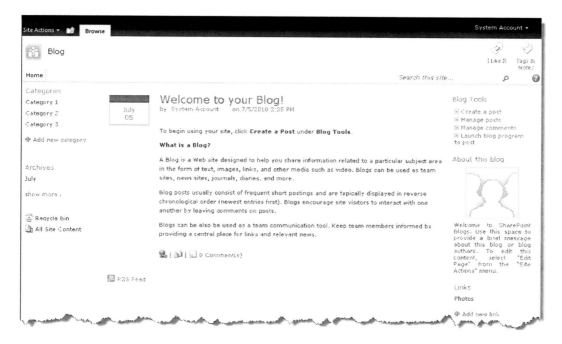

Figure 8: Blog Site

Document Center

Use this site to create, work on, and store documents. This site can become a collaborative repository for authoring documents within a team, or a knowledge base for documents across multiple teams.

Figure 9: Document Center

Visio Process Repository

This is a site for teams to quickly view, share, and store Visio process diagrams. It provides a versioned document library for storing process diagrams, and lists for managing announcements, tasks, and review discussions.

Figure 10: Visio Process Repository

Data Site

The site in this category is designed to be used as a tool in large-scale business environments.

Records Center

This template creates a site designed for records management. Records managers can configure the routing table to direct incoming files to specific locations. The site prevents records from being modified after they are added to the repository.

The records center creates a number of libraries and lists when it is started:

- Libraries
    - Hold Reports
    - Missing Properties
    - Records Pending Submission
    - Unclassified Records
- Lists
    - Holds

o   Records Routing

o   Records Center

o   Submitted E-Mail Records

o   Tasks

Meetings Sites

These sites are all geared towards setting up different types of meeting workspaces.

Basic Meeting Workspace

This is a site to plan, organize, and capture the results of a meeting. It provides lists for managing the agenda, meeting attendees, and documents.

Figure 11: Basic Meeting

Blank Meeting Workspace

The blank meeting site is for you to customize based on your requirements.

Figure 12: Blank Meeting

Decision Meeting Workspace

- This site is for meetings that track status or make decisions. It provides lists for creating tasks, storing documents, and recording decisions. The complete selection of libraries and lists are:

- Document Library

- Objectives

- Attendees

- Agenda

- Tasks

- Decisions

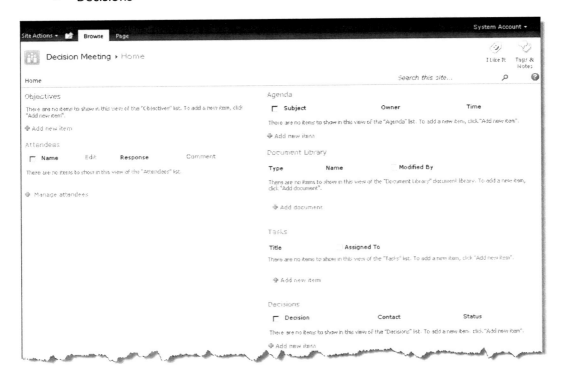

Figure 13: Decision Meeting

Social Meeting Workspace

This site is used to plan social occasions. It provides lists for tracking attendees, providing directions, and storing pictures of the event.

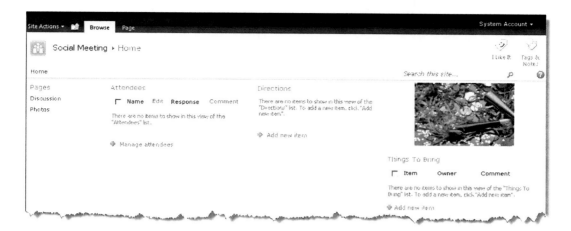

Figure 14: Social Meeting

Multipage Meeting Workspace

This site is for a person or team to post ideas, observations, and expertise that site visitors can comment on. This workspace is similar to the Decision Meeting, but has additional pages that you can add libraries and lists to if needed.

Figure 15: Multipage Meeting

Search Site

The site in this category is designed to help users find information fast.

Basic Search Center

This site is for delivering a custom search experience. The site includes pages for search results and advanced searches.

Figure 16: Basic Search Center

Enterprise Search Center

The Enterprise Search Center is a SharePoint search that includes several components, each responsible for a specific search task.

Figure 17: Enterprise Search Center

FAST Search Center

A search-oriented page that uses FAST's high-end search capabilities for SharePoint.

Web Databases

These sites contain dynamic, Access-based databases that allow you to manage business data.

Assets Web Database

This assets database will keep track of assets, including asset details and owners.

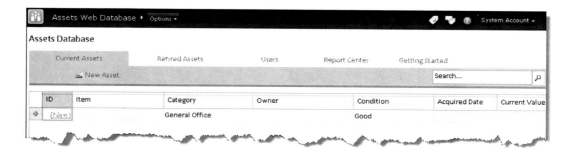

Figure 18: Assets Web Database

Charitable Contributions Web Database

This database is used to track information about fundraising campaigns, including donations made by contributors, campaign-related events, and pending tasks.

Figure 19: Charitable Contributions Web Database

Contacts Web Database

This is a database to manage information about people that your team works with, such as customers and partners.

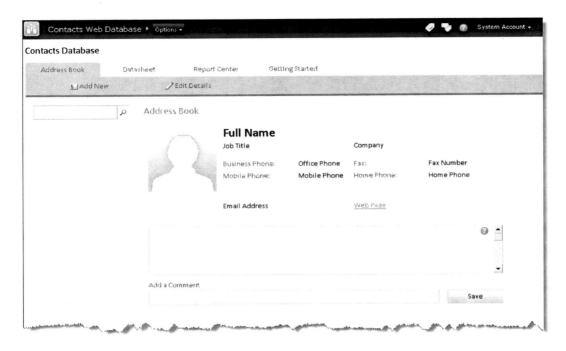

Figure 20: Contacts Web Database

Issues Web Database

This is a database to manage a set of issues or problems. You can assign, prioritize, and follow the progress of issues from start to finish.

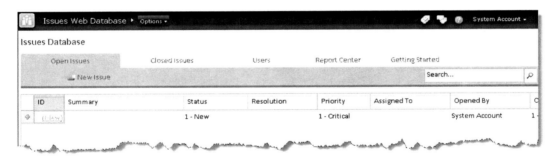

Figure 21: Issues Web Database

Projects Web Database

This is a project-tracking database to track multiple projects, and assign tasks to different people.

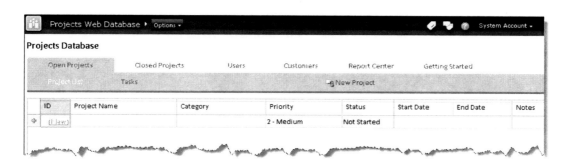

Figure 22: Projects Web Database

Publishing Sites

The two sites in this category are for publishing custom web pages, with or without a workflow process in place.

Publishing Site with Workflow

This is a site for publishing Web pages on a schedule by using approval workflows. It includes document and image libraries for storing Web publishing assets. By default, only sites with this template can be created under this site.

Home

Press Releases

Enable anonymous access
Anonymous access allows users to view the pages on this site without logging in. This is useful when creating internet facing sites or sites where you want everyone to have access to read the content without editing.

Manage navigation
Change the navigation links in this site.

Go to master page gallery
Change the page layouts and master page of this site collection.

Manage site content and structure
Reorganize content and structure in this site collection.

Set up multilingual support
Use the variations feature to manage multi-lingual sites and pages.

Add users to the Approvers and Members groups
Users in the Approvers group can publish pages, images, and documents in this site. Users in the Members group can create and edit pages, and they can upload images and documents, but they cannot publish the pages, images, or documents. Workflow is enabled in the Pages library, and content approval is enabled in the Documents and Images libraries.

Figure 23: Publishing Site with Workflow

Publishing Site

This is a blank site for expanding your Web site and quickly publishing Web pages. Contributors can work on draft versions of pages and publish them to make them visible to readers. The site includes document and image libraries for storing Web publishing assets.

Publishing Portal

A starter site hierarchy that you can use for an Internet site or a large intranet portal. You can use distinctive branding to customize this site. It includes a home page, a sample press releases site, a Search Center, and a logon page. Typically, this site has many more readers than contributors, and it is used to publish the Web pages by using approval workflows.

This site enables content approval workflows, by default, for a more formal and controlled publishing process. It also restricts the rights of anonymous users so that they can see only content pages, and they cannot see SharePoint Server 2010 application pages. This template is available only at the site collection level.

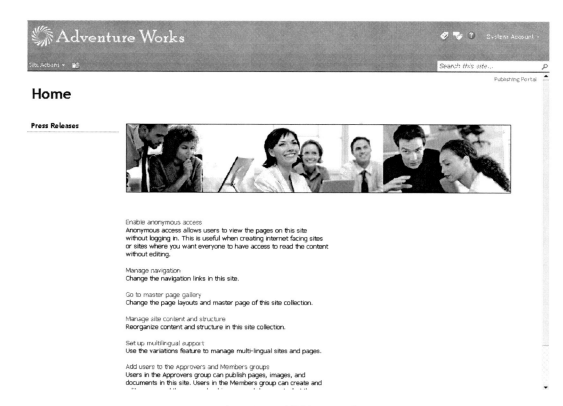

Home

Press Releases

Enable anonymous access
Anonymous access allows users to view the pages on this site
without logging in. This is useful when creating internet facing sites
or sites where you want everyone to have access to read the content
without editing.

Manage navigation
Change the navigation links in this site.

Go to master page gallery
Change the page layouts and master page of this site collection.

Manage site content and structure
Reorganize content and structure in this site collection.

Set up multilingual support
Use the variations feature to manage multi-lingual sites and pages.

Add users to the Approvers and Members groups
Users in the Approvers group can publish pages, images, and
documents in this site. Users in the Members group can create and

Figure 24: Publishing Portal

Enterprise Wiki

An Enterprise Wiki is a publishing site for sharing and updating large volumes of information across an enterprise.

Figure 25: Enterprise Wiki

Appendix B: List Definitions

Purpose: Libraries, lists, discussion boards... in SharePoint: they're all some sort of list. In this Appendix, all of the lists will be reviewed and displayed, to make your choices easier when it's time to create your own list.

Libraries

Libraries are essentially lists that have one and only one file associated with each item.

Assets Library

A library for managing and sharing digital assets, such as audio, video, and other rich media files.

Figure 1: Assets Library

Dashboards Library

A collection of business intelligence dashboards.

Figure 2: Dashboards Library

Data Connection Library

Create a Data Connection Library to make it easy to share files that contain information about external data connections.

Figure 3: Data Connection Library

Document Library

Create a document library when you have a collection of documents or other files that you want to share. Document libraries support features such as folders, versioning, and check out.

Figure 4: Document Library

Form Library

Create a form library when you have XML-based business forms, such as status reports or purchase orders, that you want to manage. These libraries are designed for use with Microsoft Office InfoPath.

The SharePoint Shepherd's Guide for End Users: 2010

Figure 5: Form Library

Picture Library

Create a picture library when you have pictures you want to share. Picture libraries provide special features for managing and displaying pictures, such as thumbnails, download options, and a slide show.

Figure 6: Picture Library

Process Diagrams Library

A collection of Visio-based process diagrams.

Figure 7: Process Diagrams Library

Report Library

A library designed to manage and share SQL reports.

Figure 8: Report Library

Slide Library

A library for managing and sharing PowerPoint presentations.

Figure 9: Slide Library

Translation Management Library

The Translation Management Library is a document library template available for SharePoint sites, designed to help organizations create, store, and manage translated documents.

Wiki Page Library

Create a Wiki page library when you want to have an interconnected collection of Wiki pages. Wiki page libraries support pictures, tables, hyperlinks, and wiki linking.

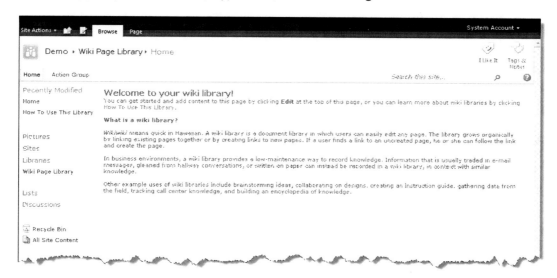

Figure 10: Wiki Page Library

Lists

Lists in this collection are designed to be used as tools in connecting with your co-workers.

Administrator Tasks

A task list for a SharePoint administrator.

Agenda

A Meeting Workspace list that creates a list of items related to the topics of a meeting.

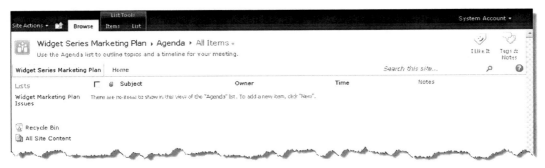

Figure 11: Agenda

Announcements

Create an announcements list when you want a place to share news, status, and other short bits of information.

Figure 12: Announcements

Calendar

Create a calendar list when you want a calendar-based view of upcoming meetings, deadlines, and other important events. You can share information between your calendar list and Windows SharePoint Services-compatible events programs.

Figure 13: Calendar

Circulations

Use this list to inform team members and request confirmation for meetings.

Figure 14: Circulations

Contacts

Create a contacts list when you want to manage information about people that your team works with, such as customers or partners. You can share information between your contacts list and Microsoft Outlook.

Figure 15: Contacts

Custom List

Create a custom list when you want to specify your own columns. The list opens as a Web page and lets you add or edit items one at a time. Your title field must be a single line of text, but it can be renamed. You can also add all of the columns that you want, as shown in "Create a List."

Figure 16: Custom List

Custom List in Datasheet View

Create a custom list when you want to specify your own columns, just like a regular custom list. In this case, the list opens in a spreadsheet-like environment for convenient data entry, editing, and formatting. It requires Microsoft Access and a browser with ActiveX control support.

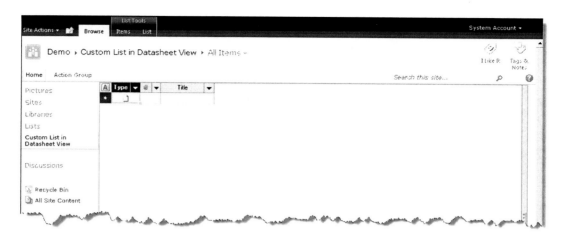

Figure 17: Custom List in Datasheet View

Decisions

A list designed to contain items for collaborative decision making.

Figure 18: Decisions

Discussion Board

Create a discussion board when you want to provide a place for newsgroup-style discussions. Discussion boards provide features for managing discussion threads and ensuring that only approved posts appear.

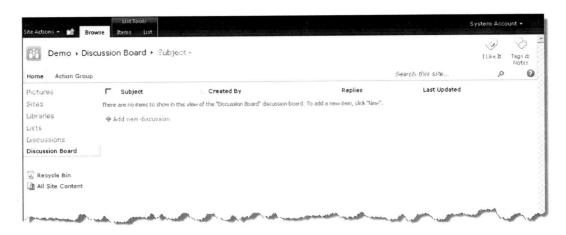

Figure 19: Discussion Board

Distribution Groups

A list of Active Directory distribution groups.

External List

Create an external list to view the data in an External Content Type.

Import Spreadsheet

Import a spreadsheet when you want to create a list that has the same columns and contents as an existing spreadsheet. Importing a spreadsheet requires Microsoft Excel.

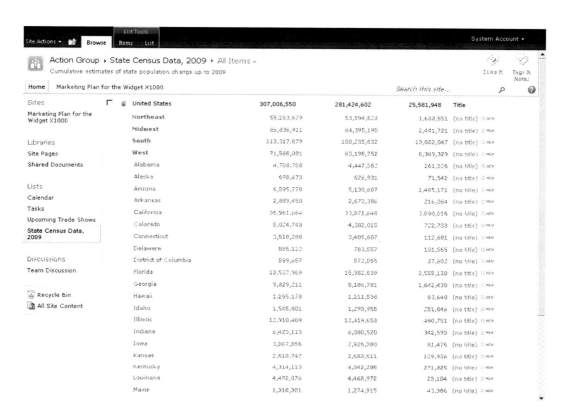

Figure 20: Import Spreadsheet

Issue Tracking

Create an issue tracking list when you want to manage a set of issues or problems. You can assign, prioritize, and follow the progress of issues from start to finish. Another key feature is that you can relate issues to one another, which makes it easier to create logical progressions of work to be done.

Figure 21: Issue Tracking

Languages and Translators

A list of languages used by the Translation Management Library. Translators for each language and languages can be added.

Links

Create a links list when you have links to Web pages or other resources that you want to share.

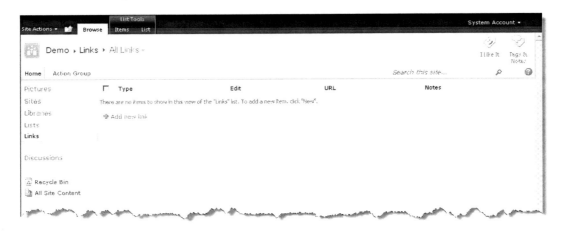

Figure 22: Links

Microsoft IME Dictionary List

The Microsoft IME Dictionary list uses items in the list as part of a Microsoft IME dictionary.

Objectives

A list of goals and objectives from a meeting. Found in the Meeting Workspace.

Figure 23: Objectives

PerformancePoint Content

PerformancePoint Services is a performance management service that you can use to monitor and analyze your business. This list contains the content for this service.

Figure 24: PerformancePoint Content

Project Tasks

Create a project tasks list when you want a graphical view (a Gantt chart) on a group of work items that you or your team needs to complete. You can open this list in Windows SharePoint Services-compatible programs, such as Microsoft Project.

Figure 25: Project Tasks

Status

A list to manage a set of goals. Colored icons track the progress of each goal's completion.

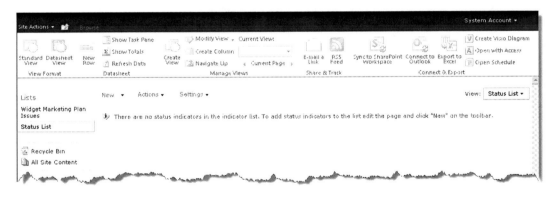

Figure 26: Status

Survey

Create a survey when you want to poll other Web site users. Surveys provide features that allow you to quickly create questions and define how users specify their answers.

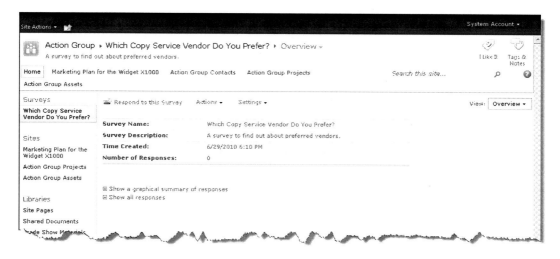

Figure 27: Survey

Tabs List

A list of items that contains multiple tabbed pages for organization purposes.

Tasks

Create a tasks list when you want to track a group of work items that you or your team needs to complete.

Figure 28: Tasks

Text Box

A list that contains rich text boxes to handle data items.

Figure 29: Text Box

Things to Bring

A meeting workspace list that details the items to bring to a meeting.

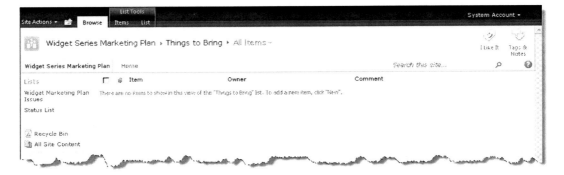

Figure 30: Things to Bring

Appendix C: Web Parts

Purpose: When you create a Web Parts page, you can easily insert content from almost any list made available in SharePoint. There are also some specialized content Web Parts. In this Appendix, the most common Web Parts will be reviewed and displayed, to make your choices easier when it's time to create your Web Parts page.

Lists and Libraries

The lists and libraries category allows for list and library functionality to be inserted within a Web page.

Content and Structure Reports

Use the reports list to customize the queries that appear in the Content and Structure Tool views.

Customized Reports

This Document library has the templates to create Web Analytics custom reports for this site collection.

Documents

This system library was created by the Publishing feature to store documents that are used on pages in this site.

Form Templates

This library contains administrator-approved form templates that were activated to this site collection.

Images

This system library was created by the Publishing feature to store images that are used on pages in this site.

Pages

This system library was created by the Publishing feature to store pages that are created in this site.

Reusable Content

Items in this list contain HTML or text content which can be inserted into Web pages. If an item has automatic update selected, the content will be inserted into Web pages as a read-only reference, and the content will update if the item is changed. If the item does not have automatic update selected, the content will be inserted as a copy in the Web page, and the content will not update if the item is changed.

Site Assets

Use this library to store files which are included on pages within this site, such as images on Wiki pages.

Site Collection Documents

This system library was created by the Publishing Resources feature to store documents that are used throughout the site collection.

Site Collection Images

This system library was created by the Publishing Resources feature to store images that are used throughout the site collection.

Site Pages

Use this library to create and store pages on this site.

Workflow Tasks

This system library was created by the Publishing feature to store workflow tasks that are created in this site.

Content Rollup

Web Parts in this category can aggregate content from a variety of sources.

Content Query

Displays a dynamic view of content from your site.

Relevant Documents

Displays documents that are relevant to the current user.

Summary Links

Allows authors to create links that can be grouped and styled.

Table of Contents

Displays the navigation hierarchy of your site.

Web Analytics

Displays the most viewed content, most frequent search queries from a site, or most frequent search queries from a search center.

XML Viewer

Transforms XML data using XSL and shows the results.

Forms

Web Parts in this category build Web page forms for users.

HTML Form

Connects simple form controls to other Web Parts.

InfoPath Form

Use this Web Part to display an InfoPath browser-enabled form.

Media and Content

Web Parts in this category display a variety of multimedia content.

Content Editor

Allows authors to enter rich text content.

Image Viewer

Displays a specified image.

Media

Use to embed media clips (video and audio) in a Web page.

Page Viewer

Displays another Web page on this Web page. The other Web page is presented in an IFrame.

Picture Library Slideshow

Use to display a slideshow of images and photos from a picture library.

Silverlight

A Web Part to display a Silverlight application.

Social Collaboration

Web Parts in this category enable user to engage in collaborative and social activities.

Site Users

Use the Site Users Web Part to see a list of the site users and their online status.

User Tasks

Displays tasks that are assigned to the current user.

SQL Server Reporting

The Web Part in this category enables SQL Server connectivity.

SQL Server Reporting Services Report Viewer

Use the Report Viewer to view SQL Server Reporting Services reports.

Appendix D: Views

Purpose: When you create a new view of a list in SharePoint, you are given a choice of six default views. In this Appendix, these views will be reviewed and displayed, to make your choices easier when it's time to customize the way you look at a list.

Standard

View data on a Web page. This view displays a standard data grid type view of the data, as seen on most Web pages and sites.

Figure 1: Standard View

Standard with Expanded Recurring Events

View data on a Web page. You can choose from a list of display styles. Use this view type to show each instance of a recurring event.

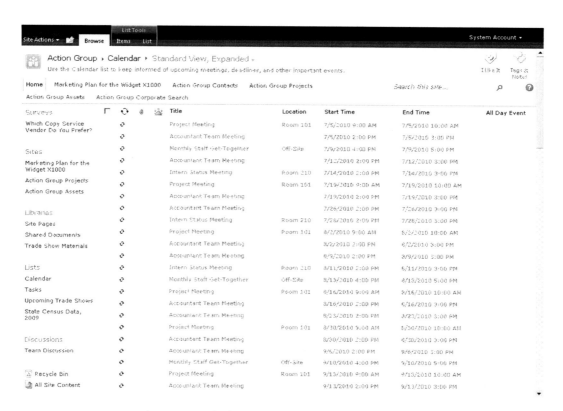

Figure 2: Standard with Expanded Recurring Events View

Calendar

View data as a daily, weekly, or monthly calendar.

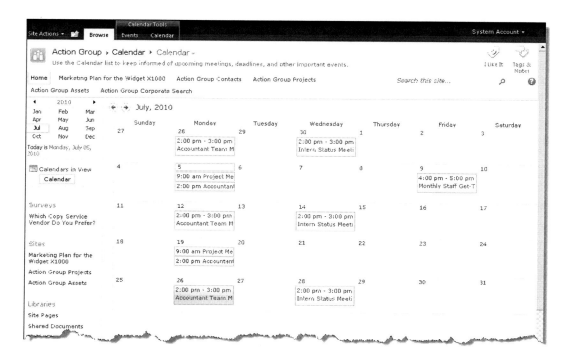

Figure 3: Calendar View

Gantt

View list items in a Gantt chart to see a graphical representation of the items related over time.

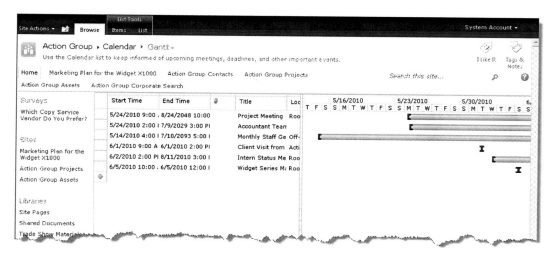

Figure 4: Gantt View

Datasheet

View data in an editable spreadsheet format that is convenient for bulk editing and quick customization. This view requires the use of an ActiveX-capable browser and Microsoft Access.

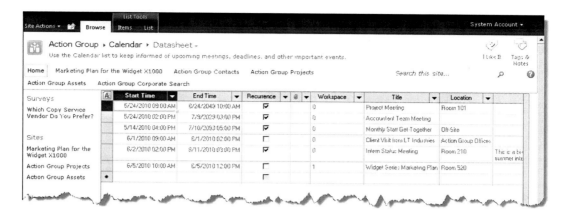

Figure 4: Datasheet View

Access

Start Microsoft Office Access to create forms and reports that are based on this list.

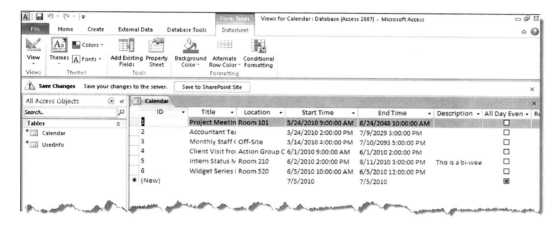

Figure 6: Access View

Appendix E: Permissions in SharePoint

Purpose: To keep documents secure in SharePoint, there are a number of permission levels that can be assigned to individual users or user groups. You can also manage permissions for a user or group at the site level, at the individual list item level, and everywhere in between within SharePoint. In this Appendix, the definitions of the various default permission levels in SharePoint are listed.

NOTE: SharePoint administrators can define additional permission levels, so there may be other permission levels defined for your organization's sites.

Permission Levels

Full Control	User has full control.
Design	User can view, add, update, delete, approve, and customize.
Manage Hierarchy	User can create sites and edit pages, list items, and documents.
Approve	User can edit and approve pages, list items, and documents.
Contribute	User can view, add, update, and delete list items and documents.
Read	User can view pages and list items and download documents.
Restricted Read	User can view pages and documents, but cannot view historical versions or user permissions.
Limited Access	User can view specific lists, document libraries, list items, folders, or documents when given permission.

Index

CPSIA information can be obtained at www.ICGtesting.com
Printed in the USA
BVOW081137160212

282909BV00007B/7/P